RENEWALS DATE DUE

WITHDRAWN
UTSA LIBRARIES

In the Name of Harmony and Prosperity

SUNY series in the Anthropology of Work
June C. Nash, Editor

In the Name of Harmony and Prosperity

Labor and Gender Politics in Taiwan's Economic Restructuring

ANRU LEE

STATE UNIVERSITY OF NEW YORK PRESS

Published by
State University of New York Press, Albany

© 2004 State University of New York

All rights reserved

Printed in the United States of America
No part of this book may be used or reproduced in any manner whatsoever without written permission. No part of this book may be stored in a retrieval system or transmitted in any form or by any means including electronic, electrostatic, magnetic tape, mechanical, photocopying, recording, or otherwise without the prior permission in writing of the publisher.

For information, address State University of New York Press, 90 State Street, Suite 700, Albany, N.Y. 12207

Production by Diane Ganeles
Marketing by Susan Petrie

Library of Congress Cataloging-in-Publication Data

Lee, Anru.
　In the name of harmony and prosperity : labor and gender politics in Taiwan's economic restructuring / Anru Lee.
　　p. cm.—(SUNY series in the anthropology of work)
　Includes bibliographical references and index.
　ISBN 0-7914-6033-9 (alk. paper).
　1. Women—Employment—Taiwan. 2. Women—Taiwan—Social conditions.
　3. Women—Taiwan—Economic conditions. 4. Sex role in the work environment—Taiwan. 5. Structural adjustment (Economic policy)—Taiwan. 6. Business ethics—Taiwan. 7. Working class—Taiwan. I. Title. II. Series.
HD6202.L44 2004
331.4′095124′9—dc21

2003052609

10 9 8 7 6 5 4 3 2 1

To my mother, Lee Lo Yu-chiao
In memory of my father, Lee Shu-jen (1934–1997)

Contents

Acknowledgments	ix
Introduction	xiii
Chapter 1. Taiwan's Great Transformation	1
Chapter 2. From Sunrise to Sunset	21
Chapter 3. The Waning of a Hard Work Ethic	49
Chapter 4. The Meaning of Work	75
Chapter 5. Between Filial Daughter and Loyal Sister	111
Chapter 6. Guests from the Tropics	131
Chapter 7. Bridging the Global and the Local: Understanding Taiwan's Economic Restructuring	151
Notes	167
References	175
Index	191

Acknowledgments

A Chinese proverb says that if you have many people to thank but cannot possibly thank them all, you thank the Heaven.

My first and foremost gratitude goes to many friends in Homei, who took me under their wings, shared their lives and work with me, and patiently and indulgently tolerated me for my often rude and senseless intrusion into their personal worlds. Their wisdom and courage toward life constituted the core pillar of my fieldwork. Without their kindness and generosity, my research and this book would not have been possible.

This book grew out of my doctoral dissertation. I owe my intellectual maturity and self-confidence to my advisors and professors at CUNY Graduate Center, who always have more faith in me than I have in myself. Dr. Burton Pasternak, with his utmost support and understanding, shepherded me through my earlier years at graduate school, when I was most doubtful about the meanings of being in academia. While I was struggling through the lone and long process of dissertation writing, it was the close supervision and continuous timely assistance of Dr. June Nash, Dr. Joan Mencher, and Dr. Michael Blim that kept me focused. June, Joan, and Michael remain as my foremost supporters to these days. I learned from all of them not only anthropological theories but also the crucial task of bridging theories with social praxis. I was extremely lucky to have had the opportunity—and blessing—to be their student. I also dedicate this book to the whole faculty in the Ph.D. Program in Anthropology at CUNY Graduate Center. Their firm belief in social justice and unwavering advocacy for public education were the center guidance of my formative years.

Many friends and colleagues helped me at various junctures of confusion and frustration during the long years of research and writing, whose names cannot possibly all be listed here. For such I plead for their forgiveness. I can only thank heaven for sending them to cross my path. Special thanks go to Julia Butterfield and Leon Arrendondo, my comrades at Room 1126 of the Graduate Center, who always kindly took the precious time off from their own writing to read my work-in-progress and indulged me on my days of excitement and dismay. This project also benefits from the comments and encouragement of Ian Skoggard, Murray Rubinstein, Scott Simon, Donald DeGlopper, Chang-hui Chi, Hill Gates, Jun Jing, Ellen Oxford, and Danning Wang, who read the whole or part of my manuscript at the different stages of its making, and the three anonymous readers who reviewed this book for SUNY Press. The remaining errors are certainly mine.

The unequivocal love of my parents, Lee Shu-jen (1934–1997) and Lee Lo Yu–chiao, is the ultimate foundation of my life. They assure me with their unreserved support that I could choose to follow my own destiny under any conditions. I am most grateful that I was able to share much of my time in Taiwan with them while collecting data for this book, after a very long absence from their life, as I was pursuing higher education—and am now teaching—in the United States. I also owe my current achievement to my husband, Keith Markus, my best intellectual and life companion, who not only humored (with the greatest patience) a wife with constant frenzy while I was finishing this book but also read most critically almost every version of this book until its completion. Keith deserves a postgraduate degree in anthropology.

Last but not the least, I thank the following funding agencies for their generous financial support that made this book possible: the Wenner-Gren Foundation for Anthropological Research, the Institute of Ethnology at the Academia Sinica in Taiwan, and the Ministry of Education of the Taiwan Government that sponsored the initial field research (September 1993–December 1995) of this project as well as my early stage of writing; the Office of Research and Sponsored Projects at California State University, Sacramento, that aided one of my summer follow-up studies (June–August 2001) and partial release from teaching in the following academic year; and, once again, the Wenner-Gren Foundation for Anthropological Research, the Chiang Ching–Kuo Foundation for International Scholarly Exchange, and a summer fellowship from the College of Social Sciences and Interdisciplinary Studies at CSU Sacramento for the last phase of manuscript preparation (2002–2003).

A different version of Chapter Five was published as "Between Filial Daughter and Loyal Sister: Global Economy and Family Politics in Taiwan," in Catherine Farris, Anru Lee, and Murray A. Rubinstein, eds. *Women in the New Taiwan: Gender Roles and Gender Consciousness in a Changing Society*. Copyright © 2004 by M. E. Sharpe. Reproduced by permission of M. E. Sharpe, Inc.

A different version of Chapter Six was published as "Guests from the Tropics: Labor Practices and Foreign Workers in Taiwan," in Esther Ngan-ling Chow, ed. *Transforming Gender and Development in East Asia*, pp. 183–202. Copyright © 2002 by Routledge. Reproduced by permission of Routledge, Inc., part of The Taylor & Francis Group.

Readers familiar with these works may find that the name of the town in my prior publications was different from that used in the current book. As I increasingly see this book as a project as much to articulate the general sociocultural configuration of the Taiwanese society as to document Taiwanese people's struggle and ingenuity in a specific historical period, I decided to use Homei, the real name of the town, instead of Hai-kou, the pseudonym that I used previously, to present my field site. To preserve the confidentiality of my informants, however, I continue to use pseudonyms for the individuals, factories, and companies whose stories are discussed in this book.

Introduction

和諧 *(ho-hsieh): harmonious; in harmony; harmony.*
Usage: 族群和諧 *(tzu-ch'un ho-hsieh;* ethnic harmony*);* 勞資和諧 *(lao-tzi ho-hsieh;* labor-capital harmony*);* 家庭和諧 *(chia-ting ho-hsieh;* family harmony*);* 和諧相處 *(ho-hsieh hsiang-ch'u;* getting along harmoniously*).*

繁榮 *(fan-jung): prosperous; flourishing; thriving.*
Usage: 國家繁榮 *(kuo-jia fan-jung;* national prosperity*);* 社會繁榮 *(sho-hui fan-jung;* social prosperity*);* 繁榮進步 *(fan-jung chin-pu;* prosperity and progress*).*

The major challenge in—and thus the chief excitement of—studying Taiwanese economy rests on its expeditious speed of change. While it took Western European societies several hundred years of formation for a large percentage of female population to eventually participate in the industrial (and now service-oriented) wage labor market (Tilly and Scott 1978), and it took nearly a hundred years for a New England town in North America to witness a shift in its textile workforce from one dominated by young single women to one with mostly married mothers with children (Lamphere 1987), similar changes took place in Taiwan in less than forty years. It was only in the 1960s that the Taiwan government adopted an export-oriented initiative to spearhead its industrialization process. By the 1980s, however, Taiwan had grown into a manufacturing powerhouse in the global economy. The success story of the "Taiwan Miracle," along with the experiences of other East Asian Newly Industrializing Countries (NICs) (namely South Korea, Hong Kong, and Singapore), has not only become a textbook case study but also has inspired emulation from policy makers in the developing world. Yet, ironically, it was also at the peak of its success that Taiwanese industrial producers began to feel the squeeze caused by changes both in the Taiwanese society and internationally. By the end of the 1990s, Taiwan had exported most of its labor-intensive industries that once made it a global fame. There are few light consumer products that are still made in Taiwan, but most of them bear a label of "Made in China" or somewhere in Southeast Asia. Young people now seek employment in the booming sector of service or the computer technology, or managerial posts in overseas Taiwanese companies. They shun factory work, which was highly sought after only a generation ago.

Great change brings great hope. It also, however, generates a tremendous amount of uncertainty. Although it may appear to many observers of the Asian Pacific economy that Taiwan is taking an inevitable course—and the aforementioned changes were merely a natural result of this progression—the transition has not been easy; nor has its effect been even or felt unequivocally. The fact that Taiwan was concomitantly experiencing a political transformation—or democratization, as it is often referred to in the media—has not helped to reduce but only aggravated the agony. Many Taiwanese since the late 1980s have learned that they need to master new skills in order to excel in the economic field, while treading the uncharted territory of national identity. This is most evident in the unceasing episodes of confrontation between Taiwanese businessmen favoring a stable and predictable investment environment and politicians of various political parties rivaling over new-found power and resources, and between companies pushing for a more open trading policy especially with the People's Republic of China and a state government trying to reach a precarious balance between global economic competitiveness, and national sovereignty and security, again, against China. This is certainly a time of contention. Nonetheless, the contention does not always occur at the national or macroeconomic level. More often than not it comes closer to home and affects individuals on a personal level. Anxiety over losing businesses, or becoming unemployed, thereby worrying about one's own and family welfare, is just one obvious example.

It is the concern over the personal anguish and the efforts individuals made to improve their situations that propelled me to begin the journey of understanding Taiwan's recent economic restructuring. After the 1980s, to reinvigorate the process of capital accumulation, Taiwanese industrial producers developed cost-effective strategies, such as reorganizing the division of labor on the shop floor, reducing the factory size, or upgrading the quality of production. They also explored new sources of cheap labor, adopting more radical practices, such as relocating their production overseas and importing foreign workers (mainly from Southeast Asia) to their shop floor in the country. With capital outflow and the introduction of foreign workers to the country, the Taiwanese economy has become increasingly internationalized and transnationalized.

Several paradoxes were apparent in Taiwan's recent economic restructuring. First and foremost were the contradictory phenomena of labor shortage and plant relocation. That is, on the one hand, industrial manufacturers asserted that they faced a problem of labor shortage, which they claimed had seriously curtailed their production capacity and therefore reduced their global competitiveness. On the other hand, manufacturers were seen closing down production in the country and relocating their businesses abroad, often leaving their employees with little compensation for the transition to another equivalent job. The question that presents itself is why those manufacturers who claimed to have difficulty finding workers did not hire those laid-off workers who could not find jobs, which would seem to be a prefect solution to the problems of both.

Centered on the paradox between the talk of labor shortage and the reality of plant closing and relocation, this book examines the labor and gender politics in the recent economic restructuring. Specifically, I focus on the latest changes in the textile industry in Homei, central Taiwan, and how the local residents responded to and engaged in the changes. Ethnographically, this book provides a detailed description of the latest phase of Taiwan's socioeconomic development, which thus far has not been discussed fully in spite of (or due to) its rapidly changing nature. Theoretically, this book contributes to our understanding of the increasingly complex but locally specific capital-labor relations in the current global economic system. As such, this book is well within the tradition of the anthropology of the global factory, whose current task, as indicated by Blim (1992:26), is to "investigate the ways in which local peoples mobilize culturally distinctive capacities to shape their unfolding economic destinies as well as [to document] their struggles to resist the world capitalist logic in whole or in part." It also acknowledges the fact that "the global factory is shaped in important ways by the actions of and conflicts between a variety of agents—from nation-states and capitalist classes to workers and communities" (Blim 1992:19).

Correspondingly, new sites of contradictions are constantly produced in the process of capitalist expansion. Beyond the task noted above, this book also attempts to show that not all of the contradictions thus produced can be subsumed by the capitalist logic of commodification (Lowe and Lloyd 1997). Furthermore, following the lead of practice theory (cf. Knauft 1996:105–140; Ortner 1989, 1999)—or perhaps due to my Taiwanese upbringing that accepts karma and reincarnation, or both—I believe that the symbolic construction of one's own world can and will be translated into reality, by being acted upon by the individual, which would eventually become the foundation of one's future action. The enactment thus planted the seed of change.

This, in turn, contributes to the theoretical pursuit of understanding Asian capitalisms. By examining how industrial production in Taiwan is organized and legitimized, and accepted by the local population, this book further affirms the view that no capitalist system is free from the sociocultural or political influence within which it is embedded (Hefner 1998). Yet, the recent challenge faced by Taiwanese producers also presents itself as an opportunity to test the limit of this theorization. As Taiwanese producers learn to adopt their new role as capital exporter in the world economy, and as the Taiwanese learn to use the newly acquired affluence in their now consumption-oriented society, we may also find more convergence to the experiences of Western advanced industrial societies.

CHAPTER 1

Taiwan's Great Transformation

Taiwan was a colony of Japan from 1895 to 1945. It was ceded to the Chinese government, led then by Chiang Kai-shek's Nationalist Party (KMT, short for Kuomingtang [國民黨]), after Japan lost the Second World War in 1945. Although only a province of the Republic of China (ROC) upon the retrocession, Taiwan became the de facto ROC after the KMT was defeated by the Chinese Communist Party in the Chinese Civil War and retreated to Taiwan in 1949. The relationship between the KMT and the local society of Taiwan has been rocky. To rid the Japanese influence and to establish its supremacy, the KMT implemented Mandarin-centered cultural and educational policy on the predominantly Japanese- and Taiwanese-speaking population. Politically, a martial law was imposed. Authoritarian rule based on repression and coercion was the norm. Epitomized by the February 28 (2–28) incident in 1947 and the subsequent White Terror in the 1950s, the KMT quickly eliminated most of the dissidents and many of the Taiwanese elites, and suppressed the rest of the society into silence. In the first few decades after WWII, the KMT had an iron grip on the Taiwanese society, under which the state, the central/national government, and the KMT were essentially synonyms. Yet, interestingly, in contrast to its tight control over the political sphere, the KMT had a rather lenient attitude toward economic activities. Despite the fact that the KMT-led government owned the majority of the large, capital-intensive enterprises in heavy industries, it left most of the small businesses unregulated and to thrive on their own. It was a widely shared sentiment among the Taiwanese then—though with a tint of cynicism, or practicality—that one could be left alone, make a lot of money, and have a good life, as long as one did not make trouble and was well behaved.

But things were gradually changing. This book tells a different story starting in the late 1980s. The late 1980s was a time of great transformation—a time of both confusion and turbulence, and new possibilities—after the past few decades of forced calm in Taiwan's post-WWII history. After several decades of struggle, with many lives lost and individuals persecuted and imprisoned, the political tension in Taiwan gradually abated. The government began to consider political rallies to be less threatening and more tolerable. Rally participants were not necessarily arrested or detained for further investigation, though they still risked being beaten by the police and were sometimes badly injured from the police violence. Prior to the lifting of martial law in 1987, the first opposition party, the Democratic Progressive Party (DPP), eventually came out in the open in 1986. Though still illegal and considered treasonous, the party campaigned for the election at the end of that year.

Protests for various social or economic causes burgeoned at the same time. This was particularly so after the lifting of martial law. Farmers or village residents protested the pollution of their lands by petrochemical companies. Workers rallied for higher pay and better annual bonuses. Environmentalists criticized the government's single-minded developmental ideology and economic policies that had resulted in serious deterioration of Taiwan's natural environment. Women's groups fought for the legal protection of young aboriginal women who were frequently coerced and sold by Han Chinese into prostitution. In addition, consumer advocates, retired and aged veterans, aborigines, farmers, teachers, and college students all added their agenda to the already highly volatile social milieu (Hsu and Sung 1989). Some of them posed a serious challenge to the legitimacy of many governmental practices based on political exclusion backed by the martial law. Also, for the first time in Taiwan's postwar history, workers were able to bargain with their employers collectively with much less fear, though they were not entirely free from the possibility of coercion or suppression. Accordingly, the number of industrial disputes rapidly rose at the end of the 1980s.

Many of these gatherings had developed spontaneously, however, without much ideological guidance or well thought out strategies to accomplish their purported goals. In the cases of farmers or villagers protesting against industrial pollution, or workers fighting for better pay and bonuses, the participants often blocked the front entrances of the alleged offending companies. They tried to force the owners or management to come to the negotiation table by stopping the production, or by making enough disruption to attract the media's attention, hoping that this would lead to the government's intervention.

Quite a few companies gave in under these confrontational circumstances. Companies agreed to compensate for the losses of farmers or local residents for the amount of money demanded, mainly because it cost much less to compensate local communities than to endure the possible loss of profit and damage to the company's public image due to disrupted production. The companies would also be able to develop better rapport with local residents by making amends with each individual. It was "to buy their hearts," as a Chinese saying goes. Many of the local communities were indeed content with the monetary retribution to individual families. They rarely pushed the companies to actually improve their environmental standards, leaving open their options to protest and be compensated again in the future, whenever new incidents or discontent arose.

Workers wrestling over annual bonuses were frequently appeased in similar ways. They sometimes won concessions from their employers, yet they were not able to make the terms of concession a permanent part of their work contracts. As a result, the Taiwanese society watched similar events recurring every year, seeing the same groups of people ceaselessly grumbling for more money, more payment, and more demands. The lack of legal means to settle civil disputes of these kinds, and the government's hesitation to intervene heavy-handedly as it used to do in previous decades, only aggravated the scale of animosity of the people involved and companies affected. These eventually became a real trial of patience for the general public in Taiwan. A derogatory term, *tsi li chiu chi* (自力救濟), literally "saving oneself through one's own action," was developed to describe these "wild-cat" events. The term addressed the irony that the Taiwan government was neither willing nor able to offer efficient redress when its citizens held legitimate grievances. Nevertheless, it was widely believed that the louder one cried, and the more annoying one became, the more likely one would be attended to and thus achieve one's goals. Thus, many Taiwanese considered the advent of democratic expressions to be lawless, particularly when compared to the earlier quiet and orderly era, when the government had tight control over the society.

While most Taiwanese citizens were experimenting with newly found freedom and rights, some of the industrial producers had become impatient with the seemingly endless demands from their workers. The industrial sector also had to face the constant disruption of production due to environmentalists' pressure for the government to enforce a stricter environmental code. A strong sentiment that the society was becoming unruly gradually developed among industrial employers and producers, and was quickly picked up by the media. In the late 1980s, right before and just after the removal of martial law, Taiwanese businesses and the media were constantly criticizing, depicting the Taiwan government as "lacking public authority and power" (*kung ch'uan li pu chang* [公權力不彰]). They charged that the government was incapable of purging troublemakers and thereby unable to reinstate the social order and harmony that were essential to the continuation of Taiwan's economic prosperity.

Changes in Taiwan's financial market evoked further complaints of industrial producers. The stagnation of the international market in the mid-1980s discouraged Taiwanese manufacturers from further investment and expansion, while at the same time the national savings rate and Taiwan's foreign reserves remained high. With an excessive amount of savings but limited channels to invest, a huge sum of these monies was channeled into the recently thriving stock market and a sprouting real estate market as well as to illegal activities of lottery (Ch'ai and Hsieh 1988; Yu 1993).

Among its many ramifications, this volatile money market provided the Taiwanese with new ways of seeking financial profit other than working for fixed wages. As such, it attracted a large population of Taiwanese who had spare money in their hands to invest. In the middle of the fervor, some people were known to quit their jobs or withdraw from their daily obligations in order to take full advantage of speculative opportunities. It was not long before the media and social pundits, soon joined by employers, began to criticize the Taiwanese' declining morale and productivity. Many industrial producers also began to cry about the shortage of dedicated workers. Concurrently, Taiwanese industrial producers faced serious challenges due both to intensified global competition and to demographic and economic changes in the society. As a result, Taiwanese manufacturers began to move their production overseas, mostly to Southeast Asia and China.

Labor and Management: Confronting the Economic Restructuring

Along with capital flight, there was a soaring number of plant closings and an increase in labor-management disputes in the country. One of the major causes of the disputes was the failure of owners/managers to render the severance pay and sometimes also past wages owed by the employers in plant-closing cases. The media frequently portrayed these workers as employees who had been betrayed by their supposedly benevolent employers. Their protests were often depicted as an expression of personal outrage or a search for cash compensation for personal loss. Seldom discussed in the media as well as in the general public were the socioeconomic circumstances in which these events took place and the bleak future in store for the majority of these laid-off workers.

When I started this research in the early 1990s, I heard few discussions about the dislocation of laborers and little expression of concern over how and where they found jobs after layoffs. As I tried to understand the seemingly indifferent attitude of Taiwanese society toward the human cost of this industrial restructuring, I gathered diverse opinions on the issue that were often contradictory. Nevertheless, there seemed to be a consensus among the people I talked to that it was not a problem for the laid-off workers to find jobs. On the contrary, I was frequently told that there was a labor shortage in Taiwan. Whether or not the new jobs that workers could find were as good or the pay was as high as those of their previous ones were separate matters.

It seemed that only labor activists were concerned about these issues. Many of those with whom I had conversations[1] indeed pointed out that the new jobs laid-off workers were able to find were usually marginal, less stable, and with lower wages. It was definitely downgrading, they said. The very few formal reports on this subject (e.g., Bo 1993; Hsia 1993), as well as my own investigation in the Taipei metropolitan area, confirmed their observations. Bo's (1993) research on the plant closings in the garment industry in Taipei County indicated that, due to their relatively advanced old age, limited educational background, and low skill level, laid-off women workers rarely found jobs in the booming service sector. Most of them stayed in the garment industry but worked in smaller or "underground" (i.e., unregistered) factories, and many became homeworkers. Needless to say, the wage and working conditions of most of these new jobs were worse than the old ones. Furthermore, labor activists with whom I talked were very concerned about the extensive scale of plant closings. They were particularly critical of the fact that many large firms in or near metropolitan areas were shut down not because the production costs were too high to be profitable, but because the lands on which these plants were built had become too valuable for industrial uses (Y. Ho 1992:18–20). The profit turnover from industrial production had become too low and too slow compared to using the land for commercial or real estate development. Owners of these large firms shut down their factories with the anticipation of converting these industrial lands to commercial uses in the near future by pressing the government to change its zoning laws.

It also became apparent that factory owners frequently used plant closings as a means to escape from paying workers' retirement pensions, which were frequently twice as much as the severance pay in plant-closing cases (Hsia 1993; You 1994). According to Taiwan's Labor Standards Law, workers are entitled to retirement pensions after staying in the same company for twenty-five years. Many entrepreneurs who started business in the early 1970s, at the beginning of Taiwan's export-oriented industrialization, were approaching this "deadline" at the end of the 1980s. They were anxious about the enormous expenditure for retirement pensions they would have to pay. They considered it to be a great financial burden, particularly under the soaring global competition. Some evaded the problem by setting up a factory in another country and gradually moving production there. When production in their Taiwan factories slackened as a result, they then announced to the workers that they could no longer obtain sufficient orders to make a profit and had to close the factories. Aging workers approaching retirement were hit the hardest. Most of these workers were in their late forties or early fifties. They were not only forced to give up their retirement pension and accept lower severance pay instead, but they also had great difficulty in finding new jobs due to their age and seniority.

Subsequently, the unemployment rate began to soar after the mid-1990s (Table 1.1); and one-fourth of the unemployed fell between age thirty-five and forty-nine (Table 1.2). Together, this gradually aroused a concern in Taiwan, where people had enjoyed nearly full employment until very recently. A newspaper article in 1997,[2] entitled "To become

Table 1.1
Unemployment Rate by Sex (%)

Average of Year	Total	Male	Female
1966	3.02	2.28	4.91
1971	1.66	1.47	2.10
1976	1.78	1.59	2.19
1981	1.36	1.21	1.65
1986	2.66	2.75	2.53
1991	1.51	1.50	1.53
1996	2.60	2.72	2.42
1997	2.72	2.94	2.37
1998	2.69	2.93	2.33
1999	2.92	3.23	2.46
2000	2.99	3.36	2.44
2001	4.57	5.16	3.17

Source: Directorate-General of Budget, Accounting, and Statistics (DGBAS) (July 2002). Adapted from *National Statistics: Social Indicators* (http://www.dgbas.gov.tw).

Table 1.2
Unemployment Rate by Educational Attainment (%)

Average of Year	Total	Primary & Below	Junior High	Senior High & Vocational	Junior College & Above
1966	3.02	—*	—*	5.03	2.58
1971	1.66	—*	—*	4.55	2.62
1976	1.78	—*	—*	4.63	3.46
1981	1.36	0.46	1.69	2.72	2.23
1986	2.66	1.12	2.85	4.41	3.76
1991	1.51	0.56	1.61	2.16	2.04
1996	2.60	1.40	2.77	3.00	3.13
1997	2.72	1.77	3.25	3.02	2.76
1998	2.69	1.65	2.97	3.09	2.80
1999	2.92	1.99	3.28	3.23	2.93
2000	2.99	2.05	3.50	3.34	2.80
2001	4.57	3.56	5.75	5.12	3.72

Source: Adapted from DGBAS (2002).
*Data not available.

middle-aged is not a mistake. The mistake was to have chosen the wrong vocation" (*Chung nien pu shi ts'uo, ts'uo tsai tang nien ju ts'uo hang?* [中年不是錯，錯在當年入錯行?]), attributed the climbing unemployment rate to an enlarged population of middle-aged male workers[3] who lost their jobs due to plant closing or factory relocation. These middle-aged workers were trapped in an awkward situation, the article continued, for they were too young to be retired yet too old to learn new knowledge and technologies. The article further stated, even if these workers' skills were still in need, very few companies would be willing to hire them, primarily for the concern that the companies would soon be burdened with their retirement pensions.

Nonetheless, the disheartening news of a mounting unemployment rate did not dominate the society's attention; neither did the labor activists' organizing efforts to counteract the impact of plant closing and relocation. There were only sporadic reports that made it to the newspaper headlines that helped to raise temporary interest of the society. For the most part, the discussion of labor shortages led the popular discourse. Taiwanese industrial producers were complaining vehemently that they could not find workers, and according to them, one of the major causes for this was the Taiwanese' declining work ethic, especially that of the New New Generation (*Hsin hsin ren lei* [新新人類]). The expression, the "New New Generation," is an adaptation of the term "the New Generation," which was coined in the mid-1980s by Japanese writer Sakaiya Taichi to describe the generation of rich and carefree urban youth born after 1965, when the Japanese excelled in the world economy.[4] In Taiwan, where the course of economic development trailed after Japan, the phrase was used to judge the generation of young people who were born after the 1970s, when Taiwan began to win the name of "economic miracle." Government statistics seemed to support this "New New Generation" moral discourse. According to the Council of Labor Affairs (1995), the labor force participation rate reached a peak of 61 percent of the whole population in 1987 but has dropped since then. Subsequently, Taiwanese employers urged the government to find workers for them. Otherwise, they would be left with no choice but to leave the country and make their investment elsewhere.

In response, the Taiwan government legalized the hiring of foreign labor in the early 1990s, but employers continued to complain that the allowed quotas were too low, and the procedures for hiring foreign laborers were too cumbersome. Under local employers' pressing threat to move overseas, the government responded by introducing more open policies regarding foreign labor employment. Even after the labor unions of some of Taiwan's leading corporations (mainly in the petrochemical industry) reported that their companies were deliberately replacing the Taiwanese workforce with foreign workers to reduce the labor cost, the government's increasingly lenient policies were not challenged. Yet, the speed of "liberation" was never fast enough as far as the industrialists were concerned. The cry for labor was becoming increasingly imperative along with the capital flight out of the country.

Theoretical Premises

What intrigues me are the ways in which the logic of capital engages the logic of culture, based on which individual decisions are made and their daily practices are informed. One may be able to explain the source of Taiwan's economic restructuring by way of a structural analysis of capitalist expansion and global competition, and see Taiwanese manufacturers' strategies as inspired by economic incentives and calculation common to all players in the global economic system. But this line of analysis is insufficient at least in two respects. Cross-culturally, a full understanding of the issue in question must elucidate the differences in response and strategy, or the different meanings associated with similar strategies as observed around the world, which distinguish the Taiwanese case from others. Concomitantly, at the societal level, one also has to be able to explain the formation of dominant discourses that allows for the rise of certain industrial strategies in spite of and according to the social stratification and differentiation.

Answers to these concerns can be obtained only by looking closely at the articulation of culture, history, and economy, as shown in the expressions of people involved (Blim 1992; Cairoli 1998; Nash 1989). A linkage between the following two theoretical endeavors, I believe, will be informative to the current pursuit.

Culture and Economy in Asian Capitalisms

Ever since the global economic restructuring after the 1960s, East Asian nations have been in the forefront of scholarly attention. The East Asian NICs witnessed not only rapid growth but also equality of income distribution, low unemployment, and the near elimination of the desolate poverty often associated with the poorest social strata in other developing countries (Deyo 1987). These impressive accomplishments have generated heated scholarly debates and produced an extensive body of literature on what factors contributed most to the East Asian "economic miracle" and whether the experiences of these countries provided qualitatively distinct forms of capitalist development from the West. In the case of Taiwan, the focus of discussion has been on an array of social, political, and economic activity lying between family and state (Bosco 1990; Skoggard 1996). Recent literature identifies the Taiwan state as a major factor because of its prodevelopment policies, and its strength and autonomy from foreign influence and from the intervention of vested interest groups in Taiwan (Deyo 1987; Gold 1986; Wade 1990; Winckler and Greenhalgh 1990). The role of the family is also acknowledged. Specifically, the desire for family security and prosperity has been recognized as a powerful motivation behind entrepreneurial activities (Harrell 1985; Niehoff 1987; Stites 1982, 1985). This has contributed to the flourishing of small businesses, the major players in Taiwan's export economy, whose versatility and flexibility prove to be essential for success in the current global economic system (Castells 1996; Gereffi and Pan 1994). Lately, the term "Network Capitalism" has been coined to illustrate the emphasis on personalistic ties (both within the family and among business partners) in Chinese societies including Taiwan (Hamilton 1998; Hefner 1998).

Labor, Gender, and Global Industrialization

Though with a different theoretical pursuit in mind, the effort to understand the culturally specifically patterns of Asian capitalisms has reinforced the recognition that these economies are part of the current global economic system typified by capital accumulation. Consequently, changes in Taiwan's industrial sector exemplify the larger process of flexible accumulation in the current global economy (Harvey 1989), which is characterized by the employment of increasingly heterogeneous workforces and the utilization of multiple modes of production. The variety of industrial situations linked to flexible accumulation raised anew questions about workers' relations with, and their responses to, capitalist transformation (Ong 1997). Specifically, as women emerged to be the major force in the global assembly line, models of regulation based on gender ideologies have been developed to control labor (Fernandez-Kelly 1994; Nash and Fernandez-Kelly 1983; Safa 1995; Ward 1990). These ranged from direct despotic labor management in large firms (Fernandez-Kelly 1983; Kim 1997; C. Lee 1998; Ong 1987) to paternalistic control in small-scale, family-centered factories (Greenhalgh 1994; Hsiung 1996). The latter is particularly common in Taiwan, where young women's role in the family made them an ideal source of cheap labor essential to Taiwan's early export-oriented industrialization (Arrigo 1980; Cheng and Hsiung 1992; Diamond 1979; R. Gallin 1984a, 1984b, 1990; Kung 1994; Salaff 1995). In response, women workers seeking improvement in the workplace and in their lives adopted strategies both within and outside the traditional realm of class struggle, drawing inspiration from their individual cultures. Despite the fact that most of the tactics adopted by women workers were ineffective in challenging the hegemony of capital, these cultural struggles often engendered a new sense of self and community for the workers, thus imposing potential challenge to the constitution of civil society (Ong 1997:86; also see Cairoli 1998; Mills 1997, 1999).

I believe that changes in gender roles and gender ideologies are keys to understand Taiwan's recent economic restructuring, mainly because labor was in the center of Taiwan's recent economic debates, and women have been the predominant work force in Taiwan's labor-intensive industries. It is through gender that production is organized; it is also through the language of gender that the labor-management relations are largely defined. Gender is therefore an interlocutor of the dynamics between culture and economy, of structure and agency, and of the processes of global, national, and local, that this book seeks to understand. To make clear these points, I will examine the labor and gender politics in the textile industry in Homei, by making connections among capital accumulation, shifting of work organization and discourse on work ethics, and the formation of women's subjectivity.

Homei: The Field Site

Homei is a small town in central Taiwan, where local residents have been engaged in textile manufacturing (mainly weaving) since the final years of the Japanese colonization (1895–1945). The choice of Homei was more a result of accidents and coincidence than a conscious selection.[5] Yet, because of its residents' extensive engagement in the textile production, Homei turned out to be an ideal site for my research. Textile production was one of the first few industries pursued by the Taiwanese in the post-WWII era, and with the assistance from the government it soon became Taiwan's leading industry. The development of Homei's textile industry thus stands for Taiwan's post-WWII economic history, signifying the process of Taiwan's incorporation into the global economy. Although the scale of production is sharply reduced, and local capital and labor have both become transnationalized, textile continues to be the most important industry in Homei even today. The local residents' long engagement in textile production, in relation to Taiwan's short history of industrialization, made the industry an integral part of the local culture and memory. Almost every individual I met in Homei had a story to tell about textile. They were either working or once worked in textile factories, or they knew someone who was or had been a textile worker. Their families might have owned or ran a textile factory, or they were suppliers of raw textile materials. Some of them sold or repaired machines. Still, there were others who were representatives of local, national, or international trading companies. Local women of almost all ages had been part of the textile workforce. Grandmothers in their sixties were veterans from the initial stage, while their teenage granddaughters just entered the trade recently. The experiences of these different generations of workers provide a rare chance in the Taiwanese context to construct a profile of women and work, and to compare changes overtime.

My experience in Homei began with a small weaving factory owned by the Wang family, whose two youngest daughters, Mei-hua and Mei-ling, became my best guides and companions during the course of my research. I treasure their friendship to these days. I spent the first month of my fieldwork with the family and learned the basics of the trade. The Wang firm presents a typical example of local production. The family began their operation in the late 1970s—the beginning of the heyday of the local export-oriented textile manufacturing—relying on family assets accumulated and converted from agriculture for initial capital. Their production scale was small (never exceeding a hundred semiautomatic looms), and the nature of their business was subcontracting. Although they had always hired workers, family members made up the most essential core of the workforce. Like the majority of their counterparts in Homei, the Wang factory has always been, and will continue to be, a family enterprise. It depends on the will and wits of family members to sail through economic ups-and-downs.

Through the introduction of the Wang family, I then moved into the dormitory of another local textile company, where I lived and studied for the next nine months. This second home of mine, which I call Treasure Island, was different from the Wang factory and atypical of the local textile industry in many respects. First and foremost, the company was not a family business but had multiple investors. Second, its size was comparatively large by the local standard. At the time of my research, Treasure Island consisted of two production units, one for spinning and the other for weaving. The company employed roughly 150 shop floor workers, a number far exceeding that of workers hired (usually fewer than 30) in most of the local settings. Third, instead of being just a subcontracting firm like most of the local operations, it had its own brand name for the yarns produced. A big sign reading "Formosa," the company's brand name, along with a drawing of the Taiwan Island, was painted high on the front gate of the company for every passer-by to see. Likewise, the company kept a trading office in Taipei City to take charge of its trading business. However, its weaving section was still under subcontracting operation. Fourth, benefiting from its relatively large size, the company was still able to attract young single women who were nearly absent in small factories. Among the company's 150 shop-floor workers, two-thirds of them were Taiwanese, with half of them young single women and the other half married women with children. The other one-third of the workforce comprised of foreign workers from Thailand, a common practice adopted by many of the local textile factories to supplement the short labor supply since the early 1990s.

In spite of these differences, the company shared many things in common with other local manufacturers in this "sunset" industry (夕陽工業)—a metaphor widely used in Taiwan to refer to its labor-intensive industries, whose best days are over and will never come back again. Local textile factories all faced intensified competition not only from entrepreneurs in the rapidly rising industrializing countries in Asia but also from their fellow Taiwanese businessmen who had relocated their production to these countries. The margin of their profit was further squeezed by the competition from these overseas Taiwanese producers, who shared the same customer base as well as a similar level of machinery, technology, and business skills as their Taiwan-based counterparts. Also, like Treasure Island, many of the textile manufacturers in Homei relied on foreign workers, at least as a temporary arrangement, to relieve them both from the pressure of rising labor costs and the difficulty of finding workers.

Studying Treasure Island granted me certain advantages. This opportunity was especially precious for me at the beginning stage of my research. Thanks to the size of the company, as the workers worked around the clock in three shifts, I could always find someone to talk to, even at three o'clock in the morning, when I was too anxious to fall asleep. Day and night I watched them work, and very soon I acquired some knowledge of textile production that helped me to talk intelligently and to ask meaningful questions to a broader audience outside the factory in the later stage of my fieldwork. Specifically, because of its relatively large production scale and seemingly more abundant financial resources, this company had more leeway to adjust to the narrowing margin of profit than that of small firms or family factories. I learned from the management of Treasure Island various tactics to cope with the current economic predicament.

The workers and management at Treasure Island became my primary informants. I became acquainted with every one of them, and as time went by, became very close to some of them and their families. Most of the workers, staff, and management personnel in this company came from different villages near Homei, with a few exceptions who came from less industrialized regions in central Taiwan. Whereas many workers had already worked at Treasure Island for more than ten years, others had just joined this company. Some of the workers never changed their jobs; Treasure Island was their first and only workplace thus far. There were still others who had rich experience with local employers, however, either because they were veterans from previous plant-closing incidents or simply because they chose to change jobs often. Therefore, even though the labor pool at Treasure Island was not big enough to be a microcosm of the larger industrial community, it certainly covered a wide range of workers and worker's experiences. Moreover, it is worth noting that mothers and/or mothers-in-law of many of the employees also worked (and some were still working at the time of my research) in textile factories. Their experiences and those of their daughters and daughters-in-law provided a valuable transgenerational comparison of the workers' profile. A cross-generational comparison of working women's lives is especially meaningful in the Taiwanese context. Taiwan witnessed a swift transformation in less than four decades, from being a poverty-stricken agrarian society, to one based on full-fledged, successful export-oriented industrialization, and now to one experiencing the decline of industrial manufacturing as well as the booming of the service sector. The experiences of different generations of women workers are thus manifestations of the evolving global economic system, as it intertwines with Taiwan's local culture and economy.

The experience I acquired from Treasure Island and the Wang family factory proved to be invaluable for my research. A comparison of the labor process in the two localities reveals the parameter of strategies each factory had in relation to their production scale, source of capital and labor, and type of product. Here I draw my inspiration from Nash (1985), who identified two categories of firms with distinct types of labor-management relations in advanced capitalist economies: those in the monopolistic sector and those in the competitive sector. In the U.S. context, the greater margin of profitability in monopolistic capitalist firms makes it possible for larger corporations to accommodate to industrial unions, whereas smaller competitive firms appropriate personalistic and paternalistic labor policies as well as rely on disadvantaged groups, such as women and minorities, for labor. Also, smaller firms depend on commonsense approaches to labor recruitment and tenure, while large corporations develop more explicit and rationalized personnel relations (Nash 1985:60). Although the difference between Treasure Island and the Wang family factory is not equivalent to that of the monopolistic and competitive sectors—both of these Taiwanese firms are in the competitive sector—the existence of multiple forms of labor control was quickly observed. These two places also had distinct sources of workers and means of labor recruitment. The Wang factory, a small family firm, relied on family members or word-of-mouth to find workers, whereas Treasure Island, a medium-sized company, used formal channels, such as advertisements or junior high school job fairs, as well as word-of-mouth, for labor recruitment. These distinctions, in addition to the fact that women workers in these two types of workplace differed in their age and marital status, formed a highly fragmented social realm within which diverse meanings concerning Taiwan's economic habitat were developed.

After Treasure Island and the Wang family, I moved around in the town and conducted interviews in various neighborhoods and villages at the later stage of my research. This later stage of fieldwork broadened my understanding of the labor and business practices I had observed in the previous two manufacturing settings. Moreover, a holistic study of the community provided me with a political, social, and cultural contextualization, which enabled me to assess the dialectical relationship between the labor processes on the shop floor and the larger society (cf. Nash 1989).

On Doing Native Anthropology

My status of being a native anthropologist—i.e., someone who was born and raised in the culture she studies—proved mostly positive in understanding the practices, motivations, and emotions of people in my research in Homei, though not without predicaments. Specifically, as my female informants and I both grew up under the influence and constraints of Chinese patrilineal culture, the contrast between my life and most of theirs reveals the important economic factors that shape one's living experience. More significantly, it is through their comparison of and comments on my ways of life that I saw most clearly their perception of rights, duties, and responsibilities, and their apprehension toward the power relations embedded in Taiwanese cultural and social systems that constituted their own lives.

The initial stage of my fieldwork went like a typical ethnographic report. My arrival raised certain curiosity and suspicion. Even though I was born and raised in Taiwan and only came to North America for postgraduate study, I was obviously different from local female workers in many major ways. People in Homei were generally amazed at the fact that I was pursuing a doctoral degree in the United States. Most of the workers I met had only junior high school diplomas, and many of them began working in their early teens. It was almost beyond their imagination that a woman in her thirties could still be at school, enjoy the freedom of traveling, and even get paid for doing "nothing." They also saw it as a major problem that, being a married woman, I came to Taiwan alone, ignoring my wifely duty by leaving my husband unattended in New York City, which included taking care of the daily chores and my husband's sexual (and to a lesser degree, emotional) need for companionship. As a matter of fact, many married women at Treasure Island signaled the possibility that my husband would have a mistress occupying my side of the bed while I was away. One friend even warned me not to hand over my grant money to my husband for deposit. She cautioned that I would never see the money again because my husband would most likely use it up for vulgar purposes.

They laughed at my calling the fieldwork "work." How could anyone call "chatting," "playing," and "fooling around" all day every day work? It was entertainment! Grant money might be an intangible concept to the female workers, but they certainly were not ignorant about the hardship one would have to endure without secure or sufficient financial support. Many of them quickly came to their first conclusion about me: "Ah, your family must be rich!"

No matter how hard I tried to fit in, there were always subtle differences that gave me away. Some women were particularly fascinated with examining my hands. "Touch it!" they liked to say, calling attention to other friends of theirs, "Her hands are so soft. Her skin color is so pale [a sign for not needing to toil under the sun]." My hands were apparently not hands of those who had to sweat for a living; nor were they hands of a wife and mother who had to labor to keep her house and children tidy. My clothes were clean and spotless; there were no oil stains on them. I often wore white T-shirts. No one else wore white on the shop floor. It would be too difficult to wash. Female workers liked to say to me, in wistful amazement, "You have a very good destiny. How could you have such a wonderful life?"

Their questions did not end there. After their initial inspection of my appearance, almost every one of them asked me about my family background: where my family lived, how many brothers and sisters I had, what they each were doing, and most important of all, what my father did for a living. In nearly every occasion, as soon as they learned that my father was a medical doctor, they comprehended with great relief: "No wonder you have a very good life."

Individual accomplishment seemed to play a lesser role in determining one's personal identity. Different from the academic world where one's institutional affiliation, publications, and research projects were frequently cited and exchanged, these women emphasized one's position in a family-centered social network. This does not simply signify, however, that Taiwan has a kin-based social organization or that the family is a critical institution of Taiwanese society. Their emphasis on one's family background derived from their deep understanding of the production and reproduction of a stratified Taiwan society. I might appear more competent or successful—and I might have worked hard for my accomplishment—but both women workers and I knew well that I would not have easily gone this far had my family not been able to provide me with financial and social support. Many of the workers did not finish high school education mainly because their labor was needed to make cash income to pay for the family debt or to feed the family. As evidenced in the life stories presented later in this book, I have very little doubt that, if these women had been given the opportunity, they would have chosen a very different life trajectory. Why should anyone choose to work in a textile factory as a teenager if she does not need to?

My closeness with Taiwanese workers, unfortunately, also diverted my attention from foreign workers. As an anthropologist who primarily relies on participant observation for information, I only feel comfortable about doing a good job when establishing a close rapport with people in my research. As such, I have to confess that I was ill prepared for meeting non-Taiwanese workers and hence did not explore the issue as much as I would have liked otherwise. Being a Taiwanese, I was naturally suspected by foreign workers as one of the unfriendly hosts in a country where they were more often than not not warmly welcomed. Also, not foreseeing the relevance of the foreign component of the current manufacturing workforce, I was not equipped with the appropriate languages (mainly Thai) before entering the field and thus unable to talk directly to most of the foreign workers I met in Homei. Without a common language to bridge the communication gap, my contact with foreign workers in Homei was mostly limited to daily greetings, although on a few occasions I did manage to engage in short but superficial conversation in English, if they happened to come from the Philippines or were educated to understand the language. Nevertheless, none of these encounters resulted in fruitful understandings.

Plan of the Book

This book consists of seven chapters. Between this Introduction and the conclusions in Chapter Seven, Chapters Two through Six address different issues, as they are related to Taiwan's recent economic restructuring. Each chapter also engages in dialogue with one theoretical concern relevant to the question of East Asian development. Together, this book intends to show that any static understanding of the relationship between culture and economy fails to capture the important dimensions of the relationship. It is precisely the fact that culture and economy change both as a result of the other and also in response to other forces outside the other that demonstrates the complexity of issues under study. As such, in the broader context of anthropological theory, this book develops a dialectic approach to culture and economy. This stands in contrast to reductionist approaches that attempt to subordinate one to the other.

Chapter Two, "From Sunrise to Sunset," deals with the development of the textile industry in Homei. This chapter aims to elucidate the rise of a decentralized production system in the local area and the specific relations of production embedded in it, a topic much discussed in the past study of the Taiwan economy. While past literature focuses mainly on the economic implications of Taiwan's decentralized production system in the country's advancement in the global economy, this chapter emphasizes the significance of its cultural ethos. The decentralized production system, itself a historical product, built up a set of dispositions from which Taiwanese factory owners and workers drew their understanding and strategies in response to the latest economic changes. It also helped to fashion dominant discourses in the society. Specifically, this chapter argues that the "black-hand becoming boss" cultural ideal, which was made into reality concurring with the success of the decentralized production system, facilitated the legitimacy of the factory owners' claim of labor shortage and the society's declining work ethic that was said to cause the labor shortage.

It is at this juncture that we begin to observe the mutually transforming effect of local cultural beliefs and economic practices, as they are affected by the conditions in the global economic system. Chapter Three, "The Waning of a Hard Work Ethic," looks at the interface of these issues. To problematize Taiwan's recent economic predicaments as an issue of work ethic not only had a cultural root but in turn implicated the strategies factory owners might adopt to solve their problems; this in turn shapes the path of their future. Yet, there was always a possibility that, knowing how labor costs could undercut one's profit, factory owners were simply exploiting the common sentiment of the society to their own advantage. Whether or not it was motivated by a calculated move, the discourse of the labor shortage and of the declining work ethic (which I named the "New New Generation" moral discourse in chapter Three) had asserted an encompassing effect—or a hegemonic status—that informed the Taiwanese' thoughts and actions. Subsequently, the discourse did not exist in a void but was continuously supported by a material reality.

On the other hand, in spite of its hegemonic nature, the New New Generation moral discourse was by no means free from challenge or oppositions. Chapter Three also examines the different accounts given by people in Homei of Taiwan's recent economic restructuring, focusing especially on the conflicting notions surrounding the moral discourse. This theme is further elaborated in Chapter Four, "The Meaning of Work," which personalizes and contextualizes these diverse views through the lives and subject formation of female textile workers. By way of the life stories of three Treasure Island employees, who differed in age and marital status and belonged to different generations, Chapter Four documents the rapid transformation in Taiwan's wage labor market, the cultural and socioeconomic forces that brought about the transformation, and the dialectical relationship between the structural change and women workers' personal lives. Most relevant to the current economic restructuring, the tight labor market has increased the employment opportunity of married women, who were previously considered as less dependable because of their domestic responsibilities but now are regarded as more reliable, since young women are no longer available. Young women who choose to work in factories also tend to have a strong sense of economic independence, for industrial employers eagerly seek after them. Some even felt that they could choose to remain unmarried and support themselves with their wages. Why these women should want to remain single, and how they managed to do it without risking being ridiculed as abnormal or antisocial—both of which are cultural questions—are two of the foci of this chapter.

As I am essentially engaging in translation between an objective world and a subjective one (Ortner 1989:18), I adopt the concepts of practice and agency to aid this task. Originally crafted by Bourdieu (1977) and later refined by Ortner (1984, 1996), practice emerged as a theoretical tool to bridge the gap between symbolic analysis and political economy, by which sociocultural life is considered to be a product of both societal structure and individual agency (Knauft 1996:105–140; Pinches 1999:5). That is, on the one hand, "individual practices are seen as constrained and orchestrated by collective structures of cultural logic or organization," but on the other hand, "individuals are also seen as agents who reinforce or resist the larger structure that encompasses them" (Knauft 1996:105–140). Borrowing Ortner's own words (1989:18),

> One observes actors in real circumstances using their cultural frames to interpret and meaningfully act upon the world, converting it from a stubborn object to a knowable and manageable life-place. At the same time one observes the other edge of their process, as actors' modes of engaging the world generate more stubborn objects (either the same or novel ones) that escape their frames and, as it were, reenter the observer's.

However powerful a culture is as a guiding force of behavior, it can at best be a partial hegemony (Ortner 1996:17), leaving sites of practices and perspectives that may become the bases for resistance and transformation. The erosion of longstanding patterns as a result of individual alternative practices is revealed in Chapter Five, "Between Filial Daughter and Loyal Sister." Chapter Five details the rise and fall of the Wang family factory, whose success relied primarily on the seamless cooperation of its family members. The family has long been an important area of research in Chinese studies, and it is often considered as a corporate unit within which members contribute to advance its collective welfare under the leadership of the household head, usually the father of the family. This chapter challenges this cultural assumption by highlighting the conflicting views and interests of people—especially the two youngest daughters—in the Wang family. In resonance with the previous chapter, the appropriate roles for women had been redefined as a result of the past economic development, which fostered a demographic recomposition in the wage labor market. This in turn challenged the existing gender ideologies that had helped to impose moral imperatives to the social division of labor until the recent economic restructuring. Yet, paradoxically, while young women have obtained more employment opportunities outside the traditional industrial sector, daughters of small-scale, family-centered factories also face new contradictions in their lives. Specifically, in a time of labor shortage, family loyalty is continuously evoked in order to keep daughters to work for their family factories. This frequently calls for an altered course of action from young women's own expectation, thus subjecting them in a moral dilemma.

If the previous chapters demonstrate the importance of culture in shaping the specific pattern that a local economy adopts to respond to the conditions in the global economy, thus suggesting the possibility of plural forms of capitalism, Chapter Six, "Guests from the Tropics," coming to a full circle, attends to Taiwan's conformity to the logic of capital accumulation in capitalism. Chapter Six tackles the issue of foreign labor, one of the most dramatic trends in Taiwan's recent economy. In spite of their constant lament of young Taiwanese' waning work ethic, textile producers in Homei articulate the hiring of foreign labor largely in economic terms. They calculated the labor cost they could save from employing foreign workers. They continued to explore new sources of foreign labor by going further inland in both continental and island Southeast Asia, where the workers were said to be cheaper, less sophisticated, and more obedient. They also urged the Taiwan government to certify foreign labor from an increasingly long list of countries including China. Unique to the current global economy is "the particular circuits of capital and labor that have resulted from competition over time" (Fernandez-Kelly 1989a:152), and labor and capital migrations across national borders represent two contemporary aspects of the same process. Taiwanese manufacturers, including those in Homei, are apparently taking advantage of both, in spite of their limitations.

CHAPTER 2

From Sunrise to Sunset

The first time I visited Yueh-mei Village, one of the earliest textile districts in Homei, I was amazed by the grandiosity of its village temple. Standing in the center of the village plaza, the temple rose up steeply on a two-story high pedestal, with a heavily decorated roof and flamboyant architectural style. It is certainly the most remarkable, if not the largest or the tallest, building in the surrounding area. In response to my surprise and fascination, my companion Mrs. Tsai, a married-in daughter-in-law from an adjacent village, sighed slightly: "Oh, yes, they have money, don't they?"

An old man in charge of the day-to-day maintenance of the temple said to us that the Yueh-mei villagers rebuilt the temple and lifted it to the current scale not long ago. A village temple is usually a showcase of the economic status of its residents, and the people in Yueh-mei demonstrate their position well. It is said that there are quite a number of rich people in Yueh-mei—or at least, people who originally came from the village. They made their fortune early on, right from the beginning of the local textile development. Yet, the village temple is also the silent witness of the vicissitude of the local economy. The plaza was quiet, and the village temple seemingly stood alone, in the afternoon on my first visit, just as on many of the afternoons on my following trips. Retired male farmers and entrepreneurs are the only regular visitors, not because the side room of the temple houses the Yueh-mei Club for the Elderly, but mainly because they are the ones left behind. Over the years Yueh-mei experienced a population decline. Many successful businessmen moved their families to nearby downtown Homei or Changhua City, in search of greater economic opportunity, better education for children, or simply a different lifestyle. They rarely come back to the village, except on occasions when they need to pay annual tribute to their ancestral halls, where the spirits and tablets of their family ancestors rest. Many of the former residences along the village's main alley are abandoned and falling apart for lack of care. The owners have established their homes as well as economic prospects elsewhere.

The dispersion of Yueh-mei's population mirrors changes in the local economy as well as in the society at large. As Taiwan's postwar industrialization accelerated, textile production also diffused widely in almost every corner of the Homei area. Yueh-mei no longer held a central place but became one of the many production sites during the swift process of rural industrialization. Yet, like the single remaining hand loom in the Homei vicinity, which was used by early-day weavers before automation and is now casually kept in a back corner of the warehouse under Yueh-mei's village temple and occasionally carried around on lantern festival parades,[1] Yueh-mei is an essential part of the local memory. It symbolizes a legendary past, from which the present stems but is no longer affected.

This chapter tells the story of Homei's textile industry that encompasses in a short time span drastic changes from a bleak period of wartime recovery, to an excessively protected, lucrative "oligopoly" of the domestic market, then to a dramatic incorporation into the international market, and finally to a recent descent due to escalating production costs and intensified world competition. These local changes exemplify the major stages of Taiwan's post-WWII integration into the global economic system. This chapter also examines how the process of economic expansion led to the emergence of a highly decentralized production system dominated by family-centered, small-scale subcontracting firms. These firms form intricate cooperative relationships, based on which textile producers in Homei are able to remain immensely resilient and hence competitive in the ever-changing international market, at least until very recently. Their community-based employment practice also fosters potential labor-management contradictions in a more covert way. Formal employer-employee relations are frequently disguised as informal relationships between fellow villagers, neighbors, or even relatives or fictive kin. Yet in the same vein, the sheer size of local factories also limits the owners' access to formal financial sources and to institutional support from the government, as well as to a larger pool of prospective labor beyond immediate neighborhoods.

The implication of Taiwan's decentralized production system, however, is far reaching beyond the economic efficiency it has shown relating to the global economy. Also nurtured, if not engendered, in this production system was a sense of optimism and understanding of reality that both young Taiwanese men and women possessed while pursuing upward social mobility. The phrase "black-hand becoming boss" (*hei shou pien t'ou chia* [黑手變頭家]) (Shieh 1989) evokes an image familiar to Taiwanese of a mechanic, whose hands were constantly dirty and greasy from working with machines, who one day owned a factory and became a boss. Although referring to a male subject, it speaks to the widely shared belief that, in spite of one's humble background, as long as one worked hard and persistently, one would eventually achieve the dream of success. This dream was in the past substantiated by the rapid expansion of Taiwan's export-oriented industry, yet it has become increasingly difficult to realize under the current economic conditions. As a result, what has been shattered is more than a chance to get rich, but also the cultural concept of fair reward for fair work, and on the personal level, a sense of purpose in life as well as the confidence in one's ability to accomplish.

Ascent: The Historical Roots

Homei has a long record of textile manufacturing within the context of Taiwan's short history of industrialization. Since the end of the Japanese colonization, Homei has been known for its weaving production. Nevertheless, none of the local residents I came to know seemed able to recount the birth of this local industry. Some speculated that it might be related to the straw-hat-weaving tradition in the coastal area of central Taiwan, where Homei is located. Straw-hat weaving was operated through a household production system, in which a middleman distributed raw materials to women in rural areas, and collected and resold the finished hats to retail shops. Cloth weaving was discouraged under the Japanese rule. In the economic blueprint of the Japanese Empire, Taiwan was designated to be the supplier of foodstuff (mainly rice and sugar) and recipient of industrial commodities from the colonial metropole. Textile manufacturing, along with some other light industries, was only developed after the Japanese military launched its invasion in Southeast Asia and needed an intermediary base for military supplies.

Nonetheless, Taiwan remained largely an agricultural society, and individual households were not allowed to weave. As a result, the local production in Homei was very small, and usually done in secrecy. Women worked on their wooden hand looms alone at home. They also had to sell their products clandestinely. Many old people described those days as a mixture of harshness and adventurousness. It was usually women, the less likely legal offenders in the eyes of law enforcement, who were selling the homemade fabric. They used the cloth to carry their children on the back, so that they could sell it in public without being noticed.

The weaving technology during this initial period was primitive. Also, it was very difficult to get cotton, the raw material needed for weaving, near the end of the Second World War. Women in Homei had to draw yarn from old quilts or hand gloves on a simple, hand-operated spinning device. Owing to the simplicity of the technology, the range of product was limited; cotton quilts, fishing nets, and foot-binding strips were some of the major items. The width of the cloth was narrow as well.

The weaving industry in Homei further developed upon the end of World War II. Beginning with the cotton threads and foot-binding strips, people in Homei gradually improved their technology and learned to produce cloth wider in size as well as for more diverse uses. But the technology remained rudimentary, and the production speed was slow. Ironically, weavers in Homei were benefiting from their low productivity. The short supply of cloth made their product scarce and therefore highly valuable. This was particularly true in the first few years of the postwar era. After the war was over, when most of the population on the island was suffering from a severe shortage of almost every item of daily goods, many people in Homei were enjoying a lucrative profit from weaving. The elderly in town remember those glorious days. With a tint of exaggeration, many of them liked to say that at the end of a day, clerks from cloth stores in nearby cities would rush in, cut off the cloth from the loom, and rush out to sell. Sometimes the cloth was only several inches long, i.e., too short to have any great use, but the demand was so pressing that cloth dealers were craving for material of any length. "Homei fabric" (和美織仔) became famous not only in central Taiwan but also in Taipei's Ti-hua cloth market, the largest fabric wholesale and retail center on Taiwan.

The ban against private textile manufacturing was lifted following the defeat of the Japanese, when Taiwan was ceded to the Chinese government led by the KMT. As the Homei people had already had substantial experience in weaving, as soon as the political circumstances allowed, many of them established workshops at home and began to hire hands to carry out the weaving activity. The technology remained simple and therefore was easy to acquire; so was the capital for setting up a workshop. Small workshops were mushrooming.

It did not take long before downtown Homei, Yueh-mei, and a few other villages turned into industrial zones. Workshop runners assembled their own machines, and set up workstations in spare rooms, storage areas, or even corners in the house. In order to meet the need for labor, in addition to those available for hiring in downtown Homei, weavers and helpers were also drawn in from surrounding villages, where agriculture (and sometimes fishing) prevailed as the major means of subsistence.

Despite the fact that a rudimentary industrialization was underway, the problem of getting cotton supplies faced by early weavers continued to be an obstacle for the emerging entrepreneurship in postwar Homei. Taiwan did not grow cotton, which had to be imported from elsewhere. Before the Chinese Civil War broke out on Mainland China, textile producers in Taiwan were able to obtain cotton supplied from the Mainland. However, after the KMT was defeated by the Chinese Communist Party and driven to Taiwan in 1949, the trading ties between the two sides of the Taiwan Strait were cut off, and Taiwan had to rely on foreign sources for industrial raw materials. At that time Taiwan was still recovering from its wartime damage. It possessed little foreign reserves to spend on the cotton imports.

The withdrawal of the KMT was a mixed blessing for Homei's manufacturers. Although the lack of raw materials impeded their operations, the influx of more than one million expatriates from China (mostly military personnel and civil servants) also made the development of Taiwan's textile industry the KMT's first priority in order to clothe these people. This generated promising business opportunities. Yet, also retreating with the KMT government were Shanghai textile producers and their more advanced production equipments (more of the former Mainland textile industrialists moved their assets to Hong Kong instead of Taiwan, however, which facilitated the inception of Hong Kong's post-WWII industrialization). The Shanghai industrialists brought in large, power-geared plants, which had much higher productivity than that of manually operated workshops in Homei. Homei producers were too slow to compete with these newcomers. Subsequently, the Shanghai industrialists gradually took over most of the market share. Furthermore, many of these "Mainlanders"—a term frequently used in Taiwan to refer to those whose families migrated to Taiwan from Mainland China after the defeat of the KMT in the Chinese Civil War—had strong ties with the KMT. They were the ones, along with a few Taiwanese businessmen, whom the government was inclined to assist in economic hard times, when resources were scarce.

Liu (1992; also see Hsiao et al. 1992) points out that many of the early economic policies of the KMT government were designed to assure the dominance of party-related capital, which served as a crucial base for the party's control over the Taiwanese society. Garment and textile manufacturing commonly represent the first stage of industrialization in both advanced industrial and industrializing countries. With part of the

Mainland textile industry transferred to Taiwan, the KMT government seemed more than eager to institute policies in favor of the textile industry (Liu 1992:206–224). Mainland industrialists and a few of their Taiwanese counterparts benefited from the government's protection policies, such as a multiple exchange rate system, import and foreign exchange controls, hidden subsidies, and rationing and administrative pricing of certain goods and services. This included cotton from the United States aid, subsidized and sold sometimes at a price less than one-third of the regular market cost.

Development aid provided by the United States government played a crucial role in Taiwan's post-WWII industrialization. Beginning in 1950 huge amounts of the U.S. assistance flowed into Taiwan; and this continued until the late 1960s (S. Ho 1978:111). Cotton was one of the most important items in the aid; it constituted almost 90 percent of the cotton imported to Taiwan in the 1950s. As described previously, cotton was a costly raw material, and cloth was a high-priced merchandise. By granting manufacturers the right to purchase subsidized U.S.-aid cotton (and the yarn made of it), the KMT government contributed greatly to the early capital accumulation of Taiwan's textile industry.

Textile producers in Homei were first discriminated against when the cotton and yarn were rationed to private manufacturers based on the number of power looms they owned. As most of the Homei producers had only wooden hand looms, they were excluded from the purchase of these heavily subsidized raw materials, and, as a result, from the extremely lucrative textile business. This problem was solved only when local leaders mobilized a fair number of factory owners and organized a Taichung County Hand-loom Textile Business Association (台中縣手紡織同業公會) and petitioned the government for the purchasing rights. They were eventually approved, and were rationed cotton and yarn based on the number of hand looms in their possession (Homei chen kung suo 1989).[2]

In addition to the cheap cotton supply, the KMT government further assisted in the accumulation of capital in the textile industry with the implementation of its Entrusted Spinning and Weaving Policy (代紡代織制). Under this policy a limited number of textile producers signed a contract to spin for the government, and they were rewarded with surplus amounts of cotton that they then used to develop their own enterprises. The yarn processed for the government was resold to textile manufacturers, again, at a heavily subsidized price. Finally, the government guaranteed to buy back a certain percentage of the cloth made from the manufacturers at a favorable rate. Under this policy, the selected textile manufacturers obtained not only cotton or processing fees from the government, but also guarantee of market share for their final products. All these fortunate manufacturers needed in order to take part in this extremely profitable business was production equipment.

The original Entrusted Spinning and Weaving Policy and its various modifications lasted for less than a decade, when its side effects (such as corruption and a black market) were seen to outweigh its benefits (Kuo 1995:93). Although only a small number of factories in Homei were directly covered by this policy, a larger population in town benefited indirectly. Some factory owners/producers were granted the rationing right but no longer produced cloth themselves. They sold the rationed cotton to other producers at a higher rate and made money from the price difference. Some others gained the rationing right with borrowed looms that belonged to their neighbors. One of the producers from a village well known for its residents' defiant spirit in the Homei area became rather excited when he recited their tricks to me. He said,

> Not everyone who got the purchasing permit had looms. We borrowed the machines from one another in order to get the permit. The government sent representatives around to count the number of looms each of us had. We all knew in advance of the arrival dates of the government representatives. On the day before they came, let's say, to your place, all of us would move our looms to yours for them to count. When the representatives went to another person's house, we moved the machines to another house, too. We moved the looms around, following the schedule of the government representatives. Many of us got a share in this way.

> My father always sent me to grocery stores to fetch sodas, so that we could treat the government representatives when they came. Sodas were very expensive in those days, and it was really a big deal to treat someone with sodas. But my father's effort was paid off. I figured that roughly fifty factories in my village got the purchasing permit, but probably only ten of us were really in the business.

The people who were not in the textile business but obtained the purchasing permit made a fortune by reselling the cotton to their fellow villagers. Those who had to purchase cotton or yarn from their neighbors were still able to make a profit because of the great need for cloth in the domestic market. Indeed, the impact of the KMT government's subsidizing policy on the local capital accumulation had been so overwhelming that even today residents in Homei continue to taunt someone who gets rich too quickly and unexpectedly as one "receiving U.S. Aid" (Huang 2000:46–47).

In terms of technology, the eventual introduction of power looms raised the productivity of Homei's producers, which enabled them to compete with big companies (such as the Shanghai firms and their Taiwanese counterparts) for the domestic market. The advancement of machinery also allowed them to produce a wide variety of commodities.

The primary product of Homei's weaving industry at this period was plaid. There was hardly any division of labor in the industry. Each factory was an all-encompassing production unit, doing tasks that included yarn dyeing, cloth weaving, and even sales. They also designed their own patterns. In fact, the pride of the craft lay in the creativity of pattern design. Those who were talented and able to design novel patterns could not only succeed in the business but also win themselves local fame. In order to maintain their supremacy in the market, factory owners always guarded their designs carefully. Looms were kept from outsiders' view, and cloth was covered on the way to market. Nonetheless, there was not much marketing involved at this time. Producers in Homei mainly carried samples of their products from shop to shop. If some of the shop owners liked their samples—or thought they would sell—they might offer a space in their shop to display the products. Sometimes they also urged the producers to replicate popular items. Rather than buying out the finished fabric from textile producers, cloth shop owners often played a middleman's role. They provided their storefronts as a showroom for the products, and they received commissions based on the quantity sold. It was usually the textile producers, not cloth shop owners, who were held accountable for the unsold fabric; they had to bear most of the business risk. In spite of the widely spread popularity of Homei fabric, very few local producers seemed to realize their own potential of becoming wholesalers or marketers. Most of them remained content with their role as successful producers and stopped short of developing marketing skills.

In a time of very low level of mechanization—i.e., the looms were largely power-geared, but the other tasks still needed to be done manually—the labor of weaving was minute and complicated, and required both patience and dexterity. With or without hired hands, family members of factory owners in Homei were deeply involved in the production. Although there was no strict sexual division of labor, men usually took care of the dyeing procedures, which required physical strength to stir the pot and hang dry the dyed yarns, as well as starching. They were also in charge of the mechanical details, such as pattern design, machine adjustment (to fit different designs), and repair and

**Table 2.1
Labor Force Participation Rate in Taiwan
by Sex (%)**

Average of Year	Total	Male	Female
1966	57.5	81.5	32.6
1971	57.1	78.4	35.4
1976	57.5	77.1	37.6
1981	57.8	76.8	38.8
1986	60.4	75.2	45.5
1991	59.1	73.8	44.4
1996	58.4	71.1	45.8
2001	57.2	68.5	46.1

Source: Adapted from DGBAS (2002).

maintenance. They were often the sales and public representatives as well. Women washed chemicals off dyed yarns, did preparation work such as warping and drafting, and handled weaving looms. They were also responsible for household chores and cooked for employees if there were any. Despite the fact that textile manufacturing gradually dominated the local economic life, most of the factory owners who had land continued to farm. There was always more work than anyone could possibly finish. Family members were fully utilized. No one's labor went wasted.

The prosperity brought about by the textile industry not only enriched factory owners, but also brought in regular and substantial incomes to those farming families whose children were able to get a job in textile factories. As the weaving industry underwent rapid growth, increasing numbers of young people were hired to carry out the production (Table 2.1). Girls were hired to tend looms. Young men usually worked as apprentices. In the beginning they mainly did heavy labor, but they would eventually learn to maintain, adjust, and repair looms and become skilled mechanics (i.e., 師傅工, the master workers). As plaid was the prevalent product, to become a skilled mechanic required one to learn to disassemble a small piece of cloth sample, comprehend its texture, and assemble the loom accordingly to replicate the pattern design—a rather complex task requiring some imagination.

The impact of this new wave of employment was far-reaching. Along with the regular income brought home by the young generation was an improved material life, repayment of debt owed from previous poor farming seasons, and ultimately a surplus for savings. Past literature has pointed out in the macroeconomic level the important contribution of private domestic savings to Taiwan's postwar economic development, which financed most of the industrial investment in the private sector nationwide (S. Ho 1978). In Homei the accumulation and formation of capital occurred not only in factory owners' but also in workers' families, albeit in different scales. It was the savings collected from young workers' wages (both boys' and girls') over time that became the primary asset at a time when sons in a family grew up and were about to have a career. Many young men in Homei worked in textile factories and acquired mechanical knowledge. Most of them opened up small weaving factories, as they pursued a career of their own. Wives of these small factory owners—many of whom were weavers before they got married—became their husbands' most important partners. Their know-how on the shop floor assured a smooth flow of production as well as an efficient management of the workforce. In fact, as a close working relationship and seamless cooperation between a husband and a wife were often the first key to one's success, many ambitious mechanics were known to actively pursue young, capable, and hard-working weavers in their factories for wives.

Peak: Little Dragon Flying High

Multiplying rapidly, small factories in Homei did not merely depend on the owner's will or skill for success. Ultimately it was the expansion of Taiwan's export-oriented economy that brought in wealth and prosperity to people in Taiwan and especially residents in Homei.

Taiwan's import substitution industrialization did not last long. The demand of the domestic market was quickly saturated in the late 1950s. In order to sustain further economic growth, it became both a necessity and an inevitability to turn to export-oriented production. Whether it was the pressure of the U.S. government or the foresight of Taiwan's own Western-educated technocrats that compelled the Taiwan government to initiate its export-oriented industrialization (EOI) campaign has been a heatedly debated subject, of which a full discussion is beyond the scope of this book. I am inclined to believe, however, that the success of Taiwan's EOI can be attributed only in part to the "liberalization" of Taiwan's macroeconomic policy in the late 1950s. This is mainly illustrated by the difficulty in identifying a particular set of industrial policies as the underlying cause of Taiwan's rapid economic growth (Aberbach et al. 1994).[3] Rather, it is the link with the global economy that I think is crucial to Taiwan's success.

Taiwan's export expansion runs parallel to the transformation in global capitalism after the 1960s, namely "flexible accumulation," i.e., a fundamental transformation in the dominant form of capital accumulation from one based on mass production to one based on the quick turnover of capital (Harvey 1989). The economic restructuring in advanced capitalist countries and the relocation of manufacturing production from these countries to other parts of the world facilitated Taiwan's EOI. In the case of the textile industry, Taiwan first benefited from Japan, when the latter was experiencing an overproduction of synthetic fiber and a rapid rise of production costs. Japan also faced growing protectionism from the United States and needed to get around this by exporting its textile industry overseas. To do so, Japanese businessmen first sold the synthetic fiber to Taiwanese producers in the late 1950s and later brought in orders for garments made of such material for them to sell in the U.S. market (Lin 1994). From then on textile manufacturers in Taiwan acquired the technology to produce fabric from synthetic fiber. Textile production increased rapidly over the course of the 1960s, and as a result, textile gradually became Taiwan's single largest product for export (Rubinstein 1999).

Taiwan's textile industry was moved further forward by U.S. retailers who were looking for cheap apparel to sell in their domestic market starting from the 1960s (Cheng and Gereffi 1994; Gereffi and Pan 1994). The relation between the garment and textile industry is evidence of backward linkage, that is, when a downstream industry (e.g., garment) is growing, it will stimulate its upper-stream industries (e.g., textile) to grow as well. When Taiwan's garment industry was booming, the demand for yarn and fabric increased, and this in turn stimulated the domestic spinning and weaving industries. At the local level, producers in Homei experienced a tremendous transformation at this juncture. New economic opportunities were brought in not only from Taiwan's fast-growing garment industry, but also from a nearby village that specialized in manufacturing umbrellas, which had a great impact on the regional development of the Homei area. This nearby village was once called "the Umbrella Empire," and it reportedly produced one-third of the world's umbrellas at its peak (Huang 2000:56–59; Skoggard 1996). Synthetic fabric was in great need as "the Empire" expanded, and to save the transportation cost, most of it came from Homei.

Both garment and umbrellas, as well as other textile-related industries, required specified manufacturing items. The standardization of cloth dramatically changed the face of Homei's textile industry. There was no more need for great imagination or talented craftspeople, or to steal ideas from others. The plentiful supply of standardized orders from overseas assured each producer a profit. It also allowed a certain degree of mass production or even overproduction. Several local producers told me that they used to have the luxury of making as much cloth as possible but not having to worry about selling it. There were always buyers with an urgent need or offering a better price.

The standardization of commodities also entailed a different kind of, if not simpler, technological know-how from the plaid period. A mechanic no longer needed to master the knowledge of how to fabricate various designs but focused on merely one single product. This was often referred to as the "Sixty-eight sixty-eight" era by local producers, named after the specification of the particular item produced at that time. The pride procured from one's creativity disappeared, and the market turned to mass production instead of craftsmanship. This transformation was a difficult time particularly for those who were highly successful in the domestic production of plaid cloth. It was not uncommon for me to hear remorse for the old days. Mrs. Tsai's husband (Mrs. Tsai accompanied me to Yueh-mei on my first visit), whose family made beautiful and originally designed plaid but failed to adjust to the later changes, often expressed his sorrow for the loss of his father's artisan identity. "My father used to say, 'Look at all these ugly and plain-looking cloths. I can't imagine anyone buying it. What are they going to use it for?'" As a consequence, he stopped short of seeing changes in the larger economic processes, which eventually cost him the momentum to adapt to the new opportunity.

Textile manufacturers also lost their control over the destiny of their final products. Unlike the plaid epoch, when producers designed their own patterns and were aware of the application of their fabric, producers in Homei who manufactured for the international market no longer had knowledge about the use of their products. Even though the sentiment of losing control ran most strongly among old, highly skilled craftsmen like Mr. Tsai's father, many producers in Homei shared the unanswered question about the fabric they were making. "We don't know for whom we are producing, where the cloths will go, or what will be made from them. Most of the time we don't bother to ask, either. We just produce, produce, and produce," so I was repeatedly told during the course of my research.

The effect of the booming textile industry was multifold. First of all, existing factories were expanding. Owners could afford to purchase more machines (power-geared, of course), and they would hire more workers. As the demand for workers increased, employers gradually exhausted the local labor supply. They had to go to farther places and more rural areas to look for potential employees. Second, as the production scale

**Table 2.2
Educational Attainment of Civilian Population
Aged 15 and Over in Taiwan (%)**

Average of Year	Total	Primary & Below	Junior High	Senior High & Vocational	Junior College & Above
1976	100.0	60.5	14.8	17.7	7.0
1981	100.0	52.1	16.6	21.6	9.8
1986	100.0	44.5	17.4	26.3	11.7
1991	100.0	37.4	17.8	29.9	14.8
1996	100.0	30.7	17.3	32.8	19.2
2001	100.0	25.5	16.3	33.7	24.5

Source: Adapted from DGBAS (2002).

was enlarged, so was the number of mechanics. As stated previously, many of these skilled workers eventually quit their jobs and established their own operations. The prosperity of the industry frequently ensured their success, which further raised younger workers' expectation of becoming entrepreneurs in the future. The textile industry in Homei reached its peak in the early 1980s. At its heyday there were more than 600 factories in town, as estimated by local observers.[4]

Concomitant with this thriving entrepreneurship was a changing labor market. Weaving is primarily a woman's job. Female workers are hired to tend looms. If the widespread poverty in the countryside in the 50s and 60s led to a demand-sided labor market, the situation was turned after the rural economic conditions improved. While there was an increasing demand for laborers, fewer young people (young women in particular) were available for hiring (Tables 2.2 and 2.3). Most of the farming families were better off. They did not need to rush their daughters to work following their graduation from elementary school. Also, parents were more accepting of the value of women's education. As a result, more girls were allowed to go to secondary schools—an issue that I will come back to later. Factory owners in Homei began experiencing a labor shortage as early as the 1980s.

One of the distinctive traits of Taiwan's postwar industrialization was its dominance by small- and medium-sized enterprises (*chung hsiao ch'i yen* [中小企業]; hereafter, SMEs) (Table 2.4).[5] The textile industry in Homei was no exception. The majority of the local factories were small (i.e., with an ownership of 100 to 200 looms), and run by individual families. Furthermore, many of these operations emerged

Table 2.3
Opportunity of Education in Taiwan by Sex (%)

School Year	Secondary Education* (Age 12–17)			Higher Education** (Age 18–21)		
	Total	Male	Female	Total	Male	Female
1976	73.6	77.6	69.3	15.7	19.3	11.9
1981	82.5	82.6	82.5	18.7	20.8	16.6
1986	92.2	90.9	93.6	25.2	26.7	23.6
1991	95.4	93.6	97.3	37.9	38.1	37.7
1996	95.8	94.1	97.6	47.7	45.7	49.8
1999	99.6	98.3	101.0	61.0	57.8	64.4
2000	99.2	98.1	100.5	68.4	65.7	71.3
2001	98.3	98.3	100.6	77.1	74.5	79.9

Source: Adapted from DGBAS (2002).
*The numerator equals the number of students attending junior and senior high schools (including night schools, special-aid schools, and schools of continuing education) and the first three years of five-year junior colleges. The denominator equals the number of people aged 12 to 17 at the end of the year in question.
**The numerator equals the number of students attending junior colleges (including colleges of distance education and the last two years of five-year junior colleges) and four-year colleges and universities. The denominator equals the number of people aged 18 to 21 at the end of the year in question.

Table 2.4
Percentage of Small- and Medium-scale Businesses in Taiwan, 1961–1991

Year	% of Businesses*	% of Value Produced*	% of Employees*	Average No. of Employees
1961	99.57	—**	64.28	5.98
1966	99.28	—**	57.30	7.04
1971	99.96	37.09	52.52	8.72
1976	98.90	32.27	53.00	8.79
1986	99.00	34.46	57.89	8.49
1991	99.24	41.23	63.82	7.94

Source: Adapted from Chou and Lin (1999:35).
*Percentage of national total.
**Data not available.

spontaneously without government planning and regulation. They were not registered and thus unlicensed. Needless to say, they were excluded from formal channels, such as banks or cooperatives, for financial support, and had to depend on their family savings, or borrowing from relatives, friends, or other informal sources, such as private loan associations or even usurers, for capital. Neither were they entitled to industry-use electricity, whose rate was subsidized by the government (Hu 1983, 1984). For those who did get a license from the Bureau of Industry, the situation was not necessarily better in terms of financial support. Very often they were denied a bank loan because of their small size and limited factory assets.

Yet, these small firms constitute the backbone of Taiwan's EOI, whose success is closely related to Taiwan's link with the global economy. Foreign buyers are primarily looking for cheap commodities. However, as the competition in their domestic as well as international market intensifies, they also ask for increasingly shorter turnaround time for the products. Taiwanese manufacturers have been highly effective at meeting these needs. They have been efficient and flexible, and very capable of maintaining quality at a given price, while ensuring reliable, on-time delivery (Gereffi and Pan 1994).

The efficiency and flexibility comes from a highly decentralized industrial system. On the top of the system are domestic trading companies and "center plants" (Hu 1983; Hsiung 1996), which directly trade with or receive orders from foreign customers. Beneath the trading companies and center plants are layers of subcontracting firms in various sizes and of different technological levels, which produce different components for specific products. Among subcontracting firms there are also vertical and horizontal relations of cooperation. A center plant usually establishes relations with several subcontracting firms and vice versa. There are rarely legal bindings between center plants and subcontracting firms. Their relationship ceases whenever one side decides to terminate it.

The vast number of subcontracting firms and the multiplicity of their interdependence sustain the stability of this industrial system. It also forms a cushion particularly for those plants on the top to fall back on during periods of economic recession. The lower a factory is situated in the subcontracting hierarchy, the more vulnerable it is in economic downtimes. On the occasions when foreign orders are sharply reduced, center factories may stop providing their subcontracting firms with work in order to retain a full production schedule in their own factories (Hu 1983:403). The ferocious competition among small subcontractors then forces them to cope with the demand of center plants, which are themselves constrained by their unequal relationship with foreign buyers. In fact, Taiwanese subcontractors constantly have to reduce their production cost and adjust their production organization to comply with increasingly stringent trading terms.

Textile manufacturers in Homei were at the bottom of the subcontracting system in their industry. The primary product of their operations was gray cloth (白胚布), likely the most rudimentary product in the textile industry that requires further processing where the higher profit lies. However, the low technological level also lowered the financial barrier for starters. No expensive machines were needed for the operation. Many of the upcoming entrepreneurs bought secondhand looms, sometimes even from their former employers. They obtained orders through the connections made in previous laboring years; and again, some became subcontractors of their former employers.[6]

Mostly acquiring their knowledge from hands-on experience, the majority of small factory owners lacked formal technical education or education in engineering, nor were they equipped with skills in foreign languages or international trade. Although this situation might have improved, as an increasing number of young men attended vocational high school or beyond—corresponding to the overall improvement in educational attainment at the societal level—through which they acquired formal technical training, many of them still depended on indirect sources for business. What they usually did in order to secure a profit was, on the one hand, to cultivate their relations with the "upper hands" (上手, those from whom one receives subcontracts), and on the other, to maximize their own productivity on the shop floor. To accomplish this, further subcontracting—or informalization—was practiced.

Before a spool of fiber is ready for weaving, many preliminary tasks need to be done. To save cost as well as to increase efficiency, it had become a common practice in Homei for different firms or individuals to specialize in different tasks and provide services to fellow producers. In order to retain orders in local hands, it was also a fairly common practice among Homei's producers to give away business to acquaintances, when the orders received exceed one's own production capacity, or to come to a friend's rescue, when he could not finish orders on time. Many of these transactions, once again, were done without a formal, written contract but based on consent derived from personal trust or past experience of collaboration. One of the local manufacturers thus proudly claimed to me during our interview that textile producers in Homei were the most cooperative and noble businessmen he had ever seen.

Descent: The Current Predicament

Textile production used to be the leading industry in Taiwan's export economy, but it has declined rapidly since the late 1980s and has become a sunset industry. Several factors account for this change. In addition to the volatile social milieu fostered by the political democratization discussed in the previous chapter, the larger socioeconomic environment of Taiwan had also changed. First of all, Taiwan was turning from the Republic of China (ROC) into a "Republic of Casino" (also ROC), as the domestic and international media mockingly called it after the country's people fervently participated in various forms of money games or investment due to their possession of overgrown yet underutilized capital. The stagnation of the international market in the mid-1980s discouraged Taiwanese manufacturers from further investment and expansion. Yet, the national savings rate[7] as well as Taiwan's foreign reserves[8] remained high. With an excessive amount of savings but limited channels to invest, a huge sum of this money was channeled into the recently thriving stock market and a sprouting real estate market (Ch'ai and Hsieh 1988; Yu 1993). As a result, Taiwan's stock index grew from several hundred points to more than twelve thousand points in a short number of years, and the price of housing and land soared many times of that prior to the mid-1980s.

Although the stock market fever cooled down, as the stock index returned to a few thousand points after the government's intervention in the early 1990s, at its peak it was indeed "an exercise of the whole nation" (*ch'uan min yun tung* [全民運動]). Regardless of their age, sex, educational background, occupation, socioeconomic status, or previous history in financial investment, many Taiwanese who had spare money in their hands were lured by the high and quick return to put their money in the stock market. Lounges of investment companies also became a popular place to hang out. People of different ages and socioeconomic backgrounds—including old retirees who had much time to kill, young and middle-aged people who quit their previous jobs to become full-time stock investors, or housewives on their way to or back from grocery shopping—gathered in front of the wall of monitors to watch the change in stock prices as well as to chat and exchange information with fellow investors. To many of them, stock market investment was not only a means for swift cash gain, but it also presented an exciting and adventurous diversion from their daily drudgery.

For Taiwanese who were short of money to invest in stocks, there were other ways to seek a quick return in Taiwan's overheated money market. Ta-chia-lo (大家樂)—literally "everyone enjoys" and an illegal form of lottery—was the best known among them. Although illegal, Ta-chia-lo was also a phenomenal "exercise of the whole nation" (as it was mockingly called by Taiwan's news media and social pundits) and attracted an even larger population than the stock market. Basing its winning numbers on those of the government-run lottery, Ta-chia-lo provided much more flexible rules of playing and thus a much better chance of winning. Furthermore, it created a social atmosphere of ferment. Combining practices of Taiwanese folk religions, people who bet on Ta-chia-lo often sought inspiration or instructions for winning numbers from every possible supernatural source, including gods who uphold traditional reverence, ghosts known for their godly power, the mentally ill or deranged who were perceived as potential mediums of spirits, or any likely signs presented by unusual events or incidents (Huang 2000:90–93; Weller 1994:148–153, 1998:93). In some occasions, particularly on the days before the winning numbers were announced, people were known to shift their attention from work to Ta-chia-lo, which irritated their employers.

This wave of capital games and investment zeal had a multifaceted impact on Taiwanese society. Industrial producers were directly affected in two important ways. First, the price of land skyrocketed beyond the means of many manufacturers to purchase or rent. This was particularly true in the areas near big cities, which as a result either compelled preexistent landowners/manufacturers to convert their land into commercial or real estate ends, or pushed upcoming entrepreneurs/producers to more remote regions to establish new production facilities. To begin a new business or to expand old ones became increasingly difficult under these circumstances. Second, the volatile money market in the late 1980s provided Taiwanese with new ways of seeking financial profit other than saving one's salary. Whether or not these new opportunities corrupted the Taiwanese work ethic and encouraged the development of a gambler's mentality, as the media and social pundits liked to claim at the time, were questions yet to be answered. Nonetheless, the newly awakened awareness of economic opportunities—mainly making money through means other than industrial manufacturing or from working for someone else for certain hours with a certain wage—did in some ways change the Taiwanese' understanding and imagination of moneymaking or management. In the long run this may lead to the development of a mature financial market within which Taiwanese have different mechanisms to invest their money. However, for a short period of time, in the middle of the fervor, some people were known to quit their jobs or become aloof about their daily obligations in order to take full advan-

Table 2.5
Fertility Rate of Taiwanese Women of Childbearing Age (Age 15–49) (per thousand)

Year	Total Fertility Rate	Net Reproduction Rate
1966	4,815	2,197.5
1971	3,705	1,715.4
1976	3,075	1,439.4
1981	2,455	1,148.2
1986	1,680	784.1
1991	1,720	799.8
1996	1,760	826.9
2001	1,400	660.8

Source: Adapted from DGBAS (2002).

tage of speculating opportunities. Employers in the industrial sector complained about the declining morale and productivity of their workers. Some of the industrial employers also began to cry about the shortage of dedicated employees.

Taiwanese manufacturers were further affected by a demographic change in the wage labor market. As mentioned earlier, a major transformation of the labor market was underway when the rural economic conditions improved and workers' families were better off. Parents no longer pushed their daughters to work at an early age. More and more young girls were able to continue their education to junior high school and beyond (Chou, Clark, & Clark 1990) (Table 2.3).[9] Subsequently, they either stayed in school longer and took factory jobs later or did not take a factory job at all. Moreover, the birth rate in Taiwan has rapidly declined since the 1960s (Table 2.5). As a consequence, there has been a decrease in the population between age twenty and twenty-four since 1984, which further aggravated the issue of short labor supply for labor-intensive industries like textile (Lin 1994:21).

As a result of the economic expansion in the past four decades, Taiwan is no longer a blue-collar society. In 1987 the industrial sector reached its peak when 35 percent of the working population had manufacturing-related jobs. After that the share of the industrial sector gradually declined. At the same time, the proportion of the workforce in the service sector increased substantially. By the end of 1995, half of the working population held jobs in the service sector (Council of Labor Affairs 1995) (Table 2.6). Simultaneously, a large number of young women who entered the wage labor market for the first time chose to

Table 2.6
Labor Force Participation in Taiwan by Sector, 1952–1998 (%)

Year	Primary	Secondary	Manufacturing	Tertiary
1952	56.1	16.9	12.4	27.0
1955	23.6	18.0	13.2	28.4
1960	50.2	20.5	14.8	29.3
1965	46.5	22.3	16.3	31.2
1970	36.7	28.0	20.9	35.3
1975	30.4	34.9	27.5	34.7
1980	19.5	42.5	32.9	38.0
1985	17.5	41.6	33.7	41.0
1990	12.8	40.8	32.0	46.3
1995	10.6	38.7	27.1	50.7
1998	8.9	37.9	28.1	53.2

Source: Adapted from Chou and Lin (1999:163).

work in the booming service sector instead of manufacturing industries. As the incoming labor force was drawn to white-collar jobs in the service sector, industrial producers suffered from both the lack of workers and, as a result, rising industrial wages.

Internationally, the huge trade surplus generated by Taiwan's successful export economy also created tremendous pressure for the appreciation of the New Taiwan (NT) dollar. In particular, the U.S. government had pushed Taiwan to appreciate its currency in order to reduce the American foreign trade deficit (Schive 1992). The exchange rate for the NT dollar vis-à-vis the US dollar plunged from forty in 1985 to twenty-six in 1990, a 42 percent and the highest percentage of increase among major Asian currencies during that period (Schive 1995:13). The rapid appreciation of the NT dollar forced labor and other production costs, calculated in US dollars, to rise dramatically. This severely impeded Taiwanese manufacturers' export capability, while they were facing more competition from industrial producers in Southeast Asia and China (Table 2.7).

Challenges precipitated by the domestic sociopolitical and international economic transformation fostered Taiwanese manufacturers' need to restructure their own industrial production system. Throughout the 1980s many Taiwanese manufacturers relocated production by investing first in Southeast Asia and later in China, mainly in search of cheap labor, inexpensive land, and raw materials (Bonacich et al. 1994; Chang and Chang 1992; Klein 1992). The capital flight was initiated by SMEs. They

Table 2.7
Average Hourly Wage in Selected Asian Countries (in US dollars)

Name of Country	Average Hourly Wage
Taiwan	$5.10
Hong Kong	$4.51
South Korea	$4.18
Thailand	$1.06
Philippines	$0.62
Indonesia	$0.34
China	$0.28

Source: Adapted from the Smithsonian Institute (1999).

were the backbone of Taiwan's export economy and major producers of downstream commodities, which made them the most vulnerable to the recent political and economic changes in Taiwan. Their move, however, triggered a backward linkage of capital outflow. Large enterprises of upper-stream industries who provided materials to these low-end producers followed suit, when a significant number of SMEs set up production overseas and created a need in their host countries, or when the host countries became rich enough to develop a domestic market for consumer commodities (Wang 1995:226).

Offshore investment was further prompted by the Taiwan government's fiscal liberalization measures in 1987, which removed almost all foreign-exchange controls except for regulations on remittances to Taiwan with the intention to prevent the influx of foreign hot money (Schive 1995:12–14). By the end of 1997, the total amount of Taiwanese investment in Southeast Asia mounted to US$36 billion.[10] Taiwan also became the second largest foreign direct investor in Southeast Asia, trailing Japan. The significant phenomenon of offshore investment has also changed the pattern and contents of Taiwan's own export-led manufacturing. First, it has become a common practice among Taiwanese manufacturers who invest overseas to split their production in parts and, according to the technology involved, to move their least competitive production units overseas while retaining the high-tech parts at home. Their remaining production in Taiwan often serves as a center for research and development. Second, Taiwanese businessmen usually maintain control over their preexisting trade networks. They receive orders through trading offices in Taiwan and then redirect the production to a third site. Third, in relation to the first two practices, machinery, raw materials (e.g., synthetic fiber), and intermediate goods have become important items on Taiwan's export list, to support their compatriots' offshore production. Known as "triangle manufacturing" (Gereffi and Pan 1994), these items are then used to produce final commodities for the markets of capitalist advanced countries, particularly the United States. This has helped Taiwan to decrease its export of light consumer products to the United States and thus relieved some of the pressure on Taiwan by the U.S. government and American businesses to reach a trade balance. Over time, however, Taiwanese firms may increase their purchase of raw materials and intermediate goods from local suppliers in their host countries, as local industries become capable of providing these goods, a process of backward linkage analogous to Taiwan's own experience of industrial development.

Southeast Asian countries were initially the destination of Taiwanese offshore production investments in the 1980s. However, this began to change after Taiwan's governing KMT undertook a new approach toward its archenemy, the People's Republic of China. After forty years of separation since the end of the Chinese Civil War, Taiwanese citizens who came to the island after 1949 were allowed to visit their families on the Mainland in the late 1980s. Later, all Taiwanese with or without relatives on the Mainland were permitted to visit China for civilian activities, such as travel and tourism. However, this latter policy also paved the way for Taiwan's swift investment in the PRC during the 1990s. Since the 1987 removal of the ban on visits from Taiwan to China, Taiwanese investments in the People's Republic of China have increased significantly.

The preference for China over Southeast Asia as the site of overseas investment is perfectly understandable from economic perspectives, however disfavored by the Taiwan government due to political concerns. Given the continuous tension and hostility between Taiwan and China, and the Chinese government's unwillingness to give up its claim over Taiwan's sovereignty, Taiwan's growing economic interdependence with China emerges as not only an economic but also as a political issue and an issue of national security. These issues have been under intense discussion in Taiwan, as high-tech and capital-intensive industries began to follow their downstream SMEs to China, and when the potential business opportunity provided by the most populous market in the world lured many big Taiwanese companies to expand there.

To divert Taiwanese investors from their focus on China, yet not to discount the predicaments faced by industrial producers, the Taiwan government tried to advocate a South Bound policy (南向政策) in the late

1990s. That is, the government openly urged Taiwanese businessmen to go south and make investments in Southeast Asia, instead of going west to invest in China. Behind this economic move there was a critical political plan. The Taiwan government was hoping that, by establishing strong and long-term economic ties with countries of the Association of Southeast Asian Nations (ASEAN), Taiwan would also win these countries' support and have a voice and influence in the region. Nevertheless, the government's attention was mainly centered on big enterprises. It retained a hands-off policy toward SMEs. Yet, the South Bound policy was never well received by large manufacturers who still saw China as the best site for investment and market expansion.

Similarly, for those Taiwanese SMEs that see Southeast Asia as too distant and alien and the supply line from Taiwan to the region too costly and unreliable, the geographical and cultural proximity of China appears to be an ideal alternative (Hsing 1998). Also, as Southeast Asian governments gradually reduced their incentive provisions, and the labor cost in those countries rose rapidly after a decade of economic growth, the region lost its original attraction to Taiwanese investors. Between 1990 and 1995, the direct investment from Taiwan to China had reached more than US$30 billion and amounted to 34 percent of Taiwan's overall outward investment, widely surpassing Taiwan's investment in any other parts of the world.[11] Taiwan is currently a major direct foreign investor in the PRC.

By the late 1980s many textile producers had closed down their plants in Taiwan and relocated production to China and Southeast Asia. In Homei, people often said, based on their impression, that more than half of the looms were removed from the production line in the early 1990s. Some of the loom owners rebuilt their plants overseas. Some others simply sold their machines to upcoming entrepreneurs in China and Southeast Asia, and reinvested their money in other businesses.

Plant closure was accompanied by a reorganization of the production system in the industry. One of the reorganizing strategies was to further informalize—or subdivide—the production process. Informalization has always been a distinctive characteristic of Taiwan's manufacturing industries, including textile. Lately, with the problem of labor shortage and an increasingly narrow margin of profit, producers in Homei put out almost all the work except weaving and machine repair and maintenance, as many of the owners were former mechanics. As a result, they formed an even more intricate network. By so doing, they split and reduced the production cost, and shared the uncertainty in a time of crisis.

Another strategy for survival that I observed was to upgrade the machinery. A small group of wealthy industrialists purchased new machines to increase their productivity, upgrade the quality of product, and save on the number of workers needed. Some sold their old machines and purchased a smaller number of new looms, which enabled them to produce new yet more sophisticated items for their newly found niche in the international market. As to the majority of small factory owners in town, they did not have the financial means to invest but just sold some of their looms and downsized the production scale to the extent that family members alone would make up for a sufficient workforce. The composition of the workforce has also changed. More and more married women are recruited to work. Many small firms even try to readjust their work schedule to accommodate the needs of "housewives," in the hope of attracting them to take a factory job.

The most dramatic change in Homei, resonating with the situation in the larger society, is the introduction of foreign workers (mainly from Thailand and the Philippines) to local industries. In order to alleviate the problem of labor shortage, the Taiwan government finally legalized the employment of foreign workers for some industries, including the textile industry, in the early 1990s. Yet, textile manufacturers in Homei, as their counterparts throughout the country, continue to complain that the quotas are too low, and the hiring procedures are too cumbersome, to meet their pressing needs. Those families who can neither find Taiwanese workers nor get the government's approval to hire foreign labor have to rely on family members more than ever before to make up for the missing workforce. However, as the younger generations have attained or are attaining higher education, and they have more alternatives other than working for their families, parents are losing control over their children's labor. They may desperately need cheap labor, but they can no longer count on the support of their children.

A Diminishing Black-Hand-Boss Dream

Coined to describe the economic pattern in the Asian Pacific region, the term "network capitalism" (Hefner 1998) speaks to the preference of doing business based on personal relationship and trust as well as the intricate web of social connections that facilitate this preference. In the Taiwan context, however, this should refer not only to the patronage and alliance among large multinational corporations in order for them to monopolize the market, but more significantly, the cooperation (and certainly competition) among the vast number of small industrial producers. Separately, they each specialize in one or a few steps of the production, but together, they form a highly flexible system in which they share both the profit and risk collectively. As a matter of fact, the SMEs and the decentralized production system that they form have been so important that their "chuan hsing"—轉型, literally "shift in form or style"—dominates much of Taiwan's public discussion. In resonance with the society's anxiety, the discussion of whether or not the SMEs are adequate to compete in today's increasingly high-tech, capital-intensive global economy has become one of the heatedly debated issues in Taiwan's academic circles (Chu and Chang 2001). Also frequently discussed is the question of how the SMEs can reinvent themselves in order to find a new niche in the international market (C. H. Chen 1999).

While much of the scholarly work focuses on the SMEs' economic relevance, here I choose to address issues related to the cultural ethos. Two issues are especially critical. First and foremost, the family has to be taken into account in order to fully understand the SMEs. This is not only because family members constitute the chief and most effective labor force in the SMEs, but also because the family puts one's effort into context and gives meaning and significance to one's accomplishment (C. Y. Chen 2001). Drawing on the rhetorical question with which Harrell entitles his article, "Why do the Chinese Work So Hard?" (1985), they work hard for the security and prosperity of their families; and this devotion should apply squarely to all family members.

Whether or not this assumption speaks fairly to the mind and interests of every family member—women in particular—has been an important issue of contemporary feminist scholarship and is the central question of Chapter Five of this book. I will leave a systematic critique until then. For the purpose of the current discussion, it is necessary to point out that, under the Chinese patrilineal system, males are the primary beneficiaries of the fruit of a family's collective labor. Also, pertinent to the situation in Homei, it is a male subject that the term "black-hand boss" (*hei shou t'ou chia* [黑手頭家]) tries to describe, whereas his equally hard-working wife is referred to as the "boss's wife" (*t'ou chia niang* [頭家娘]). While I agree with Hsiung's (1996) critique that a boss's wife is sometimes coerced to work for her husband or her husband's family as cheap labor, and she is not given the amount of recognition that she deserves to have, I also accept Kao's (1999) argument that a boss's wife does not simply contribute her labor but also her ability to coordinate the routine on the shop floor and the life inside the factory; she also serves as the boss's council, and she is frequently his most intimate ally (Kao 1999). I also agree that being a "boss's wife" may give a woman the rare opportunity, again in the context of the Chinese patriliny, to prove herself by helping manage her husband's business (Kao 1999). Not to contradict myself, although the status of "boss's wife" is subsumed under that of the boss, it may only be natural from a married Taiwanese woman's perspective that she should join her husband's effort in creating a business. After all, their destinies are bound together, for a wife "is a member of her husband's family when she is alive and a ghost of his ancestral hall when she dies," goes a Chinese saying; his success certainly benefits her and the children they bear together. The success also glorifies the name of the husband's—thus also a wife's—family (Kao 1999:56–66). The dream of "black-hand becoming boss," therefore, covers the welfare of a large number of individuals, even though it is personified by a male figure. This leads us to the second issue, one at the societal level.

In recent decades, the rise of the decentralized production system, the specific pattern in which Taiwan is integrated with the global economic system, has made the black-hand-boss dream accessible to many Taiwanese. In Homei, this fact was driven home to me by the daily ritual of business card exchange, through which I was introduced to many *tung-shi-changs* (董事長) in the local textile industry. *Tung-shi-chang*, the Chinese equivalent of board director or chair of the board of trustees, does not always carry the power and authority granted to a board director in the English-speaking world. More often than not, it is a euphemism of *lao-pan* (老闆) or boss, regardless of the scale of his operation or the number of employees under his command. Sometimes, I was introduced to so many *tung-shi-changs* on the same occasion that some of them would get rather embarrassed and begin teasing themselves by telling me if a brick came loose and fell off from the roof in Homei, it would likely hit a pedestrian who was a *tung-shi-chang*. Yet, however sheepish one might feel about calling himself a *tung-shi-chang*, he surely enjoyed the glamour associated with the title and the vanity for the recognition of his ability and achievement.

The belief in the possibility of upward social mobility through one's own deeds has been so prevalent that Gates (1979) contends it helped to thwart the class formation and the development of class consciousness in Taiwanese society, as proletarian children from working-class families considered their laboring for others as only a transitory stage in their life cycle. Shieh (1992:209) further extends this line of work and argues that Taiwanese industrial producers have in fact prevented potential labor disputes from happening by deliberately encouraging this belief among their workers. Many of them, like those in Homei, also helped their employees to start their factories—often as a spin-off of their own operations—as a means to win their employees' support as well as to strengthen their own position in the decentralized production system they participated in. Together, Shieh (1992:209) contends, workers were tamed, because they forged a "manufacturing consent" with their employers.

I shall argue, however, that the manufacturing consent entails much more than the class relations on the shop floor. It should be considered as a manifestation of the cultural hegemony of prosperity based on the belief in equal opportunity and social mobility expressed in collective terms. Hegemony in this context is understood as a worldview and moral outlook, through which "one concept of reality is diffused throughout society in all its institutional and private manifestations, informing with its spirit all taste, morality, customs, religious and political principles, and all social relations, particularly in their intellectual and moral connotations" (G. Williams 1960:587). It is from here, I propose, that we can also begin to comprehend why the New New Generation moral discourse carried so much weight in the way the recent economic plight was understood. Similar to any other hegemonic discourse, the New New Generation moral discourse was a mixture of true and false statements (Smart 1997:405). Yet, it explained the difficulties faced by the SMEs in compliance with the cultural belief in self-realization through hard work as well as by placing the blame on someone else other than the current participants of the declining industrial sector. It thus helped to preserve the self-worthiness of small factory owners and their families who had labored hard for their hitherto success. In lieu of this, it also helped to fashion a solution that was within the economic capacity of—and thus favored by—small factory owners. We shall turn to these issues in the following chapter.

CHAPTER 3

The Waning of a Hard Work Ethic

It was a hot summer afternoon, and the weather was brutal. Mr. Lin, a foreman of Treasure Island, and I were chatting, standing by the side of a water fountain for cool air and to escape from the torturing heat of the sun. As usual, our conversation centered on the recent changes in the textile industry. A twenty-five-year veteran at Treasure Island, Mr. Lin observed the changes in the company almost from its founding days. "You have seen it yourself!" he said, in a very dismal voice,

> We can no longer find workers. People aren't interested in factory jobs anymore. The young generation nowadays prefers to work in the service sector where the work is easy and they can dress beautifully. Left in the factory is a polarized workforce: the old ones and those who are too young yet to know about the outside world. Chao Shou-po [the minister of the Council of Labor Affairs then] claimed that we are going to have a "Second Spring" [for Taiwan's export economy]—No way! It's impossible, I tell you.

Our conversation, as usual, ended with Mr. Lin's disparaging words. He was not optimistic about the future.

Mr. Lin was not alone in feeling a drastic decline in the textile industry. Many of his coworkers at Treasure Island and fellow inhabitants in Homei shared his view. Textile production had been the most important economic activity in town. Riding on the wings of Taiwan's fast-growing export economy, textile had earned the local residents a fair amount of wealth over the past few decades. Yet, the rapid changes in the industry since the late 1980s have generated a common sentiment of crisis among the town's population, albeit expressed in different words from those of Mr. Lin.

As discussed in the previous chapter, the recent restructuring has to be understood in the context of the global economy and Taiwan's relationship with it. Equally important is the distinctive production system built upon the specific historical, political, and cultural dynamics in Taiwanese society that shaped the parameter of strategies adopted by Taiwanese industrial producers. Nevertheless, in spite of the complexity of issues involved in Taiwan's recent economic changes, "labor shortage" was often singled out as one of the most crucial factors for this downturn. Moreover, the decline of workers' work ethic, as implied in Mr. Lin's words, was frequently taken as a cause of the labor shortage, and this belief pervaded the popular discourse.

This chapter focuses on the paradoxical nature of the claim of labor shortage. It examines the emerging New New Generation moral discourse particularly from the perspective of labor demand and capital accumulation. Taiwan's export-oriented industrialization has been dominated by small-scale producers and depended upon cheap labor, primarily young single women, for profits. However, due to the social-economic and demographic transformation in the society, young Taiwanese women are no longer available for factory work. As such, the claim of labor shortage spoke of the reality of the lack of the traditionally sought-for workforce. Yet, the claim of labor shortage was false, in the sense that there were other Taiwanese who were neither young nor single, but who were laid off because of plant closings or relocation and thereby in need of jobs. Therefore, I contend that the moral discourse has to be understood as a cultural manifestation of small producers confronting their recent predicaments. The narrative itself addressed an economic reality, but it certainly included manufacturers' own tactics and calculation for profit and survival. Largely excluded from formal financial sources, and lacking the capability to solve problems beyond their immediate production sites, small producers in Homei were left with very few options. A labor shortage and its alleged cause, attributed to the declining work ethic of young Taiwanese, thus provided small producers a legitimate reason to ask for help from the government (especially the permission to hire foreign workers), as they did not cause their problems but had only fallen victim to the corrupted moral values in Taiwanese society.

While acknowledging the hegemonic nature of the New New Generation moral discourse, I am also fully aware of the existence of the different interpretations of and opinions about the moral discourse. It is also the purpose of this chapter to explore these alternative readings. Although a hegemonic discourse is dominant by definition, it can never be totalizing or exclusive in practice (R. Williams 1977:113). It will never be a finished ideological formation, but will always be a contested process of domination and counterdominance. To remain hegemonic, therefore, a discourse has to be constantly defended, renewed, redefined, or modified. Ironically, it is also through the same process that new or new kinds of challenge, resistance, alteration, or limitation will be engendered, thereby perpetuating the very process of recreating the hegemonic discourse (R. Williams 1977:112).

To illustrate these points, I shall begin this chapter with the local (i.e., Homei) conceptualization of labor force participation and their assumed cause of the labor shortage. The second part of this chapter examines the changing attitude of workers and their families toward textile employment. This in turn affects labor-management relations in the workplace, which leads to the final part of this chapter that focuses on local producers' efforts to retain a sufficient workforce and their strategies to recruit new sources of labor.

Defining Labor Shortage

No matter how hard you have tried to upgrade your machinery and hence reduced the demand for labor, you still need workers. There is no automated factory in an absolute sense. You always need someone to keep an eye even on the most advanced machine on earth. (A factory owner moaned to me while discussing the issue of the labor shortage.)

An adequate labor supply is essential to realize the potential of surplus accumulation in an economy. It is important from the perspective of capital to maintain a steady supply of labor and to solve any problems caused by labor scarcity. However, far from a simple notion of scarcity of "cheap labor" or labor of any kind, we need to note that "specific tendencies within the capitalist system have generated specific types of labor scarcity," whereby "[any] situation in which the characteristics of the labor supply threaten existing or foreseeable levels of accumulation can be defined as one of labor scarcity" (Sassen-Koob 1984:177). It is from this theoretical postulation that I will start my discussion of the claim of labor shortage in current Taiwanese economy.

Working in textile factories used to be the first choice, and for a long time almost the only nonagricultural job, for women who wanted paid work in the Homei area. Large numbers of girls entered local textile factories upon their graduation from elementary or, for some in a later generation, junior high school. Working in a textile factory was considered to be virtuous and almost an inescapable destiny for nearly every young woman coming of age in the late 1960s throughout most of the 1980s. In many cases, particularly in earlier years, the wages of these working girls were the only regular and reliable income of their farming families.

However, a major change in the industrial labor market was underway, when the rural economic conditions improved and workers' families were better off. As fewer and fewer young women considered jobs in the textile industry as their first choice, and even fewer were willing to work in small factories, married women in their late thirties or early forties gradually became the dominant workforce in the local industry. Young single women were rarely seen in small firms—most of the workers in such places were married women. Even in a relatively big factory like Treasure Island, which employed 150 shop floor workers in the mid-1990s and was considered to be one of the largest companies in town, young single Taiwanese women made up only one-third of the workforce. Another one-third constituted married Taiwanese women, and the other one-third of the total workforce came from Thailand. This was a big change from just a few years ago. A manager in the company told me that only in the late 1980s and early 1990s there were nearly 500 employees, and among them, the ratio between unmarried and married women was eight to two. There were, of course, no foreign workers then.

For most of the textile producers and residents in Homei, "workers" referred to young, single women, especially girls in their teens and early twenties. Even when the labor force participation of middle-aged married women increased in local factories, this stereotype remained largely unchallenged. The aging of the workforce reflected the recent predicament of the textile industry. Many local manufacturers lamented that "the old are too old, and the young will not stay long," adding that when the old cohort eventually reached their age of retirement, their businesses would also be finished. "A fault in human supply" (*jen li tuan ts'eng* [人力斷層]), in their own words, had become a matter of life and death. Local producers reasoned that a steady supply of labor was the key to their success. In the past it was the continuous waves of elementary school graduates that vitalized the local labor force. They succeeded those who left upon marriage. Factory owners in Homei never expected women to stay on after they married. It was perceived as a natural move that women quit upon marriage.

The textile labor force in Homei had been successfully reproduced by this generational replacement until the recent change. In addition to the smaller pool of prospective young workers due to Taiwan's declined birth rate, local producers were further frustrated by the fact that young people who were expected to take factory jobs upon school graduation no longer chose to do so. As for those few who did come to work in factories, most of them were also going to vocational schools in the evening. For them, factory employment was only a temporary arrangement. Consequently, factory employers could count on their labor only for a few years, for they would most likely quit the factory job and move on to better things, as soon as they finished vocational high school education.

Yet it is important to note that, despite the fact that nearly everyone I talked to agreed on the trend of labor shortage, there appeared to be a generational difference in the reasons why there was a labor shortage. People aged over thirty-five who came of age before the 1980s often informed me that it was because young people these days were lazy. They said, "Young people like to play and enjoy themselves. They prefer to work in the service sector." To support the point, some of them pointed to the fact that many restaurants hired more people (as waiters and waitresses) than did factories. Young people took this as an old folks' bias, although they seldom tried to dissuade it. The older generation's conviction was best captured in a sarcastic remark made by a middleman from a trading company in Taipei, when he commented on my question of where young people had gone. Referring to the work schedule in the booming sector of KTVs,[1] pubs, and clubs that entertained late-night customers, where many of the young generation were employed, at two o'clock in the afternoon he said: "You want to know where the young people are? Go back to sleep now and come back to me after ten o'clock tonight. I will take you to where they are then." Expressed in his words were both his mockery of calling these service jobs "jobs" and the distaste he held for the lifestyle these young people allegedly had of sleeping in during the day, when they should be working industriously. His sentiment was widely shared by middle-aged factory owners who frequently criticized the youth for being fond of taking on jobs that were easy-going, high paid, with regular days off on weekends and national holidays, and which allowed them to dress beautifully. The society had lost its virtue of diligence, they lamented.

The laziness of the young people was in fact a message permeating Taiwan's popular discourse. The media—and the society—often referred to them as "the New New Generation" (*hsin hsin jen lei* [新新人類]). Compared to previous generations, they grew up in a fairly affluent environment, and they were largely exempted from the economic burden endured by children in Taiwanese families prior to their age. Portrayed in the media as carefree, self-centered, hedonistic, and consumption-oriented, this generation was perceived as a bunch of spoiled young kids eating up the fruit of Taiwan's hard-won industrialization. The degradation of their work ethic seemed to indicate an inevitable downfall of Taiwan's economy.

The economic success of Taiwan in the past was frequently attributed to the hard-working Taiwanese people, both in the popular discourse and among scholars at home and abroad (e.g., Berger and Hsiao 1988; Redding 1990; Tai 1989). This firm belief vis-à-vis the newly emerged New New Generation discourse thus provided small producers a strong moral ground to win support from the larger society. It also shifted the society's attention away from more urgent socioeconomic issues, such as the structural changes in Taiwan's economy, the exploitative nature of manufacturing jobs, and the reality and challenge Taiwan's small industries were facing in the global economy.

Furthermore, the New New Generation discourse ignored the fact that the employment trend of young people in a restaurant or a KTV rather than in a factory echoes the change in Taiwan's consumer culture engendered by its economic prosperity. The growth of wealth in the society generated an increasing demand for imported consumer goods, specialty shops, restaurants, and recreational facilities, including KTVs, clubs and bars, and bowling alleys, spawning an increase of youth employment in service and retail businesses. What was also true, but rarely mentioned by the factory owners in my research, was that many of them liked to patronize KTVs, restaurants, and night clubs for a moment of relaxation in the evening, socializing with fellow businessmen and exchanging information, with young waitresses serving them. They might spend a fortune in one night on such outing. This peculiar taste in entertainment among Taiwanese male businessmen helped to proliferate young women's employment in such places (Shen 2002).

Contested Discourses on the Shop Floor

On the shop floor the perception about different groups of workers had changed accordingly. Before the rise of the recent labor shortage, factory owners in Homei preferred to hire young girls. Married women were not welcomed in, and in practice excluded from, the local wage labor market. Young girls were said to be better workers, for they were not burdened with family responsibilities. Because they only needed to answer to themselves, it was said that young single women would not be distracted but concentrate thoroughly on their jobs. Married women, on the contrary, were burdened with endless chores. They had to cook, wash clothes, clean the house, and take care of their husbands, children, and often parents-in-law. They were said to be inattentive workers, because they were easily distracted by what happened in their families. They were more likely to take days off, when their children were ill or something in the family needed to be done. Worst of all for the employers in Taiwanese society, it was also married women's duty to prepare food and light incense on the numerous "bai-bai" (拜拜) occasions, including the days on the Taiwanese folk-religious calendar to worship various deities and the days individual families chose to pay respect to their ancestors. On those occasions, it was inevitable for married women to either take the whole day off, or at least, to come in late or go home early. Either situation would cause employers great annoyance and inconvenience.

However, as the demography of the local industrial labor force changed dramatically, so did the perceptions about married workers and their young single counterparts. Although all of their domestic duties remain, married women are no longer viewed as slack workers. Instead, they have become the model employees. It is now widely held by both local managers and workers that married women are much better workers than young single women. It is said that they work hard—and often work overtime—and rarely take days off. When they have to take days off in order to attend personal or family matters, they often voluntarily find time to make up for the hours they were absent. They are also said to be discreet, careful, and trustworthy. In comparison, young single workers nowadays are perceived as sloppy, inattentive, irresponsible, and easily distracted—ironically, some of these words were used less than a decade ago to describe married women in contrast to their hard-working, diligent young coworkers. Older people also like to refer to this upcoming generation as "having a good life" or "born with a good destiny" (*hao ming* [好命]), the meaning of which can be either benevolent or derogatory depending on the tone of the one who says it. These changes in language use reflect the tactics of employers in response to the issue of labor shortage, although there is some truth in it, given the difference in job performance of these two groups of workers.

Young workers whom I talked to knew all about the bad names applied to them. They had their own views, however. They did not see themselves as lazy, sloppy, or irresponsible. They simply had a more relaxed attitude toward work, and they spent more time to find pleasure in their lives. They commented that, in contrast to them, married women craved for money, and because of this, they haggled over task arrangements and line leaders' record of their production outputs. They said that married women were manipulative; they were difficult to work with.

The perception about jobs has also changed. Once seen as the ultimate job for young women in Homei, textile employment is now on the bottom of their preference list. Interestingly enough, in spite of their different positions on the issue of labor shortage, young and married workers as well as factory owners all told me bad things about textile employment. To name some, the working conditions in textile factories were horrible. It was hot particularly in summers, due to the heat generated by the looms, which was made worse by Taiwan's subtropical climate. Needless to say, very few employers were willing to spend money on air conditioners to make workers comfortable. If cotton was the primary raw material used in production, the air inside the factory was usually full of cotton fibers and thus polluting. Once again, not many employers were willing to spend money on ventilation to improve the situation. It was also extremely noisy on the shop floor because of the loud noise made by the looms. Degradation of hearing ability was one of the vocational hazards textile workers had to bear (Huang 2000:54–55).

Furthermore, the working schedule in a textile factory was horrible. To make maximum use of machinery, it was the local convention that textile factories run twenty-four hours per day. As a result, textile workers were required to change shifts, which was said to be hard on one's biorhythm and unnatural to one's body (Table 3.1). It also presented a difficulty for a textile worker to arrange activities in her leisure time. She would not be able to find friends to do things with as she might be off at odd hours. To use the workers' own words, to change shifts "disrupts one's life order."

Most of the workers I talked to identified textile work as laborious. A textile worker was usually assigned twenty to thirty looms depending on the scale of the factory. The major responsibility of a loom tender was

Table 3.1
Shift Change in Textile Factories in Homei

Shift Change	Time Change	No. of Off Hours
Graveyard to Night	(Sun) midnight–8AM to (Sun) 4PM–midnight	8
Night to Day	(Sat) 4PM–midnight to (Sun) 8AM–4PM	8
Day to Graveyard	(Sat) 8AM–4PM to (Mon) midnight–8AM	32 (24 + 8)

Source: Fieldwork.

to keep an eye on looms, so that the machines could operate smoothly. When a loom stopped (for various kinds of reasons), the operator had to be able to fix the situation as quickly as possible so that the loom would be back on line in no time. Since most of the textile factories in Homei adopted a piece-rate system—to ensure workers' efficiency, of course—it was in a worker's best interest to act instantly when a loom halted. To do a good job, she dare not take a break. She also had to watch all her looms with equal attention, which entailed constantly walking around the area where her machines were stationed. It was said that a weaver would have to walk tens of miles in an eight-hour shift, and this would take too much out of one's physical strength. To avoid being subject to such strenuous condition, one could choose to work in a factory with better machines, for the more advanced a loom was, the less problem it might cause. Yet, ironically, the more advanced a loom was, the bigger the size it had. Also, an employer might likely take advantage of the fact that the machines rarely broke down and assign more looms for his/her workers to tend. As a result, a worker had the choice to work in a factory with advanced looms, but the number of looms she had to tend, as well as the area of her designated responsibility, would increase correspondingly. All things considered, textile employment had lost its attraction among young women in Homei. Instead of manufacturing, the young generation desired jobs in the service sector.

In Search of Modernity: 1990s

To show me how much Treasure Island had changed in just the past five years, Shu-fen, my roommate and pretty much the only Taiwanese who lived in the dormitory on a permanent basis, pointed at the three empty bunk beds in the room (there were four altogether) and named her ex-roommates for me: "This one here left three years ago. She went back to school. That one over there quit two years ago. She found a secretarial job in another company. The one above me married a year ago. She has a baby and is a full-time mom now. The one who used to sleep in where you are now disliked the job so much that she just wanted to get out of here. She left without telling me where she went. This room used to be full of people, but they are all gone now. Gone for better things and better lives."

Among the employees at Treasure Island, I was most curious to know about the background of young workers of the New New

Generation. After all, they were the reason that drew me to study the declining textile industry in the first place. As industrial manufacturing no longer appealed to younger generations, I was eager to learn why some still stayed. As a matter of fact, "Why did you come to work in textile factories? Why didn't you seek a job in the service sector?" were often the first two questions I started conversation with my worker-friends in Homei. None of the workers whom I talked to thought that their jobs were the greatest in the world, yet again, workers of different generations had their various concerns. Older women tended to think of the pay in the textile industry—one of the highest amongst women's manufacturing jobs—as the most important factor for their decision to stay. Younger women had more diverse reasons for their decisions. Some chose to work in textile factories because this was considered to be a transitional stage in their lives before they graduated senior high school. They were less picky about the job, as long as the pay was reasonably good. Some others were previously hired in textile factories but later left for a low-level white-collar job. They chose to come back because they did not like the long working hours they had to endure in the service sector; and the pay was usually lower, especially for those jobs involved in retail sales or customer service. They sometimes left a service job because they were the only employee in the workplace (such as those working as secretaries or business assistants in an industrial setting and where they were the only one in the office besides the boss). They were alone, and they felt lonely. They came back to the textile factory because they missed the companionship that usually developed among coworkers. There were still others who would like to leave the textile for a new vocation but hesitated to put it in action because changing jobs could be risky and scary. There was surely no guarantee that one's life would become better thereafter.

Whatever the reason might be, it was clear that employees at Treasure Island all had certain ideas about who would and should work in the textile industry. Textile factory employment was a dead-end job. And indeed, young women of ambition, means, and capability would quickly find something better to move on. Those who stayed did not leave primarily because they had no other alternatives. A close friend in the company made all of these factors apparent to me. A junior high school graduate in her mid-twenties, this friend had been struggling hard to find a life other than one in the textile industry. Reflecting upon her own experience, she was as curious as I to learn about the motivation of her coworkers. She suggested that I conduct interviews with certain people in the company, asking, for example, a new recruit who recently graduated senior high school why she chose to work as a weaver, since she had a high school diploma; asking a working student why she quit her job as a kindergarten teacher's aid and came here; or asking a newly wed worker whose husband had a well paid job why she continued working after she got married. To my friend as well as her coworkers, these were the kinds of people considered to have better options or qualifications and hence who would choose to shun textile employment. Under such assumptions, their continuous presence in the factory required explanations.

The contrast between the bright outside world and the gloomy shop floor of a textile factory could not have been made more clear than on the occasions when previous employees of Treasure Island came back for a visit. These ex-workers usually dressed beautifully and fashionably, often in floral dresses or long skirts and wearing make-up. Their outfits were clean, colorful, and stain-free, which by contrast made the greasy spots on their working friends' T-shirts and casual pants distressingly obvious. Worst of all, they often brought along promising and exciting stories of their current jobs with them. They seemed to be the embodiment of success.

In the New New Generation moral discourse, employment in the service sector was frequently depicted as easy work and quick money. Yet, in reality, jobs in the service sector can be neither accommodating nor well paid. This is particularly true in the case of young women who are high school graduates or who are currently pursuing high school education. Most of these women can only find the lowest-rank jobs in an office, most likely assistants—or "hsiao mei" (小妹), as the Taiwanese call it. The term literally means "little sister," that is, someone who is young, inexperienced, and unskilled, but precisely for these reasons she can be dictated or pushed around to do things. Another possible job is to work in the front line of customer service. Aside from the abuse or humiliation one has to bear from one's supervisor or customers, the pay of entry-level service jobs is comparably lower than those of the textile industry. In the mid-1990s, a textile worker in Homei made around NT$20,000 to 30,000 per month depending on the nature of her work (nontextile industrial workers usually made only NT$14,000 to 16,000). In comparison, young women in the local service sector were largely paid NT$16,000 or 17,000. Moreover, front-line customer service generally entails long working hours and requires stamina. It is not unusual for a sales clerk to work for eight or ten hours per day, during which she remains standing most of the time and continuously uses her charm—that is, "emotional labor" (Hochschild 1983)—and skills to attend customers. Despite the fact that people who work in front-line customer service usually get a day off each week, due to the nature of their work, they commonly work on weekends when most people rest and take days off during the week when everybody else is working. This also poses difficulty in arranging one's social activity, and, once again, "disrupts one's life order."

Likewise, many of the service sector jobs these young women are able to find are dead-end. Although the situation is gradually improving, many jobs in the service sector, like those of manufacturing industries, are gender-specific and discriminatory (C. F. Chang 1995). Women's jobs in the service sector are often of an auxiliary nature. They receive less pay and often lack promotion opportunities. Some of the employers also urge their female employees to quit upon marriage. Therefore, the service sector does not provide a promising alternative to young women turning away from traditional manufacturing employment in search of a brighter future.

It is precisely for the last reason that scholars of gender and industrialization in East Asia argue against the assumption that young female workers can improve their socioeconomic status by seeking a job in the service sector (Kung 1994; Salaff 1995). Or rather, it represents a "myth of social mobility" (Kim 1992, 1997), whereby the expectation of having a better future renders young workers more accepting of their presumably temporary, day-to-day exploitation and subordination. My own data supports these arguments. For instance, I found that not many young women in Homei had a clear idea about what they wanted to do in the service sector. When pushed, they often answered uncertainly that they would like to be a sales clerk (*tien yuan* [店員]), an accountant or bookkeeper (*kuai chi* [會計]), or a marketing assistant in a trading firm or office (*yeh wu chu li* [業務助理]), all of which were traditionally women's jobs, which led to no promising future. Only one spoke clearly that she planned to become a computer programmer because that was her major in vocational high school. Most of the other girls, however, studied "general business" (*tsung ho shang ko* [綜合商科]), which involved basic training in office work but no specific skills.

Yet, I shall also argue that to view young women's anticipation as falsely placed optimism is missing the point. Whether or not financially sensible, there have always been certain advantages to working in the service sector. For one thing, in spite of the longer hours and lesser pay, jobs in the service sector tend to be physically less demanding and safer than those in manufacturing or agriculture. The workplace is also more comfortable, and at least it is often air-conditioned. There is also the issue of symbolic capital (Bourdieu 1984). In Chinese societies, including Taiwan, mental labor has always been given more prestige than manual labor. One does not need to look far for the sign of this distinction. The difference in status between office clerks and shop-floor workers was plainly evident, if subtle, inside the walls of Treasure Island as well as other local establishments. At Treasure Island, this difference was embodied in the structure of the physical plant. While it was natural among Taiwanese manufacturing companies to separate the company's office from the shop-floor operation, Treasure Island had its office on the second floor—the only function that was so located in the company— thus spatially symbolically overseeing the movement of the rest of the company. Shop-floor workers seldom set foot in the office. On those rare occasions when they needed to do so, they had to first leave their greasy, noisy, dimly lit workplace behind, climbed a long staircase, and then entered a space that was cool, clean, and lit with broad sunlight through the dust-free glass windows. The experience could be uncomfortable even intimidating, not to mention the fact that the person one was going to see often carried some authority. Office clerks also rarely stepped down to the shop floor. There was hardly social interaction between these two groups of employees. Inside Treasure Island, they belonged to two different worlds.

This hierarchical structure was further enhanced by the routine of daily activity, one good example of which was the eating arrangement in the dining hall. As most of the employees ate lunch in the company, to accommodate the limited space of the dining hall, shop-floor workers were scheduled to eat first at 11:30 A.M. They had to finish their meal in thirty minutes and rush back to work around noon. The dining hall then served meal to people of managerial positions and office employees, who started their lunch at noon. Because of this arrangement, I often heard shop-floor workers complain that the food served to the second group was conveniently of larger quantity, better quality, and with more varieties. Also, regardless of their rank—and this included "hsiao mei," the office helper—the second group had one hour to finish their meal. In contrast to the tight schedule lived by shop-floor workers, it was not unusual to see office clerks finish eating in less than thirty minutes, leaving them more than half an hour to take a nap before resuming working in the afternoon. The status inequality between jobs in different sectors was reproduced in the implicit yet taken-for-granted dispositions of daily life.

If the young people's yearning for a white-collar service job always has a cultural root, it has now become a natural course of life in contemporary Taiwanese society. The young people's vision epitomizes the very form and concept of Taiwanese modernity, propelled by the glamorous urban consumer culture and lifestyle as well as sophisticated modern technologies (Robinson and Goodman 1996). This is by no means another piece of evidence of the New New Generation's declining morality, which was often associated with fun-loving and extravagant spending. Rather, young Taiwanese women's—and certainly also men's—inspiration to become part of the white-collar professional world should be seen as informed by "fantasies of identity," that is, "ideas about the kind of person one would like to be and the sort of person one would like to be seen to be by others" (Moore 1994:66).

While studying the impact of urban employment on young women migrants from the countryside in Thailand, Mills states the obvious yet often overlooked point when she cites Enloe (1989:16–17, in Mills 1997:39) that "young women around the globe enter and stay in new types of employment despite low wages, harsh labor discipline, and unhealthy working conditions—not solely for the money earned but also to achieve more complex social goals." Following Mills (1997, 1999), as Taiwan's current sociocultural development increasingly intersects with the global process of capitalist expansion and commodification at its present stage, the "needs, values, and worries" of young Taiwanese women no longer revolve simply around the familiar meaning of family and immediate community. They are now inspired by new imagined and imaginable needs and possibilities, which are engendered in the larger society and often congealed in the modern, cosmopolitan, and progressive image of Taiwan projected in advanced forms of communication technology. Young Taiwanese women's wish to take part in the commercial and financial world is part of these new forms of imagination. Still, new forms of imagination often have real impact on one's life. Whether or not conscious, by pursuing service-sector jobs, young Taiwanese women increase their marriage prospects and prospects for upward social mobility through marriage. Like their female counterparts, more and more ambitious young men now choose not to work in factories as a black-hand mechanic but to take advantage of the opportunity provided in fast-growing nonindustrial sectors (or in the computer industry). Therefore, young Taiwanese women staying in factories may find themselves with fewer and fewer satisfactory mates, both in number and in personal character and future prospects, in their immediate surroundings. In contrast, women working in offices or retail shops have more opportunities not only to come into contact with a greater number of potential husbands but also prospective spouses of more modern outlook and better economic potential.

Factory Regime Then and Now

To be sure, the moral criticism of a lazy, degraded workforce is not new in the modern Taiwanese history. Elder people in the countryside expressed similar criticisms of young people's declining work ethic in the late 1960s, when Taiwan began its export-oriented industrialization. At that time elder people liked to say, "The youth are too spoiled and too soft to do farm work. They are too fond of factory jobs which allow them to work indoors with a definite working schedule (though with long hours), and they like to get paid in cash" (DeGlopper 1997). Ironically, some of the people who made the comment were actually parents sending their children to work in factories precisely for the cash income they could bring home. Similarly, owners of small (handmade) furniture shops in Lukang, a neighboring town near Homei, complained about the difficulty they were facing in order to find or to keep apprentices, i.e., teenage boys who were expected to work and serve their craft masters for eighteen months without pay, while they were learning to make furniture. They said that young boys had "run away" from the opportunity to learn a real skill; they "ran off" to easy jobs in factories (DeGlopper 1997).

The tendency to reminisce about the glorious past and disapprove of the corrupted present may be human nature. The moral criticism in these cases, however, had other faces to it. Also conveyed in the criticism was the passing of an economic claim—or an entitlement—based on a particular arrangement of labor. As the conditions in the wage labor market changed, so did the patterns of production politics in the workplace (C. Lee 1998).[2]

Nostalgia for the Good Old Days

Up until the 1970s, factory owners in Homei enjoyed a great advantage over workers, mainly due to job scarcity. Since there were more young people looking for work than the number of textile jobs available, workers were generally more than happy to take whatever employment opportunity they were offered. It was a golden age for employers. Workers did not have much choice. Factory owners in Homei often spoke to me with nostalgia about those good old days. A second-generation entrepreneur whose father set up one of the very first weaving factories in the area said, "Twenty years ago, if you wanted a job [in a textile factory], you had to find someone who was respectable enough [in the community] to vouch for you, and then you could plead with the boss to give you the job."

It was not unusual then for one who needed a job to bring gifts, e.g., a chicken raised by one's family or vegetables from one's own garden, to prospective employers, in the hope to get the latter's favor. Many parents also took their daughters, who frequently had not yet graduated elementary school, to factory owners with the hope that they would get a job involving preparatory work prior to weaving. By doing this, they were hoping that their daughters would be assured a weaving job in the same factory upon graduation. Also, whenever a daughter was too tired, too discontented, or too distraught to go to work, her parents would not hesitate to drag her back to the factory. They would apologize to the boss for her misbehavior and beg the boss to keep her in the factory. "The parents would say to the boss, 'we are letting you down if our daughter can't work for you,'" a local resident explained it to me.

Textile producers and most of the workers frequently portrayed the relations an employer had with his workers as benign and paternalistic. I was often told that factory owners were highly respected, for they were rich, influential, and nearly fatherly figures who took care of their employees and their families. Young girls revered their bosses and potential employers, whose success stories had long been made into local legends. In one conversation two friends of mine—both of whom were former weavers—responded with awe after I mentioned to them about my visit to a large local company: "That company! It's quite old and famous. It's been there since we were kids. When we were young, we all liked to peep over its wall to see what's going on inside [the factory]."

At a time when poverty was the general rule, workers did not negotiate for pay or work schedule. Twelve-hour working days were the norm in the local textile industry. As a matter of fact, this practice was only terminated in the 1980s, even though some local factories continued to maintain a twelve-hour working schedule. Also, workers would not complain about having to work overtime. This was best illustrated by the experience of a former Treasure Island technician in his fifties, who said:

> [In the 1970s] people were poor, and jobs were scarce. If you wanted a job, you had to go through the right person [to get it]. We worked very diligently. If the boss said we had to work overtime, we'd all do it without a word. Nobody dared to defy him. When I was at Treasure Island, we had only six spinning machines. [To catch up with the deadlines,] we were always working overtime. From Monday to Saturday—we had only Sundays off—from early morning to nine in the evening every day, we constantly worked overtime. People began to accept it as part of a normal working day and somewhat became suspicious when we got a day or two without the need to work overtime. The wages were very low. But people were poor, and they needed [as much money as they could get]. Taiwanese worked very, very hard then.

Needless to say, this former technician was one who held a critical opinion of the falling moral standard and declining hard work ethic in the current society.

Similar manners of respect and authority were observed between workers on the shop floor, although these were more a result of the way on-the-job knowledge was transmitted than something institutional. Before the looms became automated (most of the local firms replaced their old shuttled looms with shuttleless automated ones in the early 1980s), young girls had to learn to tend looms from their older, more experienced weavers by watching or word of mouth, but mostly from hands-on experience, if the older workers allowed the girls to try tending their looms. However, many older weavers did not like others to touch their looms. Inexperienced young girls often messed up the threads and slowed down or completely shut down the looms because of their lack of familiarity with the machines. It would take considerable time for experienced weavers to untangle the threads and reestablish a normal speed of operation, which meant that their productivity would go down and their personal wage (based on a piece-rate system) would suffer tremendously. Henceforth, in order to learn the essential skills of their trade, young female workers who were new on the job usually had to be discreet and respectful to their older coworkers, or at least to remain on good terms with them. The relationship between a master technician and his young subordinates was even stricter. A master technician had great authority over beginning mechanics under his supervision. A former mechanic who later established his own firm recalled his own experience in his youth:

> It was very hard to be an "apprentice"[3] in the 1970s. You couldn't eat before the master technician ate. You had to wait for him to sit down first. If you were discovered dozing by the side of looms in a cold winter night [when you were on the night shift], the master technician would confiscate your wrench. A wrench cost more than NT$200 in those days, and [my] monthly wage was only NT$450. But a mechanic couldn't go without a wrench; you had no choice but to buy a new one. If you were found dozing twice in a month, your wage was utterly gone.
>
> Nowadays master technicians no longer have this kind of authority. Young workers don't give a damn. If you say something to them or correct them, they shout back at you. They have no respect for you.

Surely not everyone in town with whom I had conversations shared such rosy memories of the past. Some of the residents spoke critically about the highly unequal relations between an employer and his employees behind the seemingly benign surface. "Workers did not have much dignity," recalled a textile producer in his fifties, whose family factory was one of the oldest in the area:

> When I was a teenager, we were still using semiautomated looms ("pan tsi tung te [半自動的]," as they called it). That means we needed to replace the shuttle when the thread ran out. We always left about two inches of thread in the shuttle before we took the shuttle out of a loom. A kid living in a village next to us and working for my next-door neighbor once stole such a shuttle and put it in his pocket. He wanted the thread for his kite. Two inches long, the thread! You know how they punished him after he was caught? They took off his pants, and burned his belly button with a cigarette. If it had been now, the boss would have been put in jail! But the father of that kid didn't think it as wrong or unbearable. He apologized to the boss on his son's behalf. There was no such thing called human rights at that time.

Some workers told me stories about the humiliating treatment they received in a covert yet degrading manner. A soft-spoken woman in her late thirties said to me that at her first job—she began working in her early teens—the boss would line up all his employees, young and old, at the beginning of each working day. If someone came in late, the person "would have to stand there for another long moment when everybody else had begun working, until the boss told him or her to go." This served as a warning to the person so that he or she dare not be late again. She also spoke frankly about how factory owners would only hire people who would listen and obey orders: "But of course they wanted someone who was well behaved. Otherwise, with so many people looking for jobs, why should they give the job to you but not someone else? What made them hire you if you were not obedient and hard working?"

Workers Are the Bosses

The good old days acquired an almost nostalgic glow when labor shortages became an issue in Taiwan's industrial labor market. The boom in the local textile manufacturing not only brought wealth to local entrepreneurs but also the workers' families. Consequently, this lessened a family's need to send their young daughters to work, which in turn affected their notions about textile employment and employment in general. Mr. Yao, a senior clerk at the Homei Town Hall, who had been in civil service for forty years, commented on the changes in the local economy and its impact on people's lives:

> In 1956 I was a young clerk in a neighboring town hall. One of my duties was to send draft notices to local families. When I sent the draft notice to a villager's house, it was usually the young wife who received it. The husband was out working. I often saw the young wife breaking into tears as soon as she saw the notice. People got married at a very early age in those days, and they bore children right away. There were very few factories back then. If a husband went to the service, his young wife and her newborn baby would be in serious economic trouble, not to mention the extreme hardship she would have to endure as a young daughter-in-law left alone with her mother-in-law. The wife wouldn't be able to find a job.
>
> The circumstance had completely changed twenty years later. By the 1970s many girls were sent to work right after they graduated elementary school. In each family there was at least one or two daughters working in textile factories. When I sent the draft notice, young daughters in the family were usually at work. Their family economic condition had improved immensely. Young wives wouldn't be left alone without care [at least economically] if their husbands were called away. Nobody cried over draft notices anymore. You also began to see people buying cars or land.
>
> Now [in the 1990s] parents encourage their children to have as much education as possible. They even encourage their children to continue post-graduate studies or to study abroad. Money is no longer their primary concern.

Mr. Yao might have exaggerated the local parents' emphasis on children's education, for many of the local residents I met were still reluctant to educate their daughters. Nonetheless, his observation had been accurate in the general trend of the local economy and society. One of the significant changes was certainly the parents' attitude toward young daughters' employment. Lately, parents in Homei no longer feel ashamed if their daughter is unwilling to take a full-time job of any kind, let alone working in a textile factory. Mr. Yao added: "Now if a factory owner comes to fetch his young, grudging, run-away worker, her parents won't necessarily comply with the boss. The parents would say: 'It's okay if she doesn't want to work in your factory. As long as our neighbor don't gossip that she is lazy, we are okay if she takes a part-time job or no job at all.'" The prosperity of ordinary Taiwanese families, as well as the changes in the wage labor market, have certainly altered parents' expectations of their daughters, as well as of these young women's life trajectories.

Labor shortage was by no means the only predicament faced by Homei's textile producers. Yet it could become an employer's biggest nightmare, because it has a direct impact on one's shop-floor operation. Consequently, many factory owners complained to me, saying that workers were the real bosses these days: "They complain. They make demands. And they quit at any time as they wish." There was neither loyalty nor predictability. A former weaver who later became a daughter-in-law of a factory-owning family compared the days when she was a worker and when she became a boss. Resonating with the opinions of her contemporary, she said that workers begged bosses to give them a job in the old days. "See how hard it was for workers then," she said. But it had completely changed. "Now if an employee doesn't show up for work [usually a sign of quitting], we go to her house [to persuade her to come back]. If we know someone has recently quit from another factory, we go and appeal to her: 'Ah-shui ah [the person's name], please come to work for us.' It's so hard and so different now. I would kneel to our employees to plea that they stay. [Labor shortage] was very troubling."

She continued on to tell me that, only when the government allowed them to hire foreign workers, did they begin to see a way out of the problem.

Labor Recruitment and Retention

The management of Treasure Island had tried many means to secure an adequate workforce. Since the local labor pool was exhausted, they had ventured farther and farther, even to the East Coast and Green Island— allegedly the last virgin land of Taiwan that is free from industrial pollution—to find workers. "We found three workers on that trip!" the manager who ventured to the East Coast proudly announced to me. The company as well as some other larger companies in the area also tried to use "Work and Education under Cooperation" programs (*Chien chiao ho tsuo* [建教合作]). That is, Treasure Island would recruit thirty-odd junior high school graduates who would like to continue their education but could not get admission from the limited number of local public schools or could not afford to pay the tuition. The company would make arrangements with a private vocational school to have these young women admitted. The number of students recruited might vary, but the idea was to get enough students for a full-sized class (or two classes or more, depending on the number of the participants) to make it economically feasible for both the school and the company. The company would then pay the tuition and work out a schedule with the school to accommodate the production need of the company and the class time of the girls. These girls would work together as a group on one shift. Young women who participated in such programs had to sign a contract with the company, promising not to leave the company at least before their graduation. Otherwise, they would have to pay back the tuition along with other cash penalties. The company benefited from such programs by keeping a sizable stable workforce for at least three years. However, the success of these programs hinged upon the scarcity of educational opportunity as well as the poor economic condition of Taiwanese families. As an increasing number of young girls could afford their own tuition, and more and more new schools were established in recent years, such programs lost their attraction. Treasure Island could no longer find at least twenty students to make the program effective.

Later, instead of trying to recruit a group of young women at once to make the "Work and Education under Cooperation" program work, Treasure Island changed its policy to sponsor individual workers. By accepting financial aid from Treasure Island, a worker had to agree to work for the company at least during the years she was in school. Otherwise, she would be fined. This new program was not particularly successful, and the company dropped it fairly quickly. Lately, Treasure Island set up a reward for its own employees who were able to recruit new workers. During the course of my research, a Treasure Island employee would get NT$8,000 for each new person he or she introduced: NT$4,000 when the new worker started working, and another NT$4,000 six months later if he or she was still on the job.

In addition to these formal means, Treasure Island also designated the recruitment task to all of its managers. It was indeed a major responsibility of each section manager to keep an adequate number of laborers in his own department. He had to be able to maintain a sufficient workforce, using any means ranging from recruiting new employees to retaining the ones already under his supervision. Managers at Treasure Island used to go to local junior high schools and those in neighboring vicinities to give "job talks" every summer before the graduation ceremony. In recent years they even got hold of a school's yearbook and then made home visits to the graduates to persuade them to work for Treasure Island.

Traditional concepts of social relations such as "kuan-hsi" (關係, "relationship") and "jen-ching" (人情, "human emotion") had also been applied intensively by the Taiwanese to forestall workers from quitting. As discussed in the previous chapter, intricate interpersonal relationships have always been considered as an essential element of Taiwan's post-WWII industrial development (C. H. Chen 1994, 1995; Hamilton 1998). Indeed, the complex network among numerous SMEs demonstrates a great extent of flexibility and adaptability that is essential to their success in the current global economy (Castells 1996:151–200). Whereas most of the literature on Taiwanese (and Chinese) "network capitalism" (Hefner 1998) focuses on the building of ties among entrepreneurs, I would also apply the concepts of network and networking to understand labor-management relations. In Homei I heard many stories of how employers cultivated close relationships or fictive kin ties, or used already existent social ties, to reduce labor costs and to increase flexibility in production, and lately, to retain laborers. These carefully cultivated relations often proved successful (and oftentimes powerful and coercive) in the recent crisis of labor shortage.

As an example, one of the packers at Treasure Island complained to me several times that she wanted to quit, because her job was hard and tiresome and the pay was minimal. However, one year after I first met her, I still found her working in the packing department. She did try to quit once or twice, but she always came back a few days after quitting. When I asked why she continued to return, she sighed and said, "How can I succeed in quitting? The manager lives in my village! Every time after I gave in the notice, the manager always came immediately to my house to talk to me. If I insisted on quitting, he would come around again, and again, and again, until I decided to come back. Not only would he come, so would some other managers. How could you say no to all of them?"

To cultivate personal relationships with one's employees was even more crucial to small factory owners who had greater difficulty in finding workers. Moreover, employers not only fostered relationships with their employees but frequently extended close ties to the employees' families as well. The kindred-like relationships an employer established with the employees' families often served as a powerful persuasion at times when the factory owner needed his or her workers' cooperation. The story of Pei-lan, a single woman in her mid-twenties, can best illustrate the usefulness of blending different kinds of relationships.

Pei-lan was recently hired by Treasure Island to work in the preweaving preparation section, when I began my research in the company. She worked the day shift only, leaving the night and graveyard shifts to be filled by foreign workers. She told me that she would not have come to work at Treasure Island had the company not promised her a day-time-only schedule. Pei-lan used to work in weaving factories, but she said she would never again take another job requiring changing shifts. The job she had prior to that of Treasure Island had worn her out. Yet, Pei-lan continued to maintain a good relationship with her former boss, whom she called "Ta ko" (大哥), the Big Brother, a kin term with reverence and intimacy for one's own eldest brother, as well as nonkin older males who take care of one like an elder brother.

There were thirty-two looms in the factory where Pei-lan previously worked. This factory was on a twelve-hour working schedule, with two weavers on each shift. Each weaver took care of sixteen looms. Pei-lan said that, though twelve hours were long, the workload was bearable until one of the four employees of the factory quit. After that, her boss at that time decided not to look for a replacement but to change the work arrangement from two shifts to three shifts, with the three remaining employees each working on one shift. Pei-lan recalled, "The working hour was shortened to eight hours, but the number of the looms was doubled. Now we had to tend thirty-two looms each! There was so much work to be done. I was far overworked. I lost more than ten kilograms in only a few months."

Knowing that Pei-lan continued to work in this factory for almost another year after this major change in their work schedule, I asked: "Why didn't you quit right away?" For that Pei-lan answered,

> I thought about quitting. The work was just too much for anyone to endure. But he is my Big Brother. I couldn't bear to bring up the topic. Besides, how could I quit? Not only my Big Brother but also his wife visited my family often. They brought gifts to everyone in my family: to my father, to my mother, to my sister, and even to my brothers. How could I quit? Even if I insisted on doing so, my Big Brother and his wife would appeal to my parents, and my parents would in turn feel obliged to persuade me to continue working for them. My parents always said: "Your Big Brother is so nice to our family. It would be very embarrassing for us to see you quit his job to work for someone else." What could I do otherwise?

It was only when she became too ill from overworking that she finally obtained an undisputable reason to quite her job in her Big Brother's factory.

A Generational Divide

I have argued in the previous chapter that the cultural notion of "black-hand becoming boss" could be considered as a hegemonic tactic that guided the Taiwanese, when they imagined their own future and the future of their families. By extension, the "New New Generation" moral discourse drew its strength from the Taiwanese' association of success with hard work; it is hence powerful. Despite the hegemonic nature of the moral discourse, however, this chapter also attempts to show through the diverse and often contradictory readings of the moral discourse, that it was by no means free from opposition or challenges. The credibility of the New New Generation moral discourse relied largely on the connection it made among hard work, equal opportunity, and social mobility, mostly evinced in the Taiwanese male adult industrial entrepreneur (read: boss) status. This in the past was sustained by Taiwan's strong and fast-growing export-led economy, but is no longer easy to sustain under the recent economic plight. The increase in the number of unemployed middle-aged male workers and the labor advocate groups' challenge to industrial employers' claim of labor shortage, on the one hand, directly contested the validity of the moral discourse. Young Taiwanese' attraction to the service sector, on the other hand, conformed to the hard work-success nexus, if with a twist. It was precisely the expectation to succeed that turned them away from the dying manufacturing sector to service, the sector with a modern image and presumably unlimited, albeit uncertain, opportunities.

There was also a generational division in the attitude toward the New New Generation moral discourse in Homei. I found three distinct groups of workers in the local textile industry: married women in their late thirties and early forties, single women in their late twenties or early thirties, and young single women in their late teens or early twenties. These three cohorts of women constituted separate work and social groups on the shop floor. As I show in the following chapter, the separation was not simply derived from the differences in their age and marital status, but rather from the connotations carried by these differences. Work in general, and industrial work in particular, covered a wide range of meanings to these three groups of women, who differed by generation and by the time in their lives when they entered textile manufacturing (cf. Rofel 1994, 1999). As women, their gender roles defined the parameters within which particular cultural and social responsibilities had to be fulfilled. This in turn affected their participation in the wage labor market. Subsequently, they had different ideas about the causes and consequences of Taiwan's recent industrial restructuring, which indeed had a different impact on each of these groups.

CHAPTER 4

The Meaning of Work

In the early 1970s, Lydia Kung (1994) studied young factory workers in an electronics plant an hour's bus ride from Taipei. At the time of her research, Taiwan was transforming from an agricultural society to one based on industry. The export-oriented economy had just begun to take off. New employment opportunities in then-booming light industries were created in or near urban areas. Young people from the countryside all over the island migrated to cities to look for jobs. At that time, factory work represented the first stable form of employment open to Taiwanese women and was almost exclusively reserved for young single women. The size and demographic structure of the workforce in Kung's company reflected this early stage of industrialization. Half of the four thousand employees in the company that Kung studied were working daughters from a nearby market town. The other half contained farming daughters from the south who lived in factory dormitories. These young women were the first-generation industrial workers in Taiwan's postwar history.[1]

The economy and society of Taiwan have greatly changed since then. By the time that I started my research in the mid-1990s—approximately twenty years after Kung's now classic study—Taiwan had lost its status as a manufacturing powerhouse of light consumer goods to its neighboring countries in the Asian-Pacific region. The economy is much more diversified, and industries have been upgraded and become more capital intensive. Young women largely shun factory employment, leaving it to older married women who have greater family responsibility yet less education or skills needed in the contemporary service sector. The participation of married women in Taiwan's industrial labor market has indeed accelerated since the mid-1980s (DGBAS 2001).

At Treasure Island, despite the effort made to recruit young girls, after the 1980s, managers were forced to change the company's single-women-only employment policy and began to hire married women and mothers as well. Similar to the situations in other textile factories in Homei, married women have become the backbone of production at Treasure Island. Notably, most of the married women who work in Homei's textile industry are not first-timers in the industrial labor market. In fact, they were the first-generation postwar industrial workers who helped to accomplish Taiwan's "economic miracle" in the 1970s, when they were very young. They had been the core workforce of Taiwan's economic development in the past, and they continue to play an active role in today's industrial production. However, the economic environment they are now living in is very different from the past. In less than twenty years, factory women who are in their thirties or forties have witnessed rapid transformation of Taiwanese society from a poverty-stricken rural economy, to its glorious days of full-fledged export-oriented industrialization, and now to the decline of manufacturing industries, while the economy gradually becomes more directed toward finance capital and service-centered enterprises. Dramatic changes in Taiwanese women's roles and responsibilities have also occurred in a very short time span, as evidenced in these women's lives and experiences.

This chapter focuses on the meaning of work to three generations of women who came of age after Taiwan's export-oriented industrialization. The life stories of three women are chosen to highlight the socioeconomic circumstances and cultural environments each of these generations face. They all worked at Treasure Island, when I first met them. Social scientists normally compare the lives of successive generations—for example, mothers and daughters—who are twenty years apart. However, given the immense economic change Taiwan has experienced since the 1960s, I adopted industrial generations instead of kinship generations for analysis, which are generally ten or even fewer years apart (c.f. Salaff, in Kung 1994:xiii). Taiwanese women joining the wage labor market ten years apart have very different work experiences. The life stories in this chapter are thus manifestations of the evolving global system as lived by Taiwanese women, and each of the stories is closely related to the others, for the development of a later stage of the evolving system is built upon the previous one.

Yeh Ah-fong, the woman whose life story is discussed first in this chapter, was born in 1961. As the majority of the women born in the late 1950s and early 1960s and came of age in the early 1970s, Ah-fong grew up in the countryside experiencing a decline in agriculture and a swift transition from an agrarian to a manufacturing-based economy. Ah-fong was one of Taiwan's first-generation industrial workers in the post-war era. The early work and family experiences of her generation are well documented in the literature (for example, Arrigo 1980, 1984, 1985; Diamond 1979; R. Gallin 1984a, 1990; Kung 1981, 1994; Salaff 1995). Most of them began working at a very young age, sacrificing their own chance for education to support their families and the education of their younger siblings. However, unlike the previous generations of Taiwanese women who retired from paid work (if they had any) upon marriage, Ah-fong and her cohorts continued working after marriage, usually only taking time off during the first few years following their first child's birth.

Yang Ch'un-mei, the second woman discussed in this chapter, was born in 1965. As she is only four years younger than Ah-fong, Ch'un-mei shared much in common with Ah-fong in life. Both of them were filial daughters working for wages at a very young age, and both of them constituted the workforce in the early stage of Taiwan's EOI and contributed to the later accomplishment of the "economic miracle." Nonetheless, their life experiences differ in many ways. Women of Ch'un-mei's generation, who were born in the late 1960s and early 1970s and came of age throughout the 1980s, usually have more education than Ah-fong's cohorts. Despite the fact that the Taiwan government extended the mandatory education from six years (i.e., elementary school) to nine years (i.e., junior high school) in 1969, parents in the countryside tended to ignore this policy—particularly if the child in question was a daughter—until much later. Most of the women in Ah-fong's generation with whom I became friends have only elementary school education, whereas most of Ch'un-mei's cohorts went to junior high school or night vocational school or even junior college. More important than the length of education, however, is the image of progress implied in education. Early on in their working lives, women of Ch'un-mei's generation had begun to witness the burgeoning of a modern and urban society and a gradual shift of the economy to one centered on service. Many of them also began to consider possibilities of a future outside the shop floor, and some of them, even outside the traditional realm of marriage.

Born in 1975, Lin Hsiao-fen, the third woman discussed in this chapter, is one of the New New Generation who are inspired to take part in Taiwan's contemporary glamorous, modern, urban, cosmopolitan, and consumption-oriented society and economy. However, being one of the few in her generation who still remains in factories, Hsiao-fen displayed many doubts about herself and uncertainties toward the future. Her life story is illuminating in that it manifests the undercurrent of anxiety in Taiwanese society, noting a mixture of hope and skepticism.

Concomitantly, this chapter seeks to shed light on the scholarship of gender and the international division of labor. Over the past few decades, an extensive body of literature has explored the effects of global capitalism on the definition and meanings of gender. Two central and interconnected issues have been examined (Cairoli 1998:182; Nash and Fernandez-Kelly 1983; Warren and Bourque 1989, 1991). The first concerns the domestic domain, primarily the impact of women's participation in industrialization on gender and the family in local cultures. The second stresses the very nature of the current global economy and questions whether women's participation in factories worldwide is intrinsic to capitalism. After generations of pioneer studies, we now fully acknowledge that these two levels of analysis are not separable. Our current task is "to contextualize and research the interplay of transnational and local cultures as gender ideologies are negotiated, refined, and contested" (Warren and Bourque 1991:300) by various players such as multinational investors, local producers and managers, workers and their families, governments, and other social-cultural forces like religious groups.

Likely due to the brief history of industrialization in most of the developing world, much of the early literature addresses the incipient stage of transformation, when young single women are the preferred workforce. As a result, researchers often focused their investigation on the local and global interaction at the juncture when the social relations in a newly industrializing economy were first affected and reconfigured. Nevertheless, young women do not persist as the preferred or available labor force forever. As such, a case study of Taiwan proves to be significant. In a rapidly developing economy like Taiwan, not only does an ever-growing wage labor market lure away potential workers to more desirable new spheres, but the definition and meanings of gender have also been dialectically reconstructed, as the economy continuously reconstitutes its patterns of production and reproduction. Young women become unavailable because of both economic reasons and shifts in cultural expectations. This, in turn, lends opportunities for comparison with women's experience in advanced capitalist countries.

My own research in Homei certainly indicates that the process of industrial transformation involves women's interpreting and reinterpreting their productive and reproductive roles, as they are incorporated in distinct phases of capitalist accumulation. In the following sections, I shall illustrate the trend of changes that I have discussed above through the life stories of three female textile workers.

Yeh Ah-fong: From Working Daughter to Working Mother[2]

Why should I tell you about my childhood? Even if I do tell you, you wouldn't understand. You don't share the same experience with us! I had a very harsh life when I was young—you know how much abuse [from employers and older coworkers] I had undertaken when I was young?—I don't want to recall it. Why do you force these questions on me? My life is getting better and better. I work, I make money, and I have a stable and secure life. This means more to me [than lamenting for my past]. (Ah-fong lost her temper with my persistent probing of her past life history.)

Yeh Ah-fong, a line leader in her mid-thirties, took me under her wings almost on the first day we met. She was usually friendly to me and liked to have me sitting next to her while she was doing her duty. She showed me the functions of the different parts of their machines and taught me tips of becoming a successful loom keeper. She also spoke frankly about her relationships with her superiors and coworkers. In her own conceptualization of my research, she had been very helpful to me in collecting essential information. But she rarely told me about herself, and when she did, she lost her temper. I knew very little about her family, her childhood, or her early work experience. She did not see the point of my poking into these subject matters; nor was she eager to answer my questions when I pressed for these issues. Only once did she bring up reminiscence of her childhood voluntarily, after I accidentally—and probably mistakenly—told her that children in my family rarely did house chores. She said to me in a scolding tone that she had washed the clothes of her whole family to ease her mother's burden, when her mother had to take a paid job outside the home upon her father's death. She was only twelve then. Ah-fong's voice was rather soft and sentimental that day, unlike the loud and practical attitude she so often expressed in the workplace. She told me that her mother had to work very hard, taking several jobs along with farming on their small plot of land, to support the four children in the family. Only when Ah-fong left home for factory employment in Homei, and after her elder brother came back from his military service, did the family finally come out of stark poverty.

From the tidbits of information gathered from our various conversations, I was gradually able to construct a fuller picture of Ah-fong's early life experience. Born in 1961, Ah-fong grew up in Yun-lin County, where the economy was based on agriculture, and where the path to industrialization lagged behind the rest of Taiwan. There were four children in the family: she had one elder brother, one younger brother, and one younger sister. Being the second child and the eldest daughter in a poor and fatherless family, Ah-fong did not have much choice but to begin working early. She was recruited to Treasure Island at the age of fourteen by her cousin, who had already worked in the company and who was inspired by the company's effort to find workers outside the nearly exhausted local labor pool due to Homei's speedy export-oriented industrialization. Despite the fact that she was not a "native" but came from a more rural region, Ah-fong's work history closely followed the life trajectory of factory women of her age in the Homei area.

From Agriculture to Industry

Ah-fong and women of her generation grew up in a declining agricultural economy. Despite the fact that almost all of the rural households owned some land after the land reform (1949–1953), from farming "one could only get food to eat but no money to spend," [有得吃，沒得用] as many of my friends in Homei liked to say. After land reform, the old land tenure system was largely destroyed, and most of the former tenants obtained private ownership of the land they cultivated. Also, with technical assistance from the government, agricultural output had significantly increased after the war-torn years. Between 1952 and 1968 agricultural production grew vigorously at an annual rate in excess of 5 percent (S. Ho 1978:147). Nevertheless, these early accomplishments did not result in an increase of family wealth in the countryside. The increase of agricultural productivity as well as the expansion of farmland could not keep up with the growth rate of rural population. More important, however, was the government's policy of maintaining a low rice price and of developing the industrial sector at the expense of agriculture, which had severely curtailed the rural households' ability to keep the fruit of their hard labor within the family and largely inhibited the process of surplus accumulation in Taiwan's agricultural sector.

According to Liu (1992), in order to insure a sufficient supply of foodstuff to feed the huge population of civil servants and soldiers (around one million) who came to Taiwan with the defeated Nationalist government from Mainland China after the end of the Chinese Civil War in 1949, the government implemented several policies to control the price of rice and to collect rice directly from farmers. In addition to the compulsory sale of rice to the government, farmers also had to pay land taxes, government loan repayments, and payments for land purchased from the government through the "land-to-the-tiller" act (耕者有其田) in kind. All of these amounted to "hidden rice taxes," because the official purchase price was much lower than the wholesale market price of rice (T. Lee 1971; S. Ho 1978:180).

The most notorious policy, however, was the rice-fertilizer barter system (*Fei liao huan ku chi* [肥料換穀制]). The Taiwan government had been the sole source of chemical fertilizer for more than two decades since the 1950s. It controlled all fertilizer production, imports, and distribution. Until the early 1970s the barter ratio between rice and fertilizer was set consistently to favor fertilizer (whose value was highly overestimated, roughly 40 percent over its production or import cost) (Liu 1992). Taiwanese farmers paid too high a price for the fertilizer they used, particularly when compared to the price of fertilizer in the world around that time (S. Ho 1978:181). In the 1950s and 1960s the rice collected through this barter system accounted for over one-half of the rice collected by the government (S. Ho 1978:80). The high price of fertilizer was in part a consequence of the government's policy to subsidize industrialization at the expense of agriculture (S. Ho 1978:181–182).

A direct result of these highly discriminatory policies was a sharp decline in the income of farming families. Nonetheless, selling land in exchange for badly needed cash was rarely an option due to several reasons. First and foremost, most of the land was inherited from ancestors. One would not easily sell it unless the family was in dire straits. Also, farmland was not as valuable as it is today. Nobody would ever imagine becoming a millionaire by selling his farmland. Under such circumstances, young people in rural areas who were unable to find work in agricultural production were forced to seek employment outside agriculture. Most of them entered the then newly developed industrial labor market.

Young girls born throughout the 1940s and 1960s in Taiwan's countryside had witnessed the inability of agriculture to sustain a vital livelihood let alone to accumulate wealth. Subsequently, many of the farming families were in debt, either to the government or to usurers in the countryside. Furthermore, debt did not end upon the death of a father who owed the money, but was passed down to the next generation of male offspring through family inheritance, in which sons divided and inherited both family property and debt equally. Helping to pay off family debt was thus a common childhood experience borne by many women in Homei.

Young girls who came of age throughout the late 1950s and 1970s then entered textile factories in large numbers. They became the first generation of industrial workers engaged in the fast-growing export-oriented industrialization, which began in the late 1960s and started to blossom in the mid-1970s. They were the "neophyte" young workers (cf. Ong 1987), whose lives had been the focus of studies of global industrialization and its impact on gender and family relations in Taiwan (Arrigo 1980, 1984, 1985; Diamond 1979; R. Gallin 1984a, 1984b, 1990; Hu 1984; Kung 1981, 1994; for a comparative study in Hong Kong, see Salaff, 1995).

They entered the wage labor market at a very young age, generally when they were thirteen or fourteen, upon elementary school graduation. However, it was not unusual that parents arranged for their young daughters to work even one year before graduation for the purpose of securing a job. Textile employment was a common ordeal for these young girls.

Although the majority of these girls left paid work upon marriage or the birth of their first child, as the past literature has well documented, many of them also returned to the workplace as soon as they could find someone or some ways to keep an eye on their children. There are two major reasons for this. First of all, when they reached the age of marriage—usually in their twenties—in the 1980s, the Taiwan economy had transformed to an extraordinarily successful export-oriented industrial economy. The society had grown much more prosperous, and the standards of living were much higher than in the previous decades. As a result, in order to catch up with the rising living standard and living expense, many of these married women felt compelled to take paid jobs in order to increase the family income. Secondly, as the economy began to experience a squeeze in labor supply after the 1980s, specifically in the industrial sector, many employers who originally rejected the idea of hiring married women were obliged to change their policies. These women had more opportunities than those in previous generations to find employment with a married status. Thus, they were not only the first generation of industrial workers in Taiwan's postwar industrialization, but also the first generation of married Taiwanese women who participated in large numbers in the wage labor market.

Because of their early participation in the wage labor market, many of these women (born in the early 1960s) who were in their mid-thirties had only six years of schooling, while those who had reached their forties rarely went beyond elementary school, despite the fact that the Taiwan government had extended the mandatory education to its citizens from six to nine years in 1968. Education did not seem to matter much, however. In the mid-1970s when Ah-fong was first hired at Treasure Island, manufacturing industries employed the highest percentage of the working population in the Taiwan economy, in addition to a dwindling and aging population who continued to farm (Kung 1994:44–45; S. Ho 1978:131).[3] There were not many other job options open to young women, especially in the countryside. Manufacturing was pretty much the only choice regardless of one's educational attainment.

Even if a young girl of Ah-fong's modest background had wished to seek a different life trajectory, she would have been easily discouraged by the harsh economic reality that she had to overcome. In the end, she usually accepted her expected destiny. Salaff's (1995) research on the impact of industrial employment on the lives of working daughters in Hong Kong under similar economic circumstances provides an ethnographic as well as a theoretical ground to understand the predicament faced by young women. She discovered that a working daughter's position in the family depended on the economic history and other socioeconomic attributes of her family and on the daughter's birth order and the structure and cycle of her family. That is to say, family economic circumstances determined the training a daughter was able to receive and the age at which she undertook employment. In the center of Salaff's analysis was the ascendancy of the Chinese family that she called the "centripetal family regime" (Salaff 1995:7–10). In its centripetal form, the family became a power base to manipulate other institutions. It gathered in its forces "by demanding the primary loyalty of its members and mobilizing their labor power, political, and psychological allegiances on behalf of kinsmen" (Salaff 1995:8). Therefore, young women from poorer backgrounds had very few options other than to work in order to fulfill their family obligations.

In Search of Modernity: 1970s

Many women I met in Homei—particularly those who were in or had passed their thirties—expressed sentiments similar to those of their Hong Kong counterparts in Salaff's study. Yet, their memories of their early working days were not unequivocally bitter. For one thing, aside from having to work hard (which was the norm of life at that time anyway), young girls generally enjoyed the company of the peers they knew from work. Some of the fortunate ones might also benefit from the relative material affluence provided by their employers. Mei-yun, also a line leader at Treasure Island who was slightly older but nonetheless shared a very similar work and life experience with Ah-fong, once told me in a matter-of-fact way that she gained a lot of weight in her first few years working at Treasure Island. The dishes prepared by the company's kitchen were much more delicious than those of her own family, she said, and they always had plenty of food to eat.[4] A woman in another company also told me that she used to save and take home the lunch toasts provided by her company for her younger brothers to eat. She said, "[In the 1970s] you didn't see much of that toasted bread around here. You know, the kind with butter and jam on it. It smelt so good! My family couldn't afford that kind of [fancy] food. But I wanted my brothers to experience it. I usually saved the toast and took it home after work for them to eat."

If to take part in the booming service sector is the New New Generation's way of searching for modernity in the late 1990s, I would also argue that to participate in the then-prospering industrial sector should be considered in part as young girls' efforts to get away from the pitiful lifestyle centered around the doomed agricultural economy in the late 1960s and throughout the 1970s. In retrospect, Ah-fong and many of her older coworkers were grateful for the opportunities that they had to work in textile factories. Their incomes had greatly improved their families' living standard. It is by now a familiar story to students of Chinese women and industrialization that young women workers contributed their wages to the purchase of modern consumer goods (e.g., TV, radio, refrigerator, etc.) and to the education of their younger siblings. From my observation in Homei, however, I would contend that a more fundamental process toward "modernization" began in the physical structure of one's home. I was often told how working daughters' wages had helped the family to fix different parts of their houses (usually beginning with the roof), and eventually to transform their old, often mud-made and straw-roofed flat farm huts into brick or concrete, several story-high houses with tiled floor, modern kitchen, and sanitary facilities. The completion of a new house made of the latest materials not only indicated a more comfortable, better equipped, and more convenient living quarters, it also symbolized a better economic status, and more importantly, a modern outlook of life of the family.

The family house was certainly an important part of Ah-fong's self-identity. In our few conversations in which she talked about her natal family, Ah-fong usually began with the hardship her family had endured in those early days and finished with affection, as she related to how her family was eventually able to build a house of their own. She often said, "We had only a broken-down farmhouse then. [My mother] finally saved some money to build part of our house, and a few years later, she saved money again to build another part. That's how we came to own our new house!"

From Working Daughter to Working Mother[5]

Ah-fong continued to work at Treasure Island until she married at age 22. Ah-fong met her husband at Treasure Island, who was then an electrician for the company. However, a few years ago Ah-fong's husband quit his job to become an independent contractor and his own boss and employee. As such, he followed the "black-hand becoming boss" career trajectory of young Taiwanese males. Ah-fong herself stayed home upon marriage and raised three children (two boys and one girl). She returned to Treasure Island seven years later, after her youngest son was old enough to be admitted to kindergarten.

As previously stated, it was Treasure Island's policy until the late 1980s that they hire only single women. The few married women they would consider hiring before the 1990s were former employees of the company who left upon marriage. Ah-fong was rehired under such circumstances. However, the company was forced to change its recruitment policy soon afterwards, when they could no longer find sufficient numbers of young single workers. The company, as well as their counterparts in Homei and in Taiwan at large, could no longer afford to reject married women who sought employment.

Nearly all of the married women at Treasure Island, except one or two, had been experienced textile workers before they married. This was also the case of textile factories across the region. For the married women themselves, textile manufacturing was one of the best jobs they were able to find. Although it required women to change shifts, it paid much better than most other female manufacturing jobs. Other options for married women besides manufacturing were to take cleaning jobs or work in fast-food chains in the booming service sector, but these were often part-time jobs with a much lower pay.

Although males have always been, and continue to be, considered as the breadwinners in Taiwanese society, the ideology does not always conform to the reality. Some of the married workers at Treasure Island, as well as some other married working women I met during the course of my research, returned to work either because their husbands did not have a regular job or they did not make enough money to pay for the day-to-day living expense. It was also not unusual for me to hear that the husbands spent most of their earnings on drinking or gambling and ignored the needs of their families.[6] Ah-fong was among the fortunate ones. Her husband worked hard and earned a fairly good income from his independent contractor-electrician business. More importantly, he neither drank nor gambled; fishing was his ultimate pastime.

Although Ah-fong liked to say that she returned to Treasure Island because she wanted to "help out" her husband—a frequently heard expression made by married working women in explaining their reasons for reentering the wage labor market—the socioeconomic reality surrounding Ah-fong's decision was never that simple. The truth was far more complex even in her words:

> When [my husband] worked for Treasure Island, he made NT$25,000 a month. Now he works as an independent contractor; he is able to make NT$40,000 or 50,000 each month. Our

> family economic situation has greatly improved after he left Treasure Island. We are okay now.
>
> I could stay home if I wanted to. But I want to share my husband's burden. We have to pay for the mortgage, and there's also the children's education to consider . . . It's all for survival.

Conveyed in Ah-fong's words was her recognition that, even though her husband's income was sufficient to provide them with a modest yet comfortable life, it would require more money in order for the family to keep up with the current consumption level in Taiwanese society, and for her children to get ahead in the future through investment in education.

Ah-fong was not alone in her decision to return to paid work. It is increasingly common for a Taiwanese woman to continue working after marriage, or even after the birth of the first child if she can find someone (usually her mother or mother-in-law) to take care of the baby without pay or with little pay. Women working on the shop floor usually cannot afford private daycare service. Even if they could afford it, the cost often equals their wages, thereby making their employment worthless.[7] They usually have to rely on close relatives to assist them. Otherwise, they would choose to stay home for a few years and return to the workplace after their youngest child has reached school age (like Ah-fong had done). Thornton and Lin (1994) confirmed this general observation in their research of Taiwanese women of all social groups. By dividing the women into marriage cohorts, they discovered dramatic changes in Taiwanese family organization and married women's employment over time. Women married in 1955–59 were unlikely to be involved in paid work outside their husbands' families—84 percent of them reported not working between marriage and the first birth—whereas 58 percent of the 1980–84 marriage cohort (to which Ah-fong belongs) had done so (Thornton and Lin 1994:129–131). Also, although only 6 percent of the 1955–59 marriage cohort worked outside the family between their first and second childbirth, 26 percent of the 1980–84 cohort did so (Thornton and Lin 1994:132).

Married women's massive participation in the wage economy marks a new stage of capitalist development in Taiwan. The distinction between women's productive and reproductive roles has broken down, merging the focus and strategies of each domain (Nash 2000). The fact that young single women are in search of more skilled, better paid clerical and other white-collar jobs in Taiwan's expanding economy, on the one hand, opens up married women's opportunities in the wage labor market, yet on the other hand, also forces them to take paid jobs. As evidenced in other industrialized societies like the United States (Safa 1983), self-upgrading in Taiwan (e.g., the youth's prolonged learning at school) "involves a dual burden on the household: not only must they bear the costs of education [but] they must also suffer the loss of their children's earnings that would otherwise have been allocated to the family" (Safa 1983:111). Subsequently, married women (the mothers) often have to make up the forgone labor and incomes of their children, who require more years of education for skilled wage labor.

For Ah-fong, the need to rely on herself for socioeconomic improvement was even greater than most of her coworkers who were natives of Homei. Both Ah-fong and her husband were newcomers to the region. Neither of their parents nor other members of their families lived nearby (except for a nephew of her husband who followed the example set by his uncle to work at Treasure Island as an electrician before becoming an independent contractor). Henceforth, Ah-fong could not count on her mother or mother-in-law for help on childcare or domestic chores. Nor were their parents capable of assisting them financially in any way. One of Ah-fong's regrets in life was that her husband inherited nothing from his parents. She told me that her husband had four brothers. Without the means to support their five sons, she said, "[My parents-in-law] told their sons to go their own ways. They gave no help to their sons. My husband and his brothers had to find a life for themselves." Therefore, unlike most of her local coworkers, whose husbands either inherited a piece of land on which they could build a house, or inherited a ready-built house from parents, Ah-fong and her husband had to build their life in Homei from scratch. After more than ten years of hard working and savings, they finally purchased a townhouse in a government-subsidized development project in 1991.

Ah-fong took great pride in her new house. On the day I toured her house, while sitting on their genuine leather couch in the living room, she said to me:

> My mom used to be very worried about me. [For a long time] I was the only child in my family who didn't have a house of her own. Only after we purchased this house, did my mom stop worrying for me.

> It's nice to have one's own house. We used to rent our friend's place. But you don't feel stable living in others' property. Even our children feel that way, too. [Ah-fong looked around her living room before she continued on speaking, almost like a queen inspecting her kingdom.] Just the other day my daughter said to me, 'Mom, it's so wonderful to have a house.' This means a lot to them.

Ah-fong's next major purchase was a computer for her eldest son. She had consulted me many times for the different models and prices. It was a widely known fact on the shop floor that Ah-fong's son was an excellent student (with very good grades) in the local junior high school. Ah-fong's friends in the company who had children of similar age often admired her for having a gifted son who required no disciplining for him to study ("It was a blessing," they often said). Ah-fong was delighted to hear these compliments. She had good faith in her son as well. In Taiwan, where fine academic performance was believed to be a prime condition for a child's later success, Ah-fong's son's future prospect seemed to be ensured. "He is learning computer now," she said. "Five days a week, and it costs a thousand dollars! But he is very smart. He has learned everything his teacher taught him. Smart kids learn fast. His father is very fond of him; he is thinking of buying him a computer. Maybe we should buy him a computer when he's older [as a computer costs much money]. Yet he's handling it so well now."

Security, Stability, and Social Mobility

In explaining why many of the middle-aged women I met in Homei did not speak about their past, one of the employees at Treasure Island, who also claimed that she had no past memory, said to me: "How the heck can one waste time on memorizing the past? There's already enough for one to worry for the present." She emphasized that it was even more impossible for those who had troubled current lives (e.g., irresponsible husbands, disobedient children, or economic difficulties) to think back. Ah-fong did in no way belong to the category of the ill fated. Yet, she surely shared her colleague's view of seeing no value in reminiscence. Reflection on the past brought back nothing except unpleasant memories.

Ah-fong was a practical person. Now that they had established a permanent residence, what mattered to her were the continued success of her husband's business and a steady job of her own, which formed the foundation of their material and emotional well-being. They both had been working hard to maintain a comfortable life. Ah-fong would also try every means within her own reach to better her children's education, so that they could be properly equipped for the fierce competition they would have to face in the years to come. Her eldest son's high performance in school had shown that he would have a promising future, at least not one relying on hard manual labor like that of his parents. Ah-fong was content.

Yang Ch'un-mei: Woman of the Sisters' Hall

You know what you should do? You should tend looms yourself so that you can really learn how we do our jobs. ["But the company has warned me not to touch the machines for the sake of my safety," I answered.] Well, if you are not to work like us, you should at least force yourself a schedule to stay on the shop floor for eight hours every day, and not to leave for whatever reason you might have until the time is up. Then you will learn about our sadness, that we don't want to be here yet have no other choice but are forced to stay. (Ch'un-mei said to me on the first day we met.)

Yang Ch'un-mei was one of my roommates at the dormitory of Treasure Island. Before meeting her in person, I was told that she was an amazing woman and a real fighter in life. Born in 1965 to a small farmer's family and coming of age at a time when rural Taiwan was speedily industrialized, Ch'un-mei's experience of growing up exemplifies that of girls in her generation under similar circumstances. She is the oldest daughter in the family, followed by four brothers and two sisters. Her father was the sole source of economic support for the family when the children were young. The ill health of her mother, and her responsibility to take care of seven young children, prevented her from looking for a paid job outside home. With many mouths to feed but insufficient economic means to do so, Ch'un-mei's father was constantly in debt and under pressure to look for nonagricultural earnings. However, as Taiwan's export-oriented industrialization had only begun, and young boys and girls were the preferred workforce, Ch'un-mei's father could only supplement agricultural revenue with low-paid part-time jobs. Exhausted from his economic burden, Ch'un-mei's father frequently took his frustration out on his wife and children. Ch'un-mei had mixed feelings toward her father. More than once she said to me,

> I know my father had huge responsibility, and he was under tremendous pressure... but he beat my mother hard, even when my mother was already bent and knelt on the floor. I tried, coming between his fist and my mother's fragile body, and cried, begging him to stop. But he only became angrier, and beat my mother and me even harder. He so frequently shouted: "It's entirely your fault, you two. The two pei-chien-huo!"[8]

Like many girls of her generation and the generation before, to ease the family economic hardship, Ch'un-mei began working for industrial wages right after she graduated from elementary school at age twelve. She could have gone to junior high school, since the Taiwan government had by then made junior high school education mandatory and subsidized the cost of the tuition. But it was her father's plan that she should work in a weaving factory. Ch'un-mei's father had a traditional Chinese attitude toward children's education (Kung 1994; Salaff 1995; Parish and Willis 1993). He insisted that boys in the family had to have at least a junior high school diploma, because education was very important in order for them to find decent jobs. Girls, on the other hand, did not need to have much education. Furthermore, their wages from industrial work could contribute substantially to the household income, or be used to pay for younger siblings' (particularly brothers') education. Although Ch'un-mei's father later changed his mind after she appealed, Ch'un-mei gave it up herself. She said that she wanted to help her father, and she could no longer bear to see her father beating her mother. She gave up the opportunity for further schooling herself and went back to work in the textile industry. Her wage soon became the family's only stable source of income.

Ch'un-mei's understanding of the family's hardship, and her willingness to sacrifice herself to improve it, did not always go without ambivalence. Looking back, she remembers vividly those days when she was too upset to work but was dragged by her father to the factory and could only sob in the dark corner between her looms. It was not always self-pity that made her cry. Her bitterness also came from the realization that she was forced to work because she was a daughter, a culturally temporary yet economically indispensable member of the family. Ch'un-mei often said,

> My father didn't want to take a factory job. He said he couldn't bear being tied up at a workshop for many hours per day. He'd rather work in the field. He said it's freer that way. He never had a regular job, even though his income from our small plot of land was not enough to feed the family.
>
> He wanted freedom. He didn't want to be tied. Did he ever think of the consequence? I was the one who was tied. I was the one who had to work in the factory.

For more than ten years Ch'un-mei was the primary breadwinner of her family. The harshest blow came after her father's death, when she was nineteen years old and suddenly became the head and the sole wage earner of the family. Her mother relied on her to make decisions for the family. Her brothers and sisters were still in school then. They were too young to share her responsibility in a major way.[9] Ch'un-mei was only released from the responsibility a few years later, when the oldest of her younger brothers graduated from middle school, finished mandatory military service, and came home to work as a relatively well-paid mechanic. Other brothers soon followed suit, and with a middle school diploma, they each took on jobs as various kinds of technician. Ch'un-mei's family economic situation became greatly improved. A new house was built, and her responsibility as the family's eldest sister was largely lifted.

Yet, toiling from a very young age had left grown-up Ch'un-mei in ill health. Specifically, she had a weak stomach. Ch'un-mei speculated that it was the lengthy working hours and improper lunch break when she worked in weaving factories that caused it:

> Previously we were on twelve-hour shifts [in the weaving industry]. The day shift was of eleven hours, from seven in the morning till six in the evening, and the night shift was of thirteen hours, from six in the afternoon to seven in the next morning. We never ate at the proper time—three or four o'clock for dinner, and the other meal after midnight. We also rushed down our food and dashed back to work. It all caused indigestion! And the loom was high, and I was short. [To reconnect the broken threads,] I had to stand on a stool and stretched my body across the machine. My stomach was right on the frame. Doing that so often, I certainly developed a serious stomach problem.

Only after she was freed from the primary family responsibility, did Ch'un-mei begin to seek her own life. She went back to school in 1990 at age twenty-five. When I first made acquaintance with her in 1994, she was twenty-nine and recently graduated from junior high school. She planned to take senior high and vocational school entrance exams that summer. In order to prepare for the exams, she took many days off from work and only resumed working regularly after she was admitted and enrolled in a night vocational school. The management at Treasure Island was not pleased with her constant absence from work. Nonetheless, due to the tight labor market, they went along with her decision and were very glad to have her back after her exams. They also made her working hours flexible enough to accommodate her need of study both before and after her entrance exams.

Ch'un-mei often told me that she had always wanted to continue her education, a dream she was deprived of but which eventually came true. She left her previous weaving job to work at Treasure Island after she started her junior high school education a few years back. A job without the need to be on a regular shift would give her more time to study, she said. At Treasure Island, she first worked at the packing department, but later changed to tend looms on the shop floor. She explained,

> The packing job was too demanding, and the work schedule conflicted with my school schedule. I requested to be transferred [to my current department], but my supervisor was unwilling to let me go. He said that the salary at Packing was higher. Who cares about the meager wage difference? If I had wanted to make money, I would have taken a job at a weaving factory and made thirty or forty thousand dollars per month. I didn't do it because I wanted to spend time on school. I didn't want to exhaust myself. Later I threatened to quit, that's when he got concerned and arranged the transfer for me.

At Treasure Island, packers only worked during the day, from 8:00 A.M. to 5:00 P.M. with one hour of lunch break in between. The spinning department where Ch'un-mei later worked, unlike other spinning and weaving departments in the company, had only two shifts: the day shift (from 8:00 A.M. to 4:00 P.M.) and the night shift (from 4:00 P.M. to midnight). Workers changed shift every Sunday. However, due to her school schedule (her classes ran from 4:30 P.M. to 8:30 P.M.), Ch'un-mei was unable to change shift but mainly worked on the day shift. She also had to leave half an hour earlier than other workers in order to be on time for school. Yet, from time to time she either volunteered, or was asked by the management, to work on the graveyard shift with other "working students" (*kung tu sheng* [工讀生], that is, young workers who go to school in the evening or night-school students who work full-time during the day) and workers working overtime, especially when the company needed to rush for orders. She seemed to like the idea of working after school. By doing so she said she could save more time to prepare for schoolwork. Also, the climate after midnight was much more relaxing than during the day. There were no management personnel in the company except department foremen. Ch'un-mei received less attention, which gave her some latitude of freedom.

The reluctance of Ch'un-mei's supervisor at the packing department to let her go, as well as the flexible schedule allowed to her, signified the company's concern over the labor shortage. Each department supervisor was under pressure from the company to keep a full (or at least, sufficient) workforce in his department. It was his job to fill the vacancy left by workers who departed.

Ch'un-mei did not stay at Treasure Island much longer, however, even with the accommodation the company was willing to make for her. One year after she began her high school education, she left the company for a part-time job at a gas station with much lower pay but fewer working hours. The job was part of a work-study program designed for night-school students by the state-owned petroleum company, which owns the majority of gas stations in the country.[10] Ch'un-mei said that she wanted to take a break from harsh work, and she needed the time to study. She had been thinking and had drawn many plans for her future. One day not long after the semester began, she asked me how she could take the certified public account (CPA) exam. Knowing that the certification exam was reserved exclusively for college graduates and postgraduates, and that even for them the passing rate was very low, I hardly thought that Ch'un-mei as a night-school graduate stood a chance to first pass the college entrance exam and then the CPA exam. I dare not tell Ch'un-mei what I thought. Nonetheless, with her strong will and fighting spirit, who knows what she would be able to accomplish?

In the Sacred Heaven Fo-tang

To further pursue her goals, Ch'un-mei adopted another more radical means in addition to going back to school. Ch'un-mei was a follower of I-Kuan Tao (一貫道), "a syncretic, universally salvational, apocalyptic, and evangelical religion whose members practice vegetarianism and are led by charismatic masters" (Skoggard 1996:157). Ch'un-mei converted to I-Kuan Tao after she started working in the textile industry. Conversion to I-Kuan Tao had been an experience widely shared by young Taiwanese workers in the 1960s and 1970s, especially when they followed the course of rural migration to cities, where many of the then-booming industrial zones were located, and found themselves in a new and alienating environment. An I-Kuan Tao temple with a group of fellow worshippers often became a home away from home under this circumstance (Sung 2000:11–12). Also, until very recently most of the textile factories in Taiwan had dormitories to accommodate their employees. At night, after work, young factory women usually spent time together. It was on these occasions that those who had converted to I-Kuan Tao would suggest to their friends to "pai-fo" (拜佛, "pay respect to the Buddha") or "t'ing-ching" (聽經, "listen to the religious scripture")—both of which were considered as righteous things to do. Toward the end of such a night, however, newcomers were frequently eagerly persuaded by their friends and fellow worshippers to go through the initiation ritual, to which they often yielded under the peer pressure.

Ch'un-mei belonged to the Lineage of Precious Radiance (*pao-kuang tzu* [寶光組]), an influential I-Kuan Tao faction in central Taiwan under which many of her fellow villagers, ex- and current coworkers were enlisted. Ch'un-mei had developed special communion with the Sacred Heaven Fo-tang, an I-Kuan Tao temple built, inhabited, and managed by a group of single women who had by and large decided to remain single in order to devote their lives to study the Tao, the virtuous way.[11] After her brothers took over the family responsibilities, Ch'un-mei successfully persuaded her mother to allow her to move into the fo-tang. Although she did not entirely reject the possibility of marriage, neither did she eagerly pursue it. She spent most of her evenings at Sacred Heaven and returned home to visit her mother from time to time. When asked for the reason why she decided to live in the fo-tang, Ch'un-mei said:

> For many years I was the one who had to take care of my family. I had to make all the decisions and solve all the problems. I got so tired and exhausted [from both the physical and mental stress]. Besides, my brothers need to learn to make decisions. I'm glad I have this opportunity to be by myself for a while! My mother understands this, too. ["What about the pressure to get married?" I asked.] She is worried about finding me a husband. But I told her there's no guarantee that marriage will do me any good. Look at her marriage! My parents constantly quarreled, and she got beaten so often . . . My mother looks much happier and more at ease now that my father has passed away. Nobody will hit her anymore. I don't want to live like her.

The teaching of I-Kuan Tao centers on the belief that, in an effort to save mankind from an impending cataclysm, Wu-sheng Lao-mu (無生老母; the Venerable Heavenly Mother) sent Milefo (彌勒佛; the Maitreya Buddha) to spread the Tao and save mankind thereafter (Jordan and Overmyer 1986:17; Sung 1983). According to Skoggard (1996:157–158),

> Those who receive the Tao will survive the apocalypse and be freed from the endless cycle of death and rebirth for a period of ten thousand years. Followers are expected to diligently and sincerely study the Tao in order to perfect themselves and through their example lead the rest of mankind to salvation. One accumulates merit most surely by contributing time and money to the religion's proselytizing mission and bringing in new recruits.

Women of Sacred Heaven are certainly good models of this religious piety.

The Sacred Heaven Fo-tang consists of two adjacent cement buildings, with one of four floors and the other five stories; they are connected both on the first as well as the third floor. The five-story building serves as a public space for worship, religious teaching, and regular meetings. "Sisters"[12] of the fo-tang live in the four-floor building. According to Ch'un-mei, the fund for constructing the Sacred Heaven Fo-tang was solely contributed by some of the women currently living in the fo-tang. Before Sacred Heaven they had already rented a house near Homei's downtown marketplace and lived together to study the Tao. One day they decided that they could do more than simply practice the Tao themselves. They put together their own savings, purchased the land of the current site, and built the fo-tang. Presently Sacred Heaven has become a major I-Kuan Tao center in the region. The temple on the top floor is open to the public most of the time, and a general congregation is held on Sundays. During the week there are also classes and recreational activities designed for specific segments of the congregation, such as "men," "women," "children," "adolescents," and "college students." Women of Sacred Heaven are thereby both participants and facilitators of these activities.[13]

In the mid-1990s when I first met these women, there were roughly twenty of them living in the fo-tang. Their ages ranged from thirty to nearly fifty. Ch'un-mei was the youngest among them, but not the only one who was in school. Many of the "Big Sisters" (i.e., 大姊, those who are older than Ch'un-mei) did not continue their education after elementary school, but were sent by their families to work in weaving factories. Some of them who were in their mid-thirties then were going back to junior or high school at night. All of them except one had regular jobs, mostly in the local manufacturing sector. To live in the fo-tang, none of the residents paid rent (to the original builders). However, all residents pooled together a certain amount of their income to pay off the daily maintenance. Sisters at Sacred Heaven lived a very simple life. Their world was mainly centered on their religious belief. Yet, they did not vow to become nuns, as devoted women in other organized religions might choose to do. I-Kuan Tao as a sectarian religion commands neither the personal devotion nor the institutional obligation for them to do so. They participated in the day-to-day social and economic life just as much as any other ordinary Taiwanese. The majority of them also kept close ties with their families of orientation. Still, they were a special group of women. Despite the fact that there was no formal ritual to signify the transition in their status, many of the middle-aged women in the fo-tang were considered as "married" daughters in the eyes of their families. It was the very thought that they had already been "married" that kept their elderly parents in comfort, who would otherwise worry for their daughters, whose future was not taken care of. The "married" status of women at Sacred Heaven was most notable on the second day of the

Chinese New Year, customarily the day on which married daughters visit their mothers' houses (nian chia [娘家]) in the busy season of the New Year. Ch'un-mei informed me that in the morning of each lunar January second, many of the Big Sisters' paternal nephews would come to invite their aunts home. "It's the custom. Brothers should send their sons to greet their aunts. That's the respect appropriate for married-out daughters and sisters," she said.

The Legacy of Marriage Resistance

Sisters of the fo-tang did not win a wide audience outside the I-Kuan Tao circle, however. Singlehood and cohabitation of women often raise overladen suspicion and disapproval, or to say the least, curiosity in Taiwanese society. Out of coincidence, not long after I was introduced to sisters of Sacred Heaven, Ah-fong and one of her married coworkers joined the yoga class at the fo-tang. They became very interested in the life in the fo-tang and had one day probed Ch'un-mei with many questions over lunchtime. The loud voice of Ah-fong drew the attention of another married worker; she, too, joined the conversation. The three of them were most interested in issues relating to these women's single status. "Do they have to pledge not to get married in order to be admitted to the fo-tang?" Ah-fong was most eager to know. Sharing the common cultural knowledge with the three married women, and knowing well that to remain single was not quite a legitimate thing to do, Ch'un-mei eventually came to the defense of her sisters, claiming that they did not reject marriage. She said that women of the fo-tang were still waiting for their time to come, which was indeed a true enough statement. This conversation was cut short by the end of their lunch break. Nonetheless, I sensed envy in these married women's ambivalent manner. After all, like one of them said, "[women in the fo-tang] all have jobs. They all get to keep their income (which was not always true). They are all free!"

Anthropologists attempt to perceive cultures through the eyes of people living in it, directing their questions and framing theoretical understanding accordingly. Marriage is significant to Chinese women, for it serves both as a symbol of and gateway to women's ultimate existence in the Chinese patriliny. I thus share the same obsession with my three married informants over the marriage question, as many anthropologists of Chinese society did before me.

Marriage was virtually universal for women in traditional Chinese society. Yet, from the Canton Delta in the late nineteenth and early twentieth centuries came reports of a startling phenomenon: that wives refused to live with their husbands, and young women vowed never to marry (Jaschok 1984; Sankar 1984; Siu 1990; Stockard 1989; Topley 1975). Topley postulates in her landmark article, "Marriage Resistance in Rural Kwangtung" (1975), that these practices presented two forms of marriage resistance. The first was a form of "*pu lo chia*" (不落家), literally "women who do not go down to the family." Such women tried every means to prevent themselves from having to join their husbands' families. On their wedding days, they took herbal medicines to suppress urination and wrapped themselves with strips of cloth under their wedding gowns, to prevent consummation. Three days after the wedding ceremony they returned to their natal families for the traditional home visit, which they prolonged for several years but with regular visits to their husbands' families on important ceremonial occasions. Stockard (1989:3–5) disputes that this practice was a form of marriage resistance but argues instead that it was a common local custom called "delayed transfer marriage." This is because women who became pregnant on their visits to their husbands' families would have to return to their husbands and begin to assume their roles of wife and daughter-in-law. The transfer of women was delayed but nonetheless completed. However, the prolonged residence with one's natal family frequently led to real marriage resistance. Some women took a further step to stay away until they passed childbearing age and never consummated their marriage. In this case, however, a woman had to find, or pay her husband to find, a secondary wife who would assume the obligations of childbearing and serving the husband and parents-in-law. By doing so the woman who paid would be exempted from the drudgery yet still maintain her status as the first (and real) wife, thus guaranteeing her a place in her husband's ancestral hall after her death (Topley 1975:67; Stockard 1989:48–69).

In the second and more direct form of marriage resistance, *tzu-shu nu* (自梳女, literally "women who dress their own hair" [Topley 1975:67]), young women took vows, before ancestors and in front of witnesses, never to wed. The hairdressing ritual preceding the vow resembled the one traditionally performed before marriage to signal a girl's arrival at social maturity. After the vow, these "sworn spinsters" would no longer live with their natal families, but often organized themselves into sisterhoods and lived in frequently self-owned spinster houses, where their spirits after death would also be laid to rest. These spinster houses, however, were often taken care of by the spinsters' adopted daughters (Stockard 1989:70–89).

Both Topley and Stockard attribute the rise of these marriage resistance practices primarily to women's important role in the local silk industry. In the local silk industry, unwed and therefore childless young women were believed to possess smooth and nimble hands, good eyesight, and long duration of concentration and attention that were necessary to the industry. After the development of mechanization in sericulture, young and unwed women became even more important because only they were unattached, thus having the freedom to rotate among different filatures to meet the different production cycles and schedules. The silk industry provided women in the Canton Delta with a means to support them—a rare opportunity in traditional China—that became the foundation of their refusal to marry.

The marriage resistance practices in the Canton Delta challenged the dominant cultural view about marriage and women's destinies in Chinese society. Yet, women's recurrent concern over the spirit displacement after death in the case of marriage resistance, as discussed above, attested to these women's conformity to the male-centered patrilineal culture. The deeply rooted belief against the spirit tablet placement of an unmarried daughter at her father's home upon her death, and the subsequent fear of becoming an eternally wondering homeless ghost due to tablet displacement, propelled unwed women to adopt various strategies to secure their well-being in the afterlife. Hence, patterns of resistance prove to be culture laden, and those who express some forms of rebellion may have challenged some parts of the social order, yet reinforced others. Precisely for this reason, female social reformers in the early Republican period (1912–1945) were frustrated by these Cantonese women who resisted marriage but showed no interest in taking part in the larger struggle against feudal cultural beliefs and conservative Confucianism (Topley 1975:68). Yet, rebellion was often significant to individuals involved, for their personal lives had likely changed forever. Furthermore, their behavior contributed to the study of Chinese culture. It is from these women's very pattern of resistance that students of Chinese societies learn to see clearly the strengths and weaknesses of Chinese patriliny and patriarchy.

The first impression of Sacred Heaven reminded me of the legacy of marriage resistance in southern China at the turn of the twentieth century. Sisters at the fo-tang seemed to resonate with those sworn spinsters who vowed never to marry and who found ways to take care of their material and spiritual well-being. However, it would be mistaken to assume that women at the fo-tang based their choice simply on fear or resentment toward marriage and married life. Neither is it accurate to assume that their act necessarily embodied a feminist awareness. These women's religious consecration played an important role in their decisions. Yet, it was also their keen understanding of women's role in the Taiwanese family that led them to believe a total separation from married life—hence the time- and energy-consuming roles of married women—would give them the best chance to study the Tao, thus enhancing the possibility that they be exempted from the everlasting suffering of reincarnation.

In spite of the similarity, women of Sacred Heaven differ in major ways from the sworn spinsters in the Canton Delta nearly a century ago. Having arranged themselves to live in spinster houses, sworn spinsters had to work in order to support themselves but rarely pursued anything else. Unlike the sworn spinsters, "sisters" of the fo-tang did not choose to remain single simply because they feared marriage; neither did they lead a cloistered life after residing at Sacred Heaven. Rather, these women answered their own call for religious propriety by actively participating in the fo-tang's activities, which in turn provided them with opportunities to live beyond the daily terrain of family and work, which they might otherwise have little chance to do.

As Sacred Heaven was a major worship center in the local area, "sisters" of the fo-tang not only took care of the daily maintenance of the temple but also coordinated with the higher-ranking leaders to design, organize, and execute various religious or social activities. Although they did not hold (or had not yet held) any official titles—except for one who served as Sacred Heaven's Hall Chairman[14]—they were indispensable assistants in the initiation and other religious functions. As a matter of fact, because of their affiliation with Sacred Heaven, the role they had played in mobilizing local followers, and the intimate knowledge they had about I-Kuan Tao rituals and taboos, "sisters" of the fo-tang were seen as exemplary models of religious propriety and often sought after especially by women believers for advice. Likewise, many of the fo-tang's residents maintained good relationships with the I-Kuan Tao believers in their "parish," i.e., followers in the adjacent villages who regularly attended the Sunday congregation and other gatherings at Sacred Heaven. They hosted and received visitors to the fo-tang. They visited ill members of their congregation at home, attended funerals, and celebrated weddings, birthdays, and month-days of the newborn. This was in part due to the fact that single men and women in I-Kuan Tao lived a this-worldly life and continued to maintain ties with their families and communities. They rejoiced and mourned with followers of their temple—many of them were their fellow villagers—because they were good neighbors or responsible members of the local society. They also participated in these events, however, not as individuals but as representatives of the Sacred Heaven Fo-tang. Being the host of the center of their religious community, it was both essential and practical for them to have good public relations. By doing so, they established a centripetal force and confidence that drew the followers closer. In addition, women of Sacred Heaven frequently joined seasonal and emergency relief efforts organized by the I-Kuan Tao leadership (the most recent one being the relief work after the major earthquake that hit central Taiwan on September 21st, 1999 [World I-Kuan Tao Headquarters 2001]). Through these good deeds, they had created a positive image of I-Kuan Tao among the local population, which would likely aid their converting effort.

The many responsibilities that the "sisters" had were most evident on the white board hanging in the fo-tang's living room that these women used to record their monthly duties. From the number of tasks listed under each day, it was clear that most of them had a very busy schedule. To prepare themselves for the diverse roles that they were encouraged and expected to play, many of these "sisters" took courses offered by the I-Kuan Tao regional office in their free time. The purpose of many of the courses was to help them better understand the essence of the Tao in order to prepare them for a more important proselytizing mission in the future. The course materials, reflecting the syncretic nature of the religion, were adopted from various religious and literary sources, including ancient Chinese texts such as the Four Books.[15] While staying with Ch'un-mei at Sacred Heaven, I was impressed to learn about the effort these women put in to understand some of their books, which required special knowledge usually reserved for students in higher education. Despite the fact that interpretations given to these texts were to support a specific religious worldview—thus could be very different from the conventional reading—these women were introduced to the ancient literary world that they might otherwise not encounter. Moreover, they were sometimes required to write up "sermons," drawing information from their course texts, and practice them in front of the class—a skill of public speech that would certainly come handy in the future.

Some of the courses taken by the "sisters" were not directly related to their religion but were considered by them (and many Taiwanese) as good for self-improvement or refinement. These included English conversation and Chinese music instrument classes. After years of mastering the musical instruments, some of the sisters had indeed become teachers themselves and begun to give lessons to young members in their congregation.

Residents of Sacred Heaven had also been sent on short overseas missions, traveling as far as inland provinces of China and lately Southeast Asia to spread the true meanings of the Tao. Again, to prepare themselves for future missionary calls, some of them had volunteered their time, at their own expense, to study the languages of prospective countries of destination. On my latest field trip to Homei, I was surprised but utterly delighted to learn that two of the "sisters" had the ability to speak Thai, though still rudimentary. Both of them had only an elementary-school level formal education. Yet, through their own endeavor, they had managed to learn a language that very few Taiwanese can speak. Between them, one learned the language through communicating with her fellow Thai workers. The other, however, went through great trouble to enroll in a Thai-language class sponsored by the county government, which was open only to factory owners and managers. Without the proper qualification (she is neither factory owner nor manager), she had to fake her position through the help of a fellow worshipper, whose factory could care less for lending its name under this circumstance. This language skill of theirs proved to be not only useful to I-Kuan Tao's propagating effort, but also beneficial to their employers and coworkers. As foreign workers have become an essential and integral part of Taiwan's industrial workforce, the language barrier between Taiwanese producers and their foreign employees has also become a major problem for the management on the shop floor. However, only recently the Chang-hua county government in which Homei is located began to offer Thai language lessons for factory owners and managers. The language skill these two "sisters" had was thus readily applied to facilitate the communication within each of their factories. Not only did the management in their workplaces gain from their expertise, their Thai coworkers also benefited from it by having someone to translate for them and answer their questions of how to better live in an alien society.

In all of these occasions, women at Sacred Heaven were able to learn new knowledge and skills, as well as to explore new life experiences. This was indeed a luxury or privilege usually associated only with urban middle-class women that most of the working wives or full-time housewives in Homei were deprived of either because of their lack of appropriate economic means or of their preoccupation with the perpetual family obligations.

Ch'un-mei's Brave New World

Being the youngest and newest member of the Sacred Heaven Fo-tang, Ch'un-mei had not yet developed her religious devotion to the extent that some of the Big Sisters had, although she had taken part in the fo-tang's routine activities. Her goal in life was largely inspired by the world of mortals. Yet, Sacred Heaven served a major function in her life. It helped her to secure a legitimate social position before she got married. Furthermore, it provided her with an alternative life trajectory with which she could choose to follow and create her own destination.

A friendly wage labor market supported Ch'un-mei's optimism. She was still young and thus a desirable worker for employers in the waning local textile industry. Her recent release from family economic responsibility and her current student status both contributed to her willingness to accept lower-paying jobs with flexible working schedules in the service sector. Nevertheless, this might prove to be only a temporary solution, with her prospect linked to the changing conditions in the local wage labor market and depending on the course of Taiwan's economy.

Lin Hsiao-fen: The Youngest Child with the Best Life

There are so many "o-ba-sans"[16] *in my village. I don't like them! They have nothing important to do but sit together talking all day every day. They gossip! They have such an idea about young girls that they should all go to work right after junior high school. It is useless for girls to have too much education, they say. And only jobs in textile factories are "jobs." Jobs in the service sector? They think that's the root of the world's sin.* (Hsiao-fen complained to me while I was riding on the back seat of her motorcycle, going home with her to interview her mother.)

The mothers of many young workers at Treasure Island also worked for the textile industry when they were younger. One day I went home with such a young worker, who had just celebrated her twentieth birthday, to interview her mother. That night, my friend Lin Hsiao-fen, her mother, and I were sitting on the bed, while I was tape recording her mother's account of her weaving experience. Hsiao-fen, lying comfortably on the bed with her head on her mother's lap, would make comments from time to time when she disagreed with her mother or when her mother mentioned something unknown to her. In the course of our interview, the mother did not say anything critical about her daughter. Only once she looked down at Hsiao-fen and said with a smile on her face: "She is the laziest, the one with the best life. She doesn't do any housework." Hsiao-fen protested mildly, saying that she did sometimes help her mother cooking and doing dishes.

Most of our conversation was in Taiwanese, the language used most locally—especially by the older generations who had hardly any formal or at most elementary school education. Hsiao-fen's mother had limited proficiency in understanding Mandarin Chinese, the official language taught at school since KMT took over Taiwan at the end of WWII. In the middle of our conversation, Hsiao-fen suddenly turned to me and said in Mandarin Chinese: "Anru, why don't you ask my mom about my going to school again? I bet she will say no to you." I did what she asked me to do. Her mother did not say anything but slightly shook her head. She still looked at her daughter indulgently, with a big smile on her face.

Hsiao-fen's family lived in a coastal town approximately thirty minutes bus ride from downtown Homei. Despite the short distance, this town never caught up with Homei's fervent textile industrialization. It remains largely agricultural to this day. Garlic is the main crop, for the local soil is too salt-soaked to grow rice. Because of the lack of nonagricultural opportunities in the town—there are only a few factories—many of the town residents have moved away, or at least, looked for jobs either in Homei or in an industrial park near the other side of the town. People in their fifties or older folks are the major population left and engaged in farming.

Hsiao-fen's family was one of the few who stayed. Hsiao-fen's parents, who were both in their fifties, grew garlic, but in idle seasons they had to find other revenues to supplement the family income. Hsiao-fen's father used to be a plasterer, until he injured his back. Her mother worked for others as a seasonal farm laborer. Sometimes she also took temporary factory jobs, although this meant that she had to travel outside the town to find work.

Hsiao-fen was the third child in her family. She had one elder brother, one elder sister, and one younger brother. Among the four children, only the youngest brother went to senior high school; the other three had only junior high school diplomas. At the time when I met the family, Hsiao-fen's elder brother had come back from his military service and was working as an apprentice to a local furniture maker. Hsiao-fen's sister, who was two years older than she, worked in a weaving factory out of town. She lived in the dormitory of the factory and only came home once a week or less. Hsiao-fen's youngest brother was still going to school. Knowing that going back to school was one of the two fancies occupying Hsiao-fen's mind—the other was to become a sales clerk in adjacent Taichung City, the largest city in central Taiwan—I spent quite some time discussing her children's education with Hsiao-fen's mother. She explained to me why only one of her four children went to senior high school:

> We encouraged my first-born [to continue his schooling.] My husband urged him to stay in school as long as he could. He said he would sell the land to pay for his tuition. But my son didn't want to. We couldn't do much to force him. ["What about the girls?" I asked] Girls? Oh, no. [When Hsiao-fen's sister

graduated junior high,] it was the time my first-born was doing his military service. Our family budget was tight. Since our first-born didn't go to high school, it wouldn't be right for the girls to go. I said to my daughter: "Your brother is in the military. Why don't you take a job to help our family?" This daughter of mine was a good girl. She has been working in the same weaving company since then. Now Hsiao-fen wants to go to senior high school—It wouldn't be fair to my first daughter if I let Hsiao-fen go. She would be embittered, wouldn't she? I have to be fair ...

None of Hsiao-fen's female cousins go to high school. My sister- and cousins-in-law all said girls don't need much schooling. I have more than ten cousins-in-law. We are a big family. We all used to live together. They all said it'd be sufficient for girls to go to junior high and make money right after. ["So you can't do otherwise?" I asked.] That's right. We can't be different. [Hsiao-fen's] grandma and grandaunts also said junior high is sufficient for girls. Let the girls make some money, they said.

The implementation of nine-year mandatory education might have changed Hsiao-fen's elder relatives' idea about the appropriate length of girls' education—now it was accepted as nine years instead of the six years in Ah-fong's or Ch'un-mei's days. Nonetheless, it had not changed the deeply entrenched belief in women's inadequacy to accomplish, and more fundamentally, in their inability to contribute to the long-term welfare of their parents' families. Thus, despite Hsiao-fen's mother's affection for Hsiao-fen, she followed the local tradition to seek a more practical destiny for and immediate return from her daughters. With only a junior high school diploma in hand, however, young girls like Hsiao-fen did not have much choice in the current economy but had their best chance in local factories, just as Hsiao-fen's elder female relatives had triumphantly predicted. Yet, a vicious cycle had been perpetuated by first depriving girls of the opportunity (e.g., education) to broaden their options and later blaming them for their inability to achieve. This further reinforced the preexisting conviction that a woman "could best cook, do laundry, bear and raise children for her husband's family," who thereby did not deserve much investment.

A New New Generation in an Old Vocation

Hsiao-fen was one of the girls in her junior high school recruited by Treasure Island before graduation. She was also one of the few who remained on the job, when most of her coworkers hired under the same circumstance had left for various sorts of reasons. Hsiao-fen was born in 1975. When I first met her in 1994, she was only nineteen years old but had been working at Treasure Island for five years. "I used to be the youngest in the company," she said to me when we first met, "but not anymore." Some of the working students who just came in were younger than Hsiao-fen. Nonetheless, this did not change the general impression of Hsiao-fen's older workers that she was the "baby" among them. This is not to say that she was too young or too spoiled to be responsible—after all, young workers these days were irresponsible by definition!—but only that Hsiao-fen shared the habits of her cohort in the New New Generation, such as enjoying regular days off, preferring not to work overtime, taking it easy on the job (e.g., not rushing to restart the looms after they halted), sometimes coming in late because of oversleeping from a previous day's outing, and not hesitating to spend money on fashionable items—that is, cheap imitations of fancy, brand-named clothes or jewelry. Hsiao-fen's spending behavior was never as extravagant as that of those urban middle-class youth hanging out in the Eastern District of Taipei City (台北東區), one of the major shopping centers in Asia, which has acquired a bad name for the New New Generation. She did not feel comfortable, for instance, spending money on a McDonald's value meal. However, she definitely differed from her older coworkers in her relative freedom in spending her own income, even though she, as well as other young workers of her age, might not be completely relieved from family economic duties.

Kung (1994:116) reported in her research nearly twenty years ago that, although there was no explicit and precise arrangement of income transfer from daughters to parents, young female workers were expected to turn over minimally 50 to 80 percent of their earnings to parents. A daughter who turned over all her wage would be considered as the most filial. A daughter's contribution to her natal family was mainly rewarded through the dowry provided by her parents on her wedding day. Twenty years after Kung's study, this perception of filial piety continued to be strong while I was conducting research in Homei. Yet, I also noticed several changes in the fulfillment of family obligations and daughters' own consumption from Hsiao-fen and young people of her age that deviated from Kung's past observation. A direct change involved the appropriate percentage of wage turned over to one's parents. The percentage had generally fallen, with 50 percent as the most frequently cited number. In some cases, young women turned little or none of their wages to parents, but they had to pay for their own high school tuition, which usually amounted to NT$10,000 or NT$15,000 per semester, as well as other related spending. It is important to note, however, even though there seemed to be little change in percentage, the actual amount of money at young women's own disposal and its worth were both greatly enhanced due to the increase in wage scales and real wages. In addition, parents nowadays seemed more relaxed about allowing their grown-up yet unmarried daughters (particularly those having reached their mid- or late twenties) entire control over their own incomes. Instead of saving for their daughters (usually by joining credit clubs) and giving the sum (often partial after home use) to them as dowry on marriage, more and more parents gave their grown-up daughters full autonomy over their money. However, this was very likely related to the fact that Taiwanese women in the 1990s married at a later age than that of their counterparts twenty years ago. Therefore, their parents felt compelled to attend to their daughters' rights and needs as adult women by granting them more financial liberty.

How Hsiao-fen spent her income represented a mixture of an old mode of obligation and a new pattern of consumption. Before Hsiao-fen was promoted to the position of assistant line leader at the end of 1994,[17] she made around NT$17,000 to NT$18,000. One month she proudly announced to me that she had made almost NT$20,000 by working thirty full days without taking any time off. Her monthly wage rose to NT$20,000 or NT$21,000 after the promotion, depending on the number of days she worked. She gave her parents NT$10,000 every month, she said, before she turned twenty. The money she turned over to her parents, along with that of her sister's, had been a great help to her family. Hsiao-fen's parents were able to use the family savings to rebuild their old, one-story brick house into a concrete, three-story, two-family house just two years before. After turning twenty, however, Hsiao-fen got to keep all the salary for herself. "Wow, you are rich! You have a lot of money to spend," I teased her. "Nah, half of the money goes to a [monthly] credit club. And I have purchased a life insurance policy, which costs me three thousand dollars per month. That leaves me only six or seven thousand to use," Hsiao-fen said. "Do you get your insurance money back sometime in the future?" I asked. "Of course! [Otherwise, who would do such an investment?]" Hsiao-fen obviously thought that my question was pretty stupid; nonetheless, she patiently explained to me that she would get all her money back after reaching a certain age. Moreover, her insurance policy also included benefits around her life cycle, that is, the insurance company would cover costs on the occasions such as her wedding or childbirth.

To purchase a life insurance policy is indeed a new way to invest and save one's money in Taiwanese society. It is a very recent phenomenon that has only flourished since the Taiwan government lessened its regulation over the financial sector of the economy in the late 1980s.

What really distinguished Hsiao-fen from her older coworkers, however, was the sense of purpose and self-worth they each carried with themselves. As one of the kind who was in fast extinction, Hsiao-fen was keenly aware of the derogatory undertone attached to her job and her current state of life, even though she rarely articulated her comprehension—and apprehension—in a clear, straightforward way. What she did instead was to denigrate her own ability. In numerous occasions my daily greeting with Hsiao-fen began with her self-disparaging remark: "Anru, I am so stupid! [I don't continue schooling because] I am dumb." I was never sure whether she believed in what she said about herself. The only thing I could do—and frequently did—was to dispute her remark to assure her self-confidence. Nonetheless, I was partly to be blamed for reinforcing the local depreciation of textile factory employment by repeatedly asking its young employees whether they ever considered taking another (read: better) job. The answers I received for that question were almost unanimous: Yes, of course, they would like to have another job. The question that mattered to them was never "whether," but "how," "what," and "when."

A Dream Yet to Come

Like many of the young workers I had come to know well, Hsiao-fen became more discreet and less playful after she celebrated her twentieth birthday. She was seen working overtime often and was more attentive to her job. To respond to my curiosity about her sudden change, Hsiao-fen said: "I am no longer a kid. I am twenty now. I have to be responsible. I have to save some money for myself, and take care of my future."

While transforming herself into a respectful employee, Hsiao-fen also became more critical toward her job. She began to describe her job as—using her own words—"purely manual labor, requiring no brainwork. And one becomes dumber and dumber as one goes along." It was an open secret on the shop floor that Hsiao-fen wished to become a sales clerk—one of the few vocations in the service sector that Hsiao-fen thought as both decent and attainable. Yet, the doubt about her ability as well as the prospect of a new job continued to linger. Whenever this topic entered our conversation, Hsiao-fen always immediately dissuaded herself by saying that she would never get a good sales clerk job, that is, in a brand-named shop, where employees received a monthly bonus based on their sales performance on top of their wages, and where they had opportunities for promotion. This was because, she said, "they only hire people with a senior high school diploma."

Hsiao-fen's limited education had become the primary obstacle to both her self-motivation and realization. In order to have a major change in her life, she would have either to enhance her educational credential or to find a nonmanufacturing job that she could feel happy about in the present job market. Neither choice sounded as if it would be an attainable option under the current circumstances. Moreover, her parents were not particularly supportive of the idea of her finding another job. Hsiao-fen was not terribly distressed by her inability to act, however. After all, she was still young. She had not yet formed a definite idea about her coming years.

Reassessing Working Women's Experience

Although gender has been identified as a key factor in understanding the current global industrialization insofar as it reveals fundamental aspects in the organization of production and labor, gender by itself is not sufficient to explain the experience of women. It is the articulation of gender and other social institutions (in this case, the patrilineal kinship system and the family along with relations in production) that has to be examined. Being a woman at various stages of the life cycle entails very different rights and responsibilities. Also, gender is not a system of determined cultural beliefs and social interactions, but a process characterized by heterogeneity and instability. Furthermore, multiple patterns of capitalist accumulation coexist in each social formation by appropriating a population segmented by varied productive and reproductive roles. Women are thus labeled as different kinds of workers or potential labor force and integrated into the wage labor market at different times and in different forms. To study the relationship of the economy and the formation of women's subjectivity, a new analytical framework is urgently needed, which requires not only recognition but also keen knowledge of the historical dynamics, social complexity, and cultural heterogeneity of any society under study. We need to address the wide range of women's experiences, as they are products of a specific historical-economic period intersecting with different stages of life cycle encoded within a culture.

The life stories presented in this chapter are examples of the transition of patriarchy from the private to the public domain (cf. Safa 1995). That is, the three women's earning ability in the industrial labor market had won them recognition from their families, and in the case of Yeh

The Meaning of Work

Ah-fong and Yang Ch'un-mei, it also granted them a greater voice at home. Yet, their wage-earning power had not fundamentally challenged the traditional perception of gender roles in the workplace. Rather, exactly because of Taiwanese textile producers' dependence on cheap labor, and of women's designation as secondary wage earners, young and middle-aged women in Homei were continuously sought out to be the desired workforce. Much of these women's optimism, therefore, was at present supported by a worker-friendly labor market, within which female labor was desperately in need.

The three women discussed in this chapter all worked for others. The specific pattern of their labor market participation—that is, being someone else's employee—reflects the way their families related to the Taiwanese economy, which in turn affected the dynamics within their families, as well as how each of their gender roles and family obligations were defined and claimed. As a comparison, in the following chapter, I will focus on the story of the Wang family, an industrial-entrepreneurial family struggling to overcome the difficulties brought about by the rising competition in the international market and the changing labor market in the country. The problem of labor shortage drove the males in the Wang family to intensively deploy the labor of their daughters and sisters, who had traditionally been the core workforce in their family's textile factory. Compared to Ah-fong, Ch'un-mei and Hsiao-fen, who were hired by others and whose families did not own a factory, young women in the Wang family were in a much more awkward situation when trying to break away from the family in order to pursue their own dreams.

CHAPTER 5

Between Filial Daughter and Loyal Sister

My brother-in-law didn't invest in his children's education. He keeps his daughters working in his factory. That is why he can still manage without downsizing. Our kids have higher education. They won't be interested in running a textile factory in the future. [Thus] We don't have any plan to upgrade or enlarge our production. I think we will close our factory after our retirement. (A mother/factory owner in her fifties, Homei, 1994)

I am really grateful to my daughters. They have done so much! In those days [when they were in elementary schools], on weekends I always enjoined them repeatedly: "Don't go away. Don't go play. You have to make the woof shuttles. You have to tie the threads." [laughter] They were all overwhelmed by the work then! Now they complain to me that they weren't able to go to school because they had to help me out. I tell them our family was not rich, it was enough for them to graduate vocational schools ... It is exactly because they have worked so hard in our textile factory that I don't want my daughters to marry into textile families. I don't want them to labor any more. (A woman/factory owner in her seventies, Homei, 1995)

    A close relationship exists between the organization of the family and the mode of production both in the family and in the larger society. This chapter investigates textile manufacturing in small-scale, family-centered factories, the dominant type of production in Homei as well as in Taiwan's industrial sector. When Taiwan began its EOI in the 1960s, many farmers set up factories on their own land and mobilized their family members to perform production tasks. Although family acting as a corporate unit and family members working together for a common future are not new in

Chinese culture, the newly emerged economic opportunities give the cooperation a new meaning. Family labor proves crucial in the success of Taiwan's small-scale industry. It provides a cheap, steady, flexible, and efficient workforce, which enables Taiwanese manufacturers to produce goods at a low price while ensuring reliable, on-time delivery.

Under the recent predicament of labor shortage, family labor becomes even more important than before. Yet, when family labor is desperately in need, the elderly in the family can no longer count on their children for help. As discussed in previous chapters, the socioeconomic changes in the past few decades have created new opportunities for upcoming generations. Young people—and young women in particular—have attained higher education, and they are more inclined to acquire jobs in the booming service sector rather than in declining manufacturing industries. Conflicts between generations in a small producer's family have likely been exacerbated when the family factory manager—usually the household head, frequently the father (or the eldest male) but sometimes the eldest son—would prefer his whole family working under the rubric of the family business, but daughters of the family wish to pursue a career of their own.

In light of the story of the Wang family, who owned a small textile factory in Homei, this chapter examines the dilemma faced by young Taiwanese women in small producers' families, who are caught in between better opportunities for personal advancement and increasing family needs for labor. I begin with a brief history of the Wang family when they joined in the local textile production in the late 1970s. I then turn to the gender aspect of family production and its ramification to men and women of the Wang family. This chapter aims to challenge the long-standing concept of the Chinese corporate family, as the notion often emphasizes the "cooperation" aspect and overlooks the gender and generational inequalities embedded in the Chinese family hierarchy, which makes the cooperation possible. I do not, however, call for an alternative vision by simply adding the gender dimension, but one with a careful analysis of the dialectical relationship among gender, culture, and economy. Without such sensitivity, any gendered critique could run the risk of ignoring the dynamic process and only assume a flat, unchangeable concept of gender inequality. To illustrate this, I shall begin with a discussion of the "family" question.

The Family Question

In the first few weeks of my field research, I lived with the Wang family who owned a small weaving factory and spent most of my time with Mei-ling, the family's youngest daughter. Wang Mei-ling had already passed her thirtieth birthday and was the only daughter still unmarried. She worked in her brother's factory from nine o'clock in the morning to 5:30 P.M. and attended a local junior college at night. During my first few days there, I watched Mei-ling work during the day and then went to school with her in the evening.

It was the beginning of June, and the semester was about over. The school gave all students three days off, so that they could study for the final exam. On the first day of this "study vacation," Mei-ling worked in the factory as usual. In the late afternoon, one of her married sisters, Mei-hua, visited her parents and stayed for dinner. After dinner, Mei-hua immediately left, telling her parents that she had to go back to look after her computer shop in Chang-hua City. Right after Mei-hua's departure, Mei-ling threw her book bag in the back seat of her car and told me it was time to go. "Where?" I asked. Mei-ling did not answer me but only jumped into her car and urged me to join her. After she started the car, I was surprised to learn that we were not taking our usual route to school. Instead, we were driving toward Chang-hua City in the opposite direction. "Where are we going?" I asked again. "To my sister's shop," Mei-ling finally answered. Noticing my confusion, Mei-ling explained that she had arranged to spend the night with her sister. She said,

> You asked me where we were going at dinner. Well, I didn't want to tell you there, because I didn't want my parents to know that I have three days off. If they knew I didn't have to go to school today, they would ask me to work more hours at night. They would be very upset to see me not going to school but also not working in the factory. To keep them from knowing, my sister and I had arranged to leave home several minutes apart. But I wonder whether they have already guessed just by watching Mei-hua and me whispering at the dinner table.

We spent that evening at Mei-hua and her husband's computer shop, watching TV and chatting. A different Mei-ling emerged that evening. She was nothing like the daughter I had seen at home and in the factory, the woman who rarely talked to her parents and usually wore a gloomy look on her face. This evening Mei-ling suddenly brightened up. She talked spiritedly to her sister, haggled with her brother-in-law, and laughed heartily at his jokes and silly remarks. She was animated, quick to express her opinions, and sometimes even argue with her sister. Watching Mei-ling, I could not help but think that she must have felt free here. Yet at the same time, the image of a daughter who considered herself unjustly treated and constrained by her family came to my mind.

Mei-ling and I first met two weeks before I began to live with the Wangs, when I was taken by Mei-hua to see her family. Mei-hua was a classmate of the sister of a friend of mine from college; she kindly volunteered to help me to start my research. As soon as Mei-ling learned that I was a university graduate—that is, someone who studied at a "t'a-hsueh" (大學), a four-year university, as opposed and superior to someone who went to a "chuan-k'o" (專科), a junior (two- or three-year) college—and I was pursuing an advanced degree in the United States, she started plying me with questions about the universities in Taiwan, such as the sorts of departments different schools had, the test scores needed to get into a particular department, strategies and tactics to study for the university entrance exam. She was particularly interested in my experience in college and abroad. "You have such a wonderful life! You always get to do what you want. You are so free," Mei-ling concluded in an astonished yet distressed tone at the end of our conversation. She told me that she wished to study at a university someday, although she suspected that it was only a fading dream in reality. Mei-ling did manage to attend junior college, eight years after she graduated high school, but she still had to endure the disapproval of her family. She said, "None of my family supported my decision to go to junior college. They don't see any value of my going back to school. They want me to get married, or at least, to work for the family. I have always worked for the family, first for my father, now for my brother. But why do I have to do so? Why do I have to sacrifice myself for the family? Why me? Is it fair? Do you think it's fair?"

Wang Mei-ling's anguished voice has echoed through my research since then. Her indignant questioning has also challenged the popular belief that the Chinese are invariably willing to sacrifice themselves for the economic betterment of their families, a belief shared both by Taiwanese people and scholars at home and abroad. This is not to say that Mei-ling was not hardworking or that she was not willing to meet the family needs. As a matter of fact, she had worked in her father's weaving factory since graduating from junior high school. The issue at stake is the gap between the expectations of those who are in charge and those who work under them. Emphasis on the collective aspect of the family economy tends to conceal the fact that different family members usually endure different strains and are often rewarded unevenly. Mei-ling's call for fairness raises the often overlooked issue of gender inequality in a modern industrial family such as the Wang's, which bases its economic success on the labor of children, sons and daughters alike, yet perpetuates a patrilineal practice that rewards mostly the labor of sons.

The family has long captured the imagination of scholars of Chinese societies. A common view sees the Chinese family as a corporate unit to which family members contribute labor and income, under the authority of the household head, usually the eldest male (Cohen 1976; Freeman 1966; Harrell 1982, 1985; Skinner, 1957). Widely discussed in the literature is the careful economic calculation in a household division of labor that maximizes family prosperity (Cohen 1976, 1978, 1992; Oxfeld 1993). The effects of such a calculation on family organization and demographic composition in rural communities are also frequently noted (Chuang 1994; Pasternak 1972, 1983; Pasternak and Salaff 1993). Recent studies of Taiwan's industrialization highlight the continued importance of family in these regards. Family ties and kin relations are seen as still providing the security, motivation, and networks that have made Taiwan's industrialization possible (B. Gallin 1966; Gallin & Gallin 1985; Gates 1987; Greenhalgh 1990; Hu 1983, 1984; Ka 1993; Niehoff 1987; Stites 1982, 1985).

Hidden under the claim of a collaborative welfare, and less discussed, is the diversity and conflict of interests of individuals. The presumed family solidarity also affects the analysis of women and industrial work in the Chinese context. For instance, in Kung's (1994) and Salaff's (1995) pioneering and seminal studies of Chinese working women, both authors stress the subordination of working daughters' personal desires to the needs of their families. Both authors state that young factory women in Taiwan and Hong Kong did not resent the fact that they had to sacrifice themselves to achieve a higher living standard for the family and to pay for the education of sons in the family. These authors contend that this situation was compatible with the Chinese value placed on the family as a joint venture for survival and continuity. Furthermore, Salaff (1990, 1992, 1995) suggests that the extent to which a daughter is allowed to enjoy her own wage depends on the "dependence ratio" (the ratio of dependents to wage earners) in her family.

Nevertheless, several authors have challenged the corporate family ideology by highlighting the difference in comprehension and action that they observed among family members. Cohen (1976) reports that an adult son's calculation of self-interests will affect the timing of family division, often allegedly instigated by their wives. The wives are then blamed for disrupting the family unity. With this rationale, the family salvages the disgrace brought about by greedy sons who are considered to be the true members of the family. Another example is the creation of "uterine family" by married women, which Wolf (1972) argues indicates these women's efforts to secure their own position in their husbands' families. This very behavior, however, can also be argued as submissive to the patrilineal principle and thus reproduces a society in which males are highly privileged. Hu (1985) shows in her study of rural Taiwanese families that the authority of male household heads has been undermined by the employment of the younger generations, especially under the circumstances when sons and daughters-in-law manage to retain the income they earn. Recently, more direct and critical critiques of the corporate family ideology have emerged as a result of surging feminist scholarship. Li and Ka's study (1994) of a garment district in Taipei City shows that the success of small-scale manufacturers depends heavily on the (sometimes unwilling) participation of unpaid or underpaid female family members. By the same token, several scholars state that the collusion of Taiwan's subcontracting firms and the Chinese family system proves to be crucial for the former to remain competitive in the world market (Cheng and Hsiung 1992; R. Gallin 1984b; Hsiung 1996). Furthermore, Greenhalgh (1985, 1994) argues that "by valorizing family collectivism and obfuscating the gender inequality on which it is based, the ideology not only reproduces Orientalist constructions of Chinese culture, but it also discourages the discovery of subjugated knowledge and lends support to a new, flexible form of capitalist accumulation that is based on gender and other social inequalities" (Greenhalgh 1994:746).

In spite of these efforts, the degree to which women's awareness of gender inequality affects the labor deployment and resource distribution is yet to be explored. Equally important is the historical evolution of Taiwan's industrialization, its connection with the global economy at each stage and the social change—especially changes in family and gender dynamics—that occurred over the course of this industrial process. Previous literature has attempted to answer these questions by pointing out that the new job opportunity and wealth engendered by the recent industrialization facilitated changes in the family as well as between two sexes, although the changes have come slowly and frequently with serious cultural and political drawbacks (Arrigo 1980, 1984, 1985; Diamond, 1979; R. Gallin 1984a, 1990; Kung 1981, 1994; Salaff, 1995). My research shows, however, the direction of change is far from linear. Revealed in the life stories of the daughters in the Wang family is the multifarious and often conflictual consequences brought about by this process. A close look at the Wang family dynamics over time illustrates a conflation of economic strategic planning and women's submission to traditional family values at the early stage of Taiwan's export-oriented industrialization. Nonetheless, it also discloses a later departure when the society becomes more affluent (along with a changing economic structure and rising wage scales), while the competition in the international market has intensified. As a result, on the one hand, young women have more opportunities to pursue a life of their own, but on the other, they are burdened with the demand of family loyalty in a time of waning manufacturing industries.

The Entrepreneurial Wang Family

Like most of their industrial-producer neighbors, the Wang family's weaving factory and living quarters were built on the same site. Their house was located in the middle of farmland. It was a three-story, big, gray, cement building—downstairs was the weaving factory and the top two floors were the family's living space. A brook ran through the back yard of the house. Behind the brook was the Wang family's asparagus field.

The Wang family was one of the major asparagus growers in the region. Asparagus used to be the family's primary source of income. Thirty years ago, in the late 1960s, when Mei-hua and Mei-ling's grandfather was still alive and in charge of the family, asparagus was an important cash crop in the local economy and a major item in Taiwan's agricultural exports to Japan and the West. In the heyday of asparagus cultivation, the Wang family hired some hands to help them with the daily harvest. Mei-hua and Mei-ling's father, along with his brothers and sisters, was acting like a modern factory line leader in the asparagus field. Each of them was assigned to an area and worked with the four or five hired hands in his or her designated territory. The Wang family was quite well known for its asparagus business. Once an old neighbor of the Wang family told me that Mei-hua and Mei-ling's aunts were called the "Asparagus Princesses" in the region before they married. The family made quite a fortune out of this asparagus business.

However, the good days of asparagus seemed to be gone with Mei-hua and Mei-ling's grandfather, when he died in 1975. After his death, following the local tradition, the three sons, Mei-ling's father and his two younger brothers, divided the family farmland and other property, and went their own way. They continued to grow asparagus for a while, but the profit quickly declined. It was a result of both the competition from other Asian countries in the 1970s and the fact that the European Economic Community cancelled Taiwan's quota and gave it to China in 1979 (Wu 1993:436–437). The youngest brother gave up asparagus first. He started a small factory making small, assembled parts for faucets. The second brother soon followed. He began a weaving factory. Mei-ling's father, the eldest brother, continued to grow asparagus, until the profit one could make from textile appeared to be too tempting for him to pass up. He purchased twenty-four looms and began to weave in 1978. A few years later he acquired more machines in order to take advantage of the opportunity provided by the rapidly expanded local textile industry. At its peak the Wang family owned sixty-eight looms and hired fifteen workers.

Although the Wang's had hired workers from the very beginning, children of the family always constituted an essential part of its workforce. There were four of them. Mei-hua and Mei-ling's eldest sister, with the best "mathematic mind" in the family, became the factory accountant. She also cooked for workers and tended looms when labor was short. She did that until she married at age 25. Mei-hua and Mei-ling's elder brother first worked as a mechanic, but he gradually took over his father's supervisory role on the shop floor. As the only son, he would eventually inherit the family business, so that it was taken for granted by the rest of the family that he should learn to run the factory. Mei-hua and Mei-ling, the two younger daughters, were still going to vocational high school at night when their father started the factory. They normally worked for four hours in the morning and took a nap in the afternoon before going to school. However, if there was any worker taking a day off, they had to make up for the absent labor by working long hours at night after they came back from school.

Family members working together under the supervision of a patriarch is not a novel arrangement in Chinese culture. However, the introduction of industrial production provides new ways to accumulate wealth and therefore gives family cooperation new meanings. Industrial production also brought in a new form of labor. A major factor responsible for Taiwan's export expansion is the international subcontracting system. Most of the subcontract work is labor-intensive; it requires little capital investment to start and mainly relies on continuous labor input to create higher output (Skoggard 1996). Unlike agriculture, whose productivity is limited by the availability of land and the length of growing season, there is virtually no limit in industrial production. Machines can operate day and night, as long as the market continues to absorb their products (Skoggard 1996). As Taiwan's industrialization proceeded rapidly, surplus agricultural labor, particularly young women, became an invaluable potential workforce. For the first time in Taiwan's history, far from being a burden, daughters became the backbone of their family's economy. Girls from landless families worked for other factory owners and brought home regular and urgently needed cash income. Daughters of factory-owning families were even more indispensable. They not only worked full-time side by side with hired workers, but also had to work overtime if there was a need to make up for the absent hired labor.

The importance of family labor was made even clearer by the unequal relationship between Taiwanese manufacturers and buyers from advanced capitalist countries. Foreign buyers are primarily looking for cheap commodities. However, as the competition in their domestic markets as well as the international market intensifies, they also ask for increasingly shorter turn-around time. Taiwanese manufacturers have proven themselves highly effective in meeting these demands. They are efficient and flexible, and very capable of maintaining quality at a given price, while ensuring reliable, on-time delivery (Gereffi and Pan 1994). To accomplish this, manufacturers need to have the cooperation of a workforce willing to work cheaply around the production cycle, that is, working overtime for days or even weeks to meet a deadline and taking unpaid time off when the market is slow. Who could be more likely to satisfy these needs than a manufacturer's own family?

Therefore, many new industrialists like Mei-hua and Mei-ling's father heavily rely on family labor to assure a profit and a smooth flow of production. Family members provide a steady source of labor; factory owners can always count on them to work overtime whenever necessary. More importantly, the labor of family members is cheap. In many family factories, they are not paid but receive a "monthly stipend" with a value much less than the wage they could otherwise make in the wage labor market. In the case of the Wang's, the children received NT$5,000 per month when the factory just started, and only in the early 1990s had their "salary" risen to NT$15,000. In comparison, weavers in Homei usually made NT$27,000 or more each month in 1996.

It had become a tradition in the Wang family that children stayed home and worked for the family after graduating vocational high school. Given the fact that many young women of Mei-hua and Mei-ling's age (both of them were born in the early 1960s, with two years apart) in Homei have only junior high or even elementary school education, daughters of the Wang's were in fact in a prestigious position. Ironically, although they might enjoy a better material life, Mei-ling and her sisters were largely bound by family duty and had less free time than working daughters in less affluent families.

Mei-hua and Mei-ling both came of age at a time when Taiwanese society was gradually becoming richer, and the job market was expanding beyond manufacturing. Because of this, they had expressed their wish to continue with their education, so that they would have a better chance to enter other occupations than weaving. But their parents discouraged them. Apart from the fact that the family factory needed their labor, their parents shared the popular notion that women did not need much education. As previously discussed, it was a widely spread perception in Homei that it was useless for women to attain higher education. No matter how much a woman had accomplished in school, she would eventually marry into someone else's family, cook for them, and bear children for them, as women had always done before and would always do in the future. The life trajectory the Wang parents assumed for their daughters was that they would stay home, work, and then marry. Their primary responsibility as parents was therefore to find a respectable family for their daughters to marry into, and there was no need for their daughters to think otherwise. While this had been the practice of many generations of Chinese parents in the past, it has different implications now. In the past, Taiwanese society considered young daughters to be of no economic value but to waste the rice owned by their natal families. As the logic went, a daughter could not help to increase the wealth of her natal family, nor could she bear grandsons to continue her father's family line. Naturally, she should not be entitled to inherit the property of her natal family. However, daughters nowadays are no longer idle family members but valuable workers. Their labor contributes to the accumulation of family wealth. Yet, even though by Taiwanese law both sons and daughters have equal rights in inheritance, it is still widely practiced in Homei and many parts of Taiwan that only sons are the rightful heirs. Daughters, on the other hand, are given a dowry as a form of inheritance when they marry out.

One may argue that this practice is based on the logic of "exchange." That is, although a daughter is not entitled to the fruit of her own labor, after marriage, she can enjoy the fruit of her husband's sisters' labor, just as her own brothers and their wives are enjoying the result of her labor. This may sound fair, but in reality, inequality runs along the gender line. Although young men and women in the family may work equally hard, only males can inherit the family property. As a result, a son has a much better idea of what the future holds for him. In fact, he sees his future materialized day after day, as he works on the shop floor. If the family factory makes a profit, he will have a better future prospect; if the family business loses money, he knows that he will have to work harder in the years to come. Daughters, in contrast, will not be able to foresee their future while working for their parents. Who knows what kind of family they will eventually marry into? Their future is always uncertain and beyond their control, even after they get married.

Mei-ling's eldest sister married out, as expected. She married into a local family who also owned a weaving factory and became a hardworking weaver along with her sisters-in-law under the supervision of her father-in-law. Mei-hua and Mei-ling were still in vocational high school when their eldest sister married. After the family lost their eldest daughter upon her marriage, the labor of the two younger sisters became much more important to the family factory. However, it was around the same time that the life course of the two younger sisters began to divert.

Sisters Telling Stories

Despite their effort to thwart their daughters' wishes for a college diploma, the Wang parents had to change their mind and allowed Mei-hua to attend junior college after years of Mei-hua's insistence. Mei-hua thus became the first child in her family who was permitted to go to college. She returned to school in 1984, three years after she graduated from vocational high school. She was twenty-one years old then, and Mei-ling was nineteen. Mei-ling expressed her wish to go to school with her sister, but her parents refused. They told Mei-ling that they could not afford at the same time to pay for two college tuitions. But this was only one of their reasons. They were also concerned about the issue of labor supply. They could not bear to lose two workers concomitantly; they could at best allow one daughter to go at a time. Yet, Mei-ling's parents did not send her back to school, even after Mei-hua graduated from junior college. This time they had a more serious concern. Mei-hua was about to get married, and because of that, the Wang family would lose her labor permanently. As a result, Mei-ling's labor became even more indispensable. Once again, the family could not afford to let her go.

The parents' differential treatment with the two sisters had caused Mei-ling much bitterness. After all, Mei-hua was allowed, if not blessed, to continue schooling, whereas Mei-ling was denied several times to do just the same. Furthermore, Mei-ling's attitude toward courtship and marriage did not help to ease the tension she had with her family. While Mei-hua married in 1990, a few years after her graduation from junior college, Mei-ling refused to consider any such possibility and eventually became an "old lady" and nuisance at home and a headache to her parents.

One may question why the Wang parents made such different decisions with regard to their daughters' similar wish. One may also be tempted to attribute this to the different relations the parents had with the two daughters due to their very different personalities. Mei-hua was outgoing, adventurous, full of curiosity and eager to try out new things; she was good at, as well as enjoying, talking to strangers. In comparison, Mei-ling was quieter, more focused, and seemingly more stubborn and less easy to reach a compromise with. There seemed to be little wonder that Mei-hua would maintain close ties with her parents even after she married, while Mei-ling was constantly in a row with them and had finally reached a point where she almost refused to talk to them. The personal experience Mei-hua and Mei-ling had with their parents had certainly helped to shape their interpretations of the past and their expectations about the future. Yet, to fully appreciate the life stories of the two sisters, we cannot merely resort to the individual idiosyncrasies involved and the specific dynamics among the Wang family for explanation. It is important to see the two sisters' relationships with their family in light of the Chinese patrilineal and patriarchal culture, and the constraints embedded in Taiwan's small-scale industrial structure.

Wang Mei-hua: The Daughter Who's Married Out

> When I was in high school, I disliked weekends so much. Whenever it was Saturday, my classmates all became very excited because they were going to have a day and half off. They always planned to have fun after school. I didn't get excited at all. My life was very different from theirs. I just went straight home and worked in the factory. I knew I wouldn't have time off. I was doubly busy on weekends.

Mei-hua once told me so when I was sitting in her computer shop and sipping the tea she made for me, while we were both watching high-school students—her main group of customers—coming in and out of her shop. This was probably one of the most solemn comments she made about her life before marriage, although she had a big smile on her face while she said it. Mei-hua usually spoke in a light-hearted tone when talking about those "old days." Despite the fact that she had been working so hard and was often forced to juggle her time among school, factory, and her job in the insurance company after her graduation from junior college in 1987—and later, dating her boyfriend in secrecy—she rarely showed hard feelings toward her parents. She usually laughed at the silly things she did before. The one story she loved to tell was how she "stole" half an hour daily on the way home from the insurance company in order to meet her boyfriend.

> I had to sign in at 8:00 in the morning, and went to the routine meeting that followed after. The meeting usually ended around 10:30, and I would immediately leave the company and rush home to tend looms. I worked at home till 4:30 in the afternoon, and hurried back to the company at five, signed out, and hurried

out again to meet my boyfriend. We met around 5:15, and had a bowl of shaved ice or a glass of juice together. I had to say goodbye to him at 5:45, that left me fifteen minutes to rush home so I wouldn't be late for my 6:00 shift, and nobody would be suspicious about my movement. And we did it all over again the next day!

After she came back from the insurance company at 6:00 in the evening, Mei-hua continued to work on the shop floor usually till midnight. "I was always working, working, and working. There was no time left for me to think of anything else," she said to me.

Mei-hua not only lived an extremely busy life but also a life with a "double" identity: she was an insurance sales person in the professional world and a weaver in her father's factory. Pursuing her own career did not release her from her duty in the family business. She was expected to fulfill her family role first before she could do other things. Despite the fact that she had been deliberately arranging her daily schedule around the family demand, her job eventually caused tension in the family. Her brother, the supervisor on the shop floor, frequently complained to their father that Mei-hua was irresponsible because she did not do her share of work until it was too late, i.e. in the late afternoon after she came back from the insurance company. He wanted their father to force Mei-hua to quit. But Mei-hua insisted on keeping her job. According to her sister Mei-ling, the more the father and the brother pushed, the more determined Mei-hua became. Consequently, the brother and sister were in disagreement all the time.

As the time went by, the family's objection seemingly waned, and they gradually accepted Mei-hua's divergent attention as part of the reality they had to live with, although they were never happy about it. On Mei-hua's part, by taking a job outside the family in the first place and later resisting the pressure from the elders, she was negotiating for more space of her own, although the family duty was still an important guideline for her decisions and actions. The recognition that she had her own idea about life did not come easily, however, and the tension was continuously simmering beneath the compromise made by the family. The conflict of interests was only solved after Mei-hua married.

It seemed rather amusing to Mei-hua to look back now. After all, she is a daughter who has been "married out." She is no longer obliged to work for her natal family. Instead, as a married woman, her fate is linked with her husband—or rather, her husband's family—so is her labor. She helped her husband take care of his computer shop. In her free time she continued to take part in Taiwan's booming insurance industry, working as a sales person and making her own money from commission. Mei-hua was fortunate. Her parents-in-law were both retired farmers. They neither ran a factory nor owned a company and were not desperately in need of her labor. Furthermore, her parents-in-law had much leisure time to take care of Mei-hua's children, which set her free to explore new possibilities for herself and her husband. Mei-hua and her husband also decided to close their shop on Sundays. No more working on weekends!

Wang Mei-ling: The Daughter Who's Left Behind

Compared to Mei-hua, Mei-ling had a very different yet much more bitter story to tell. Not long after Mei-hua married in 1990, the Wang family underwent many changes. First of all, Mei-ling became the only daughter still working for her parents, along with her brother. Second, like their counterparts nationwide, the Wang factory was affected by the recent economic crisis and suffering from lack of labor. Third, Mei-ling's father had reached an age of retirement; he was about to pass their family business to his son, the heir of the family. Last but not least, Mei-ling was approaching her thirties, an age at which most Taiwanese women would have already married.

Mei-ling eventually became a big headache for her parents, when she passed her thirtieth birthday but still remained single. She was under a tremendous pressure from not only her family but also relatives and neighbors who all urged her to marry. Mei-ling always became demoralized when we touched on this topic in our conversation.

> Do you know how gossipy those old women are in the village? They often tease my mother by asking her how much longer she is going to keep me at home. They say I must be a treasured daughter so that she is reluctant to marry me out even though I have passed the age already. My mother said that if I don't get married soon, she will have no face to live in the village anymore.

Mei-ling's parents were bearing the stigma of having a middle-aged unmarried daughter.

Aside from the social pressure, Mei-ling's parents had a practical reason for their concern. As they viewed it, Mei-ling should have married and joined another family long before the age of thirty. Mei-ling's future was to be bound with her husband, not with them. Her husband or his family, not her parents, should be the ones who provided for her and took care of her material well-being. Since she was not married, who was going to do this for her? Mei-ling's situation clearly reveals the dilemma faced by young Taiwanese women, if they choose a life trajectory deviant from the cultural expectation.

Much worse than being old and remaining unmarried, however, was Mei-ling's insistence upon going back to school. After many years of waiting, Mei-ling eventually managed to go back to school in 1990. She did not ask for her parents' permission this time, but only told them the day before she was to register. Her father could not force her to quit but had to accept it as a fact. Mei-ling's determination to go back to school at a relatively old age was perceived by her family as the cause of her refusal of marriage. Yet, Mei-ling told me it was her parents' need to keep the factory going and their biased attitude of seeing sons as more important than daughters that prevented her from going to school earlier. She said that her parents had worked hard and pushed their daughters to work hard, in order to save as much money as possible for their only son. "I've told my parents many times that I am not going to marry unless I graduate from college, but they just don't listen," and she became really upset when she said this to me.

> It's entirely their fault that I am still in school and haven't yet got married. I always wanted to study, and I have expressed myself very clearly to them ever since Mei-hua graduated college. And they kept saying yes to me, but never really supported my decision in action. But even if they had been willing to let me go, with a constant problem of labor shortage, what could they have done otherwise? They had no choice but to keep me working in the factory!

Mei-ling explained to me why she insisted on schooling first and marriage second. She said, "Eventually I will be married out. If I don't get my education now, I won't have any chance at all after I get married. My own parents don't even support me on such matters, who else in the world do you think will support me? My husband's family? Ha, in your dream!"

Family Welfare vs. Individual Interest—But Whose Family Is It Anyway?

Around the time when Mei-hua became married and Mei-ling returned to school, their father was hit hard by the changes in Taiwan's economy and decided that he was too old to endure anymore of the pressure. He retired in 1991 and passed the business to his son. To solve the constant headache of labor shortage and to upgrade the quality of products, Mei-ling's brother decided to downsize the factory. He sold all the old machines and bought six more advanced ones. According to his plan, supported by his parents, he would now only need one worker on each shift. Besides being the "sales manager" of his own factory, he would also be the mechanic. With Mei-ling working on one shift, he only needed two more weavers to take care of the other two shifts. Mei-ling's labor was obviously seen as a factory or family asset transferred from the father to the son as part of his inheritance. As long as Mei-ling was not married, she belonged to the family, and so did her labor. She was paid NT$15,000 each month by her brother, as in the past, when her father was in charge of the family business.

After her brother took over the factory, and while she was attending school in the evening, Mei-ling continued to work the day shift in her brother's factory. But she had her own plan. To work for her brother was only a temporary arrangement. She hoped to find a job and have a career of her own after graduating from junior college.

Mei-ling's brother did not find two more workers, as he had planned. In a time of labor shortage, jobs on the night and graveyard shifts were the least attractive even with higher wages than any of the daytime jobs. In any case, Mei-ling became her brother's only weaver. Although he had to turn off the machines at night to accommodate Mei-ling's schedule, he also tried to keep Mei-ling at work as long as possible, except for the time he had to let her go to school.

It was a necessary strategy on the part of Mei-ling's brother to keep the factory going. However, Mei-ling spoke bitterly to me about it. She was always urged to work overtime whenever she was off from school. Her brother's wedding in 1992 seemed only to exacerbate her bitterness. Mei-ling's sister-in-law did not come from a textile family. She knew nothing about weaving, and she was not eager to learn. Mei-ling's brother rarely asked his wife to work in the factory. "Tending looms is a lot of hard work, and he loves her very much," said Mei-ling sarcastically. Mei-ling's parents did not push their daughter-in-law to help, either. It seemed that Mei-ling's mother was more concerned about the fact that her daughter-in-law get pregnant right away. She had been occupied with finding a means—mostly by consulting deities in local temples—to get her daughter-in-law pregnant, thus insuring the family at least an heir. At any rate, it became painfully obvious that Mei-ling's brother totally depended on her for factory operation. She was responsible for the success of the business, and she would be blamed if she did not do her "share," even on those occasions when she had to take time off for school or personal reasons. Mei-ling felt particularly angry that her labor was taken for granted by her family. Her family did not appreciate her contribution, nor did they support her decisions. She said,

> If I were a hired worker, I would just brush off the dust on my hips and leave at the end of a day after eight hours of work. I wouldn't care less about the progress of the production. It would be the boss's problem. But I am his sister! My mom always presses me, saying: "If you don't help your brother, whom else are you going to help?" It is taken for granted that I should work as much as possible to help out my brother. It never occurs to them that I also have my own things to do. I need to have my own time.

Mei-ling's relationship with her brother and parents began to sour when she insisted upon going back to school. It became even worse when she asked to have Sundays off in addition to her school time. Apart from expressing discontent directly to Mei-ling, Mei-ling's brother also complained to their parents, calling upon their authority and influence to dissuade her. There was a long struggle before her brother and parents finally yielded to her will. At the end, it was Mei-ling's action of going out every Sunday that forced them to accept her decision.

But Mei-ling also endured an emotional hardship for her persistence. She said,

> My mother was particularly upset. She was offended by my request. She felt that I was letting down the family by taking Sundays off. Without me there, my brother would either have to tend the looms himself or shut down the production completely. Either way, it would require him to work more or cut back his profit. How could I do this to my brother, particularly in such a difficult time? She refused to talk to me for a very long time.

> But they only care about their son! This is their son's factory, not mine. I won't be able to live under my brother's roof for all my life, even if I want to. I will have to find something for myself.

For a Better Future, or Not?

While Chinese family norms defined the proper behavior of family members, thus placing Mei-ling under her parents' authority working in their factory a filial daughter, the same norms also granted her an opportunity to escape from her ordeal, when the family business passed from her father to her brother. He, too, had authority over her, but his authority was never as powerful and absolute as that of her parents.

The boundary of family was opened up for different interpretations, when part of the family estate (i.e., the factory but not the farmland) was transmitted from the older generation to the younger one. Mei-ling's "old" age, in combination with her unmarried status, further added to the cultural ambiguity. Thus, on the one hand, Mei-ling was considered as one of the "family" by her parents and brother, particularly when they were desperately in need of her labor, and family loyalty appeared to be a powerful justification to appeal for her sacrifice. On the other hand, they also recognized the fact that Mei-ling was not, and could never be, a permanent member of the Wang family. Under the patrilineal principle, she was not to carry the family name, neither was she to inherit the family property. She would marry out. Given the fact that she was over thirty but still single, and she had refused her mother's matchmaking efforts, it seemed that Mei-ling's prospect for marriage was getting increasingly dimmer. Culturally she became a nuisance at home, particularly as her brother was about to build his own family. She had neither obligation nor full rights to stay with her brother. It seemed to the parents that they had no other choice but to let her go, which was also her personal wish.

Mei-ling graduated from junior college in June 1994. She was determined to leave her brother's factory and find a life of her own. Her parents continued to push her to work for her brother or to get married, although their efforts usually went in vein. The tension in the family continued to build. Mei-ling left home to stay with her friends several times during that summer after quarreling with her parents. This seemed to become her way of protest and resistance, whenever her communication with her parents failed. She no longer worked for her brother, who continued to be haunted by the problem of labor shortage. Losing Mei-ling's labor put him in a fairly difficult situation. He had tried to cover the day shift himself and find another weaver to work at night, but none of the workers he hired stayed long. When he was asked about his sister, he usually shrugged and muttered: "She does not want to do it. What more can I say to her?" He did not feel that he was in the position to demand her cooperation.

Mei-ling decided to take the civil service exam at the end of that year, as the first step to search for her new life, and she spent most of her time studying for it. However, she was also worried about her future. She was hoping to find a job related to her training in junior college, so that she could start building her career. But she also feared that to work full-time would take time away from studying and diminish her chance of passing the civil service exam. Nevertheless, being a woman in her thirties, she was hardly favored in the wage labor market. She was too old for entry-level jobs, which were usually reserved for women in their early twenties. Conventionally, women of Mei-ling's age are either married or about to marry. Employers perceive them as fading out of the labor market, and thus often hesitate to hire them. But Mei-ling was not qualified for advanced-level jobs either. She had no previous work experience other than in the Wang family factory. After a few unsuccessful attempts, she eventually worked for her sister Mei-hua, helping her and her husband to run their computer shop.

Mei-ling obtained her "freedom" at a high price. She continued to live with her parents. But she came to work at Mei-hua's shop in the early morning and went home at nearly midnight. She avoided spending time at home. She seldom talked to her parents or brother. It seemed that she was "dividing" herself from the family. In contrast to her married sisters, unmarried Mei-ling had a far uncertain future. In the process of searching for a career, she traded her freedom and "autonomy" with the security she would otherwise have had, had she chosen to stay with her parents and brother. It seemed that her parents were not going to change their mind about the rightful course of her destiny; and the job market continued to be unfriendly. Her future was hardly promising at this particular moment. From time to time she was extremely demoralized about not being able to find a real job and feared the possibility that she might have to go back to the textile industry.

Nonetheless, for all the uncertainty she was facing, Mei-ling was still glad for the choice she made. A few years after she left her brother's factory, I asked her whether she ever regretted her decision to leave home, and a big smile immediately burst on her face. She said: "Yes, I am happy. As long as I do not need to work for them, I am happy!"

In a Subversive Voice

One of the goals of feminist scholarship is to "[make] the invisible visible, [bring] the margin to the center, [render] the trivial important, [put] the spotlight on women as competent actors [and understand] women as subjects in their own right rather than objects for men" (Reinharz 1992:248–249). This chapter and the previous one followed this tradition. However, more than revealing the conflictual dimension in the Chinese family, in this chapter I also pushed ahead to the important task of contextualizing the emergence of these women's voices and the particular messages they convey. Compared to the Wang sisters, daughters of the previous generations might not have had the luxury of dreaming a future other than making money for the family and then getting married. The poverty that pervaded Taiwan at the time and the scarcity of employment opportunity largely prevented them from pursuing an alternative path. However, rather than inferring the "liberating" effects of a modern, industrializing economy on Taiwanese women, I also showed, through the eyes of Mei-hua and Mei-ling, the complex and often contradicting forces that affect a young woman's life.

On a collective level, it is also through the two sisters' alternative understanding of their role in the family that we observe a possibility for change. The Chinese family as both a social institution and a cultural ideal is extremely powerful. However, echoing the point that I made at the beginning of Chapter Three about the hegemonic New New Generation moral discourse, the Chinese family is neither static nor invulnerable. The economic opportunity rendered by Taiwan's post-WWII integration into the global economic system brought new prospects to the Taiwanese family, but it also made it a site of new contradictions and contention. Yet, reiterating once again a point I previously made, not all of the contradictions thus produced could be reckoned by the logic of capital in spite of their economic roots. Rather, as manifested in Mei-ling's struggles with her family, the contradictions often gave rise to new notions of rights, obligations, and entitlement, thus helping to shape a new sense of self, particularly for the subalterns. This, in turn, posed challenges to the foundation of culture and society, but not necessarily to the hegemony of capital.

CHAPTER 6

Guests from the Tropics

I have shown in previous chapters how nascent industrial production in Taiwan depended on the labor of women (often as daughters and wives). In order to continually maintain high levels of accumulation, Taiwanese entrepreneurs adopted strategies of relocating production overseas as well as importing foreign workers into the country. In response to the crisis of labor scarcity, the Taiwan government lifted its ban on foreign labor employment in the late 1980s. The introduction of foreign workers has a multifarious impact on Taiwanese society. This chapter focuses on the economic aspect of the impact. Drawing from my observation of the textile industry in Homei and conversations with local factory owners and workers, this chapter explores the intersection of government policies and business practices. Debates regarding the employment of foreign labor reveal the growing contradictions in Taiwanese society. While some tended to see foreign labor as both a temporary yet an urgent solution for Taiwan's continuous economic prosperity, some others saw it as a potential cause for labor disruption. Disputes arose over the labor practice on the shop floor in Homei's textile factories that fully exploits the vulnerable legal status of foreign workers. Varying perceptions held by Homei's residents about foreign labor will be analyzed in the context of their different economic situations and needs.[1]

The Foreign Labor Policy

International migration is a ubiquitous phenomenon in human history, increasing particularly after the European expansion since the sixteenth century. Whether coerced or spontaneous, population movements from one location to another in recent times demonstrate a structural inter-

Table 6.1
Foreign Labor Force in Taiwan*

	Quota Available	Quota Approved	Actual no. as in Taiwan
1992	35,864	14,707	15,924
1993	124,900	93,039	97,565
1994	212,254	140,696	151,989
1995	257,226	181,463	189,051
1996	270,131	226,868	236,555
1997	302,014	226,202	248,396
1998	337,430	251,893	270,620
10/1999	349,137	273,287	291,437
Agricultural (including sailors)	1,310	866	959
Industrial	199,783	164,058	171,744
Textile**	38,456	32,607	33,839
Construction	56,753	45,472	48,752
Service	91,291	62,891	69,982

Source: Employment and Vocation Training Administration (EVTA) (2000b).
*Data provided by EVTA does not differentiate the gender of foreign workers.
**The textile industry has the second largest number of foreign workers.

connectedness of societies under global economic forces (Goss and Lindquist 1995; Kearney 1986; Massey, et al. 1993; Sassen-Koob 1984, 1988). Although Europe and North America have been historically the primary destinations for most international migrants, lately other regions with high economic growth or expanding labor markets such as oil-exporting Arab countries and East Asian NICs, including Taiwan, also experience a major influx of migrant workers (S. Cheng 1999; Nash 2000; Raghaven 1996).

A system of migrant labor is characterized by the separation of processes of renewal from those of maintenance. Certain costs of labor-force renewal are externalized to an alternate economy and/or state (Burawoy 1976:1050), thereby increasing "the level of profits of certain firms and [of] capital as a whole by lowering the cost of labor and the cost of the reproduction of the labor force" (Sassen-Koob 1984:181). In the case of international migration, the separation is often facilitated by the governments of labor-receiving countries (S. Cheng 1999:52), that intervene in the functioning of the market by enforcing specific legal and political mechanisms, which regulate geographical movement and impose restrictions on the occupational mobility of migrants and often their length of residence in the receiving societies (Burawoy 1976:1050).

The political status of migrant laborers is a key factor here. It is their relation to the state, i.e., the denial of legal, political, and civil rights, that distinguishes them from native workers. As a result, migrant workers are deprived of the rights and abilities, as individuals or as a group, to influence the institutions that subject them to the employer as well as to other factions of the labor force (Burawoy 1976:1061).

The recent legalization of foreign workers in Taiwan faithfully reflects the general pattern discussed above. It has been clear since the very beginning that foreign workers are primarily introduced to ease Taiwanese employers' urgency for cheap and disposable labor, resonating with the phenomenon of capital outflow, as a strategy to reinsure surplus accumulation. Nevertheless, it is also the general public's consensus that foreign workers' stay has to be short and temporary. They cannot become a permanent burden of the society; neither can they be allowed to exert pressure by organizing unions and thus gaining social welfare benefits. Many Taiwanese are concerned about the potential problems that may be brought about by foreign workers. These include "rising unemployment rates and lower wage scales, rising crime rates, disruption of social harmony and aggravation of social tensions due to sharpened class and cultural differentiation, higher population density and the subsequent crowdedness and worsened environmental and living quality" (C. H. Chang 1995:589–590). It also threatens to disrupt the political entente between capital and government that leaves workers out of the power structure. Most of the policy recommendations thereby focused on the maximization of economic efficiency of foreign labor, yet the minimization of its social and cultural costs as well as possible benefits in raising working class standards (cf. Nash 2000). Some economists further recommended that the government publicly auction the foreign labor quota, and then use the revenue obtained to fund job training programs for unskilled and low-skilled Taiwanese workers who may be replaced by foreign workers (e.g., C. H. Chang 1995). Consequently, underlying the Taiwan government's foreign labor policy is the concern to protect the job security of Taiwanese, particularly disadvantaged groups, such as Taiwanese aborigines or the disabled, and to prevent foreign laborers (legal and illegal) from becoming permanent residents and a cause of social problems (*Liberty Times, U.S.A.* 1998).

In order to regulate the inflow of foreign workers efficiently, the Taiwan government signed bilateral agreements with several foreign governments (mainly in Southeast Asia) and only allows citizens from those countries to be legally employed in Taiwan (Table 6.2). The Taiwan government, as well as the governments that signed the bilateral agreements with Taiwan, license a limited number of labor placement agen-

Table 6.2
Foreign Workers by Nationality

Nationality	Percentage
Thailand	45%
Philippines	35%
Indonesia	18%
Vietnam and Malaysia	2%

Source: Council of Labor Affairs (2002).

cies to be in charge of related matters, such as customs processing, health examination, travel fares, document translation, and other measures designed to screen for disqualification before a foreigner is allowed to enter Taiwan as a legal worker (Sobieszczyk 1999). Each foreign worker will have to pay up to NT$60,000—a ceiling imposed by the Council of Labor Affairs, though in reality the fee commonly exceeds double this amount (Tierney n.d.:9)—for the services provided by these agencies. The money is usually deducted from the worker's wage, in the amount of "a maximum of NT$1,800 per month in the first year of placement, falling to NT$1,700 in the second year, and to NT$1,500 in the third" to pay off the debt (Tierney n.d.:9).

Under the current policy, the number of foreign workers hired in one single factory cannot exceed 30 percent of the total workforce in that factory. This can rise up to 35 percent, if an employer also hires aborigine(s) or disabled individual(s) (EVTA 2000a). However, as the unemployment rate has been on the rise since the early 1990s (EVTA 2000b), the Council of Labor Affairs also announced its intention to gradually reduce the number of foreign workers. Each foreign worker is allowed to work in Taiwan only once for two years, with an extension of another year. During their tenure in Taiwan, foreign workers are prohibited from changing employers. They can only work for the employer who brought them to the country. They are prohibited from marrying Taiwanese, nor does such a marriage grant them permanent resident status or citizenship. They still must return to their countries of origin at the end of their contracts (EVTA 2000a).

These legal and political measures have a profound impact on foreign workers' experience both in Taiwan's wage labor market and on the shop floor. In the following section, I will illustrate the impact through a discussion of labor practices in the textile industry in the Homei area, using Treasure Island as a primary example.

On the Shop Floor

Most of the Thai workers at Treasure Island were women, and few of them were men. Although the management never explicitly explained to me why they hired more Thai women than men, it was implicit in the many conversations I had with them that women were considered as more conventional and appropriate workers for the jobs involved. This was evident in the ways work was assigned. The Thai workers were divided into small groups and assigned to both weaving and spinning sections as well as to different shifts. Their tasks varied, but the division between men and women mainly followed the traditional pattern in the textile industry, i.e., men maintained and repaired machines or carried heavy objects, and women tended looms or assisted loom tenders. However, the management would occasionally ask Thai men to assist in loom tending.

By and large, the Thai workers played an auxiliary role. In particular, they were not involved in the last phase of production, which has a decisive effect on the quality of final products and is assigned to Taiwanese only. Taiwanese workers were believed to be more skilled, for many of them had many years of experience and had learned to do the job from their line leaders and peers. In contrast, the language barrier between Taiwanese and the Thai inhibited effective communication and thus transfer of knowledge between the two groups. The management at Treasure Island could not speak directly with the Thai—or vice versa. Both sides relied on the few ethnic Chinese to be their mediators and translators. Yet, the ethnic Chinese Thais were also foreign workers at Treasure Island; they were hired to be production workers but not translators. They had their own duties to perform and could not possibly keep up with the needs of the management. Hence, the communication between the management and the Thai workers was indirect and constantly delayed. Many important messages and subtle information were lost in the process. As a result, the delivery of commands and transmission of technological know-how were difficult and incomplete, which in turn prevented the company from placing trust in its foreign workers for important tasks.

Given the fact that the majority of foreign labor in Chang-hua County, where Homei is located, came from Thailand, the Bureau of Industry at the Chung-hua County government offered some Thai language classes to factory managerial personnel in the county. Yet, no one at Treasure Island seemed eager to take this opportunity, probably for the reason that the company did not provide enough incentive for any individual to invest the considerable amount of time needed to master this new and difficult language.

The Thai workers lived in the company's dormitory during their two-year stay. The company did not build the dormitory specifically for the Thai. The dormitory had always been part of the company's facility since its founding days in the late 1970s, to house its workers from out of town, as well as those who came off from night or graveyard shifts and needed a place to sleep before going home. In the company's peak days, the dormitory was the home for a few hundred young women. However, since the number of female workers had shrunk rapidly in the past few years, and most of the remaining employees possessed motorcycles and thus preferred to commute daily, the Thai were almost the only regular residents in the dormitory. The Thai women resided on the third floor of the women's dormitory. Male Thai workers resided in the men's dormitory, to which I had no access.

In their off-hours the Thai liked to go out, shopping, visiting night markets, or meeting and socializing with friends who were also guest workers in Taiwan. But they were not encouraged to stay out overnight. The company kept a close eye on them and checked their whereabouts every night. The Thai workers needed to have permission from their direct supervisor in order to leave the company even in their off hours, although their requests were rarely turned down. One of the functions of the security office by the company's front gate was thus to stop unauthorized foreign workers from going out.

The Thai workers had very little spare time to spend, however. Textile workers do not have weekends. They work seven days a work. The only extended off-time that textile workers have, Taiwanese and the Thai alike, is between the hours they are off from the day shift on Saturday afternoon and going back to work on the graveyard shift at midnight on Monday, which gives them thirty-two hours for recuperation (Table 3.1). For the Taiwanese at Treasure Island, this was their "Grand Weekend" (*Ta li pai* [大禮拜]), a time for sleeping late or catching up with personal and family duties. But the Thai usually preferred being busy. They rarely took the time off and often asked the management for overtime work.

One of the major differences between the Taiwanese and foreign workers at Treasure Island was the way they were paid. The former was on a piece-rate wage system, and the latter was paid at a fixed monthly rate. When I first started this research in the mid-1990s, without overtime pay, a Taiwanese loom tender made around NT$22,000 to NT$30,000 per month depending on the nature of her work, and the monthly wage of a mechanic, usually a male, ranged from NT$30,000 to NT$40,000. In com-

**Table 6.3
Wage in the Textile Industry in 1999
(in NT dollars)**

	Average	Minimum
Skilled labor	$25,875	$20,700
Non-skilled labor	$22,508	$18,000

Source: EVTA (2000a).

parison, regardless of their sex, a Thai was paid around NT$14,000. This amount was originally required by the Labor Standards Law to be the minimum wage for all workers, domestic and foreign, but it often became the standard wage for foreign workers. The wages have increased since then (Table 6.3). However, the practice of paying foreign workers minimum wages largely remains unchanged. Foreign workers come to Taiwan primarily to make money. As their monthly wage is fixed under the system, the only way they can make more money is to work overtime. Typically, foreign workers are highly motivated to do so in order to pay off the brokers' fees. They frequently labored two consecutive shifts (i.e., sixteen hours), without a break in between. As a result, the foreign workers "suffer constant tiredness and emotional grief, engendering lapses in concentration which can eventuate in serious injuries or worse" (Tierney n.d.:13–14).

The differences in pay and work assignments between Taiwanese and foreign workers usually became the subject of complaint among the Thai. Conflicts and struggles between the management and the Thai workers played out on the shop floor in various forms on a daily basis. Although most of the Thai (except the few ethnic Chinese) did not speak Mandarin and Minanese/Taiwanese, and could not understand the conversation among their Taiwanese coworkers, they were not deprived of the ability to watch and observe. It did not take them long to realize the differential, and often discriminatory, practices toward them. They complained about the different pay scale and work assignments from time to time. The Thai at Treasure Island, as in many other companies, were often allocated night and graveyard shifts, because most Taiwanese were not willing to work at night and often demanded during their job interviews that they work the day shift only. As a result, foreign workers had to work the two night shifts, consuming more physical strength and rarely getting a chance to see sunlight because they needed to sleep during the day.

It was usually the ethnic Chinese, who understood both Mandarin and Minanese/Taiwanese, who picked up information on the shop floor and informed their Thai compatriots about the discriminatory practices. Sometimes they also negotiated with the company on behalf of the Thai workers. From my limited conversation with the management of Treasure Island on this subject, I was given the impression that the managers had an ambivalent attitude toward their ethnic Chinese employees. For one thing, ethnic Chinese were usually better workers because they communicated with the management directly and learned the essential production knowledge more quickly. They were also indispensable for their language skills. Yet, they were often the "trouble makers" and leaders of dissent among foreign workers.

In spite of all the grievances they had against the company, foreign workers could not do much to change their situation. The company always had the power to send them home if they were alleged to be slow workers or troublemakers. Subsequently, their protest and resistance was often in a covert form, but could cause continual disruption to the daily routine of production. Mr. Chen, a foreman of Treasure Island, said to me, "They would complain, complain, and complain. It gives me a big headache! Sometimes they also slow down their work, and stagnate the whole production process. They even threatened to have a strike once." "What did you do then?" I asked. "Well, I warned them that if they didn't keep quiet and work hard, I would bar them from any opportunity of working overtime. They all love to work overtime. That's the only chance they have in order to make more money. They can't afford to lose that." Mr. Chen continued on to tell me that the Thai came from different regions in their own country. They were not a unified group. The management of Treasure Island often played on the fact that there were factions among them and gave overtime work only to those considered to be cooperative. This strategy aggravated ill feelings among the Thai and prevented them from forming solidarity. It also created competition among them, which in turn forced them to drop their grievances and cooperate with the management.

Foreign Labor Across the Region

The situation of foreign workers at Treasure Island is neither a norm nor a universal. Great variations exist among factories in the Homei area with regard to the number of foreign workers hired, their national origin, sex ratio, work assignment, living arrangement, food preparation, and life after work. Not every factory has a ready-built dormitory to accommodate foreign labor. Some firms put together temporary huts, and some others—particularly those family-centered small factories—spared unused space in the factory owners' houses to board these workers.

The sex ratio of foreign labor varies greatly from factory to factory, depending on the nature of production and products. Some factory owners hire only males or females, most others have a mixture of both. Although the tasks assigned to male and female foreign workers are mainly in the realm of tradition, it seems that more and more factory owners discovered the advantage of using foreign males to do both "men's" and "women's" jobs. Among Taiwanese, the sexual division of labor is strictly prescribed and rarely crossed, though more so for men than for women. Women may occasionally become mechanics, but men will never choose to tend looms; neither would any sensible factory owners ask their male employees to do such tasks. "That's a woman's job," I was often told. Nonetheless, the introduction of foreign labor also began to introduce new ways of labor deployment. During the course of my research, I observed more than once that factory owners assigned their male foreign workers to tend looms, without shame or hesitation. When asked for the reason, their answers were usually simple and straightforward: "It's perfect. Men can do both, tending looms and uploading and downloading fabric." Or "But why not? They don't complain."

Sometimes I was told that men were just as good as women. Yet, a close look beyond this phenomenon reveals a strong economic incentive that did not exist when the workforce was merely Taiwanese. The labor market in Taiwan is gender biased. Men's labor is usually valued more than women's, even if they are performing the same task. A textile factory owner will have to pay much more to hire a Taiwanese man to tend looms, assuming that there are willing candidates. Hence, based on both cultural sanction and economics, it is a better deal for Taiwanese factory owners to hire a female loom tender and a male mover. The introduction of foreign labor presents a more flexible as well as cheaper option. As male and female foreign workers are paid the same wage, it appears to be a shrewd business decision to have foreign males do both tasks. The concept that loom tending is a woman's job does not apply to foreign workers. A job is gender-specifically-labeled only when there is an economic impetus.

Nevertheless, assigning foreign male workers to do "women's" work was still rare. While I was in the field, factory owners who did so often had to answer questions from fellow employers about this unusual work arrangement. It is yet to be observed whether or not deploying foreign males to do "women's work" will become a trend or "convention" in the near future, thus fostering a breakdown of gender distinctions among Taiwanese.

Aside from the differences, there are common patterns underlying foreign workers' situations in Homei. First of all, like the management of Treasure Island, employers across the region generally do not entrust their foreign employees with crucial production procedures. Foreign workers are frequently assigned to the dirtiest, most laborious (and smelly, like dyeing), and least skillful tasks that very few Taiwanese are willing to do nowadays. In an industry like textile, in which machines operate twenty-four hours per day, but where fewer and fewer Taiwanese are willing to endure the hardship of changing shifts or being on late shifts, foreign workers become the main workforce on night or graveyard shifts in many local factories. Also, although the policy varies from company to company, most employers developed strict codes in regulating the movement of their foreign workers. The Thai at Treasure Island were required to report to their immediate superior before leaving the company in their off hours. This was rather a benevolent rule compared to some of the harshest in the area. A Taiwanese weaver in another company told me that foreign workers in her workplace were prohibited from leaving the company at all. She said,

> My company has very rigid rules toward foreign workers. The company hired a couple [husband and wife] to keep an eye on the Thai. The couple lives in the dormitory, so they can watch the Thai twenty-four hours a day. Day and night! The Thai resent it.
>
> The Thai are not allowed to go out—not on any occasions. The company doesn't want them to communicate with foreign workers in other companies. They don't want the foreign workers to exchange information and compare with others. ["Are they allowed to have visitors?" I asked.] Only if the visitor is their brother, sister, or spouse . . . The Thai like to drink. They drink a lot.

A Model Company in Foreign Labor Management

How to effectively manage foreign workers emerges as one of the newest challenges not only to Taiwanese factory employers but also to government officials in related agencies, such as the Council of Labor Affairs. The widely used phrase "foreign labor management"—i.e., *Wai chi lao kung kuan li* (外籍勞工管理) or *Wai lao kuan li* (外勞管理)—in the manufacturing circle, government's guidelines, and scholarly literature of labor and human resource exemplifies their collective concern and anxiety to be in control. Two issues are frequently emphasized in the general discussion of foreign labor management: the custody of foreign labor and enhancement of their productivity. The fact that all companies have developed policies to control foreign workers' movement shows the magnitude of the former concern. As to the issue of productivity, factory employers commonly complained that two years are too short, because they have to waste the first several months to train their foreign workers. Their foreign workers can only reach a satisfactory level of productivity after six months or longer on the job. By the time foreign workers have familiarized themselves with their tasks, they are almost about to go home. Taiwanese employers constantly complained that they would have to hire new foreign workers and start the training cycle all over again. Also, many factories adopt a fixed wage system, like that of Treasure Island, whose nature impedes foreign workers' incentive to be quick learners and efficient producers; they do not have much to gain from improving their productivity. How to motivate foreign workers to learn and yield a high efficiency has therefore become an urgent issue for the companies involved.

E&P, standing for "Excellence and Prosperity," and one of the largest tire-producing companies in Taiwan, was chosen by the Council of Labor Affairs to be a model company in foreign labor management and listed on the emulation tour for factory owners and managers in central Taiwan. According to a manager of Treasure Island who participated in the tour, foreign workers at E&P (also from Thailand) could apply to the company only once a week regarding the time they wished to go out the following week. Otherwise, they would have to be escorted by their fellow Taiwanese workers if they were to leave the company. The Taiwanese served both to protect the Thai from troubles and to prevent them from escaping. Also, the management of E&P enforced the rule that those living in the same room were held jointly responsible for one another's actions—a traditional East Asian control measure. All of the roommates would be sent back to Thailand as a punishment, if any fleeing occurred among them. This strategy turned foreign workers into their own guards. In fact, this strategy was so effective that none of the Thai at E&P have run away in recent years.

In contrast to most of the local companies in Homei, foreign workers at E&P were on a piece-rate wage system. Instead of paying a fixed monthly salary for all, the company only rewarded a full wage and bonus to those who accomplished a prescribed target production quota.

Also, their pay was reduced for any products that might be of substandard quality in order to compensate for the company's loss. The company also expected them to reach a satisfactory level of productivity within a given time, and the workers were told they would be sent back to Thailand if they failed to do so.

Amazed by the strictness of E&P's codes, I asked the manager at Treasure Island how E&P's management could afford to send back their workers even for the purpose of enforcing the rules, given my understanding that it took both time and money—and time in particular—to hire a foreign worker. The manager answered that the company's forcefulness was its key to a successful foreign labor management. He said that E&P's policy was to send back a few foreign workers to set an example. Not many would risk their jobs to challenge the company's authority. Nevertheless, the manager at Treasure Island also pointed out the fact that E&P had established its overseas firm in northern Thailand for a decade. They knew the region, and they drew workers to Taiwan mainly from that region. Unlike most of the Taiwanese employers, who relied on recruitment and placement agencies to facilitate the hiring and were blind regarding the selection process, "they [E&P] get to choose better workers," said the manager at Treasure Island.

The case of E&P presents a renewed phase in the global economy. The company's very pattern of capital and labor flow exemplifies a recomposition of world capital, in which Taiwan gradually becomes a major player in shaping the structure of the Asian-Pacific regional economy, if not the global economy. As more and more Taiwanese companies invested or relocated their production overseas, hiring practices like that of E&P have become increasingly common. The transnational link between Taiwanese companies and their overseas plants not only signals the most recent development of Taiwan's capital accumulation, but also facilitates a flow of labor in both directions. For those who manufacture in both Taiwan and abroad, they arrange for workers from the region of their overseas investment to supplement or reduce the labor cost back home. Some of the foreign workers hired under this circumstance have already worked for their Taiwanese employers in Thailand before being transferred to Taiwan. They have familiarized themselves with the production and discipline codes of their factories, so that they are able to fit into their new workplaces without much disruption. Furthermore, since Taiwanese companies usually move the least complex and most mass-produced part in their production overseas and leave the more technologically advanced and complicated procedures in Taiwan, their Taiwan operations often serve as a training ground for employees from overseas. Taiwanese manufacturers recruit foreign workers and train them in Taiwan. After they complete their two-year contracts, these foreign workers go home and become line leaders or foremen in the overseas factories of their Taiwanese employers.

The Runaway Incident

The vulnerability of foreign workers is particularly evident on the occasion when they transgress the legal boundaries set up by the government of their receiving country. The runaway incident I witnessed while staying at the dormitory of Treasure Island was a clear illustration. According to the Taiwan government's regulations, each foreign worker is allowed to work in Taiwan once for two years. After that they cannot renew their contracts and must return to their countries of origin, although many Taiwanese employers did manage to manipulate the official rules and rehire the same foreign workers. Some of the Thai workers at Treasure Island came nearly two years ago. The company would have to send them back very soon.

I was away for one weekend. When I came back on Sunday evening, Mrs. Lin, the chaperone of the women's dormitory, informed me that something "big" had happened. Over the weekend two Thai women went out but did not return. "They must have gone to look for other jobs," Mrs. Lin said. "They have to go back [to Thailand] in a few months. But they want to stay. They want to make more money."[2] Mrs. Lin then pointed out to me the photos of the two runaway women from the chart of pictures she had placed on her desktop, and said, "This one! This one is particularly a troublemaker. She constantly came in late after going out. We had to look for her for several times in the past. I always had the hunch sooner or later she was going to cause us a serious problem."

Mrs. Lin continued on to tell me that this was not the first time foreign workers at Treasure Island ran away before their contract ended. A male worker, also from Thailand, ran away a year ago. He was recently caught by the police and sent to a detention center for illegal migrants waiting for deportation. "Life is not easy [in the detention center]. They are treated like criminals!" Mrs. Lin shook her head, expressing her incomprehension of Thai workers' runaway behavior. She informed me that the company had acted quietly this time and hired a private investigator to look into the whereabouts of the two Thai women. According to the government's rules, employers of runaway foreign workers have to report the missing to their local police stations at once, so that the police would be able to assist in the search. Missing foreign workers are considered potential law offenders and pose a serious threat to the society at large. Nonetheless, many Taiwanese companies choose not to report to the police, mainly out of the concern that they will be held responsible and even sanctioned for the runaway behavior. The government may take away a company's foreign labor quota, if such a missing person case occurs. Thus, the management of Treasure Island decided to act on their own.

A week passed. A rumor spread in the company saying that the two runaway workers were seen working in a factory in an industrial park near Homei. Before the weekend was over, however, the two women came back. Employees at Treasure Island gossiped that the factory owner who hired them a week ago was concerned with their illegal status and decided to fire them. They had nowhere else to go but to come back. At any rate, they quietly sneaked back in the dormitory and reappeared on the shop floor at their presumed working hours, as if they had always been there.

Life went on at Treasure Island for two peaceful days. On the third morning, while typing up field notes in my room, I heard swift steps and men's voice in the hallway. Men were not allowed in the women's dormitory! I stuck my head out of the window and saw several Thai males carrying big luggage and walking down the stairs. They were leaving the dormitory, followed by the two runaways and some other Thai women. I followed the group to the front gate of the company and saw that a crowd of Thai workers had been waiting. The two runaways went to see the personnel manager for the last time. After they came out of the office, they were immediately taken away by a staff from the recruitment and placement agency that had facilitated the hiring of these Thai for Treasure Island. There was only time for the crowd gathering at the front gate to say good-bye.

Later during that day the general manager of Treasure Island informed me that the two runaways were flying back to Thailand, at their own expense, that afternoon. The staff from the recruitment agency would see to their departure. "We have to act quickly," the general manager said,

> We have no other choice. We don't want to turn them in to the police [which we are supposed to do according to the law]. We don't want to send them to the detention center. It's like a prison! But we can't keep them in the company, either. We couldn't confine them. If we don't send them back right away, who knows what other troubles they might bring us? They have run away once. They will try it again.

Voices of the Taiwanese

The "deportation" of the runaways became a popular topic in the company's conversation for days to come. None of the Taiwanese employees were affected by the incident, but it provided them an entertainment in their boring daily routine, as well as an excellent opportunity for a researcher like me to ask about their opinions on foreign labor. In addition to the runaway incident, several other events regarding the Thai occurred lately. A woman requested the company terminate her contract and send her back to Thailand. She received a letter from home, telling her that her husband was having an affair. "Why should I work so hard here and make money for him to have fun in Thailand?" she said to the company. Another man who was considered as a troublemaker by the company and who was said to not take orders from his superior, had been sent back not long before the runaway incident. A close working relationship with the recruitment and placement agency on these events seemed to indicate that Treasure Island as a customer was entitled to full warranty for their purchase of foreign labor. The recruitment agency had to agree to replace the returned goods with satisfactory commodities. They supplied Treasure Island with new workers to replace those who had failed to follow the rules.

Factory Owners—Employers

Foreign labor running away is a potential problem faced by all factory owners who employ guest workers. They are thus interested in and sympathetic to other owners when runaway incidents occur. After listening to my recitation of the incident at Treasure Island, a friend who owned a local weaving factory and hired fifteen Thai workers quickly responded: "Did they [the Thai] have to go back soon? ["Yes," I nodded.] That will do. It's in fact very bad to foreign workers themselves that they try to run away. Their employers will only develop worse rules to control their movement. The best strategy [for foreign workers] is to stay where they are. [If they do so,] their employers won't restrict them that much, and both sides will be happy."

He spoke from his own experience. The Thai workers in his factory were not restrained from going around. They moved freely between their workplace, living quarters, and shopping areas in downtown Homei. By granting his workers unconstrained freedom, this friend seemed able to establish mutual trust with his workers, thus exempting himself from the worry that his foreign workers might attempt to flee.

The Middle-Level Management

The middle-level management at Treasure Island—i.e., those who are themselves employees of the company, but who are in charge of the shop-floor production and have direct contact with the foreign workers—had the most negative things to say about foreign labor. Primarily because of their supervisory role, and responsibility for efficiency and productivity, the middle-level management tended to see the Thai as slow, lazy, and stubborn workers who did not want to learn. Mr. Huang, a foreman at Treasure Island, said to me in a conversation after the runaways were deported:

> If it were up to me to decide, I wouldn't like to hire any foreign labor. See how many of them have been sent back since your short stay here? ("Four," I raised four fingers.) That's right. Four! They say foreign labor won't cause any problems because they will go back after two years. It's okay only when there are a few of them. Now their number has increased to such an extent, that we will have many problems to come.

One of the criticisms made by the middle-level management at Treasure Island was that the Thai did not learn the proper ways to take care of the production. Mr. Huang continued,

> As I said, when there are only a handful of them, they follow your instructions. When their number increases, they stop listening to you, [and instead,] start teaching one another wrong ways to do things. They don't learn the good things, but only the bad. When our company began to hire foreign workers, we lost money on them in the first few months on the job. Their products were only of inferior quality. Now they don't even bother to learn from you. They don't care whether their final products are in perfect shape. We completely rely on the Taiwanese [who work in the packing section and serve as the last gatekeeper before the products leave the company] for quality control.

Nevertheless, the language barrier was the key to the problem here. As stated earlier, unable to communicate directly with the Thai, the management had to rely on the few ethnic Chinese Thais to translate for them. Thus the communication was indirect and constantly delayed. Many important messages and subtle information were lost in the process, adding more barriers to already existent cultural misunderstanding.

"But how do you feel about foreign workers? Do you resent their presence here in Taiwan? Are they replacing Taiwanese in textile factories?" I always asked people in the company. Given the popular impression that foreign workers are taking over the Taiwanese jobs, these questions were of fundamental importance. As I asked the middle-level managers at Treasure Island this question, instead of expressing their concerns over the potential replacement effect of foreign labor, some chose to make comments on the problem of labor shortage and the decline of work ethics among the New New Generation as its major cause. Resonating with the larger discourse, they moaned that the society had lost its virtue of diligence, and that this foretells the downfall of the Taiwanese economy.

Shop-floor Workers

Young women workers at Treasure Island had very different views about themselves, their future, and foreign workers. Most of them were going to night vocational school while working during the day. They considered their jobs in textile factories as temporary and expected to move on to better ones upon graduation. In answering my questions regarding foreign labor, one of the young workers thought hard for a while, as though answering an exam question, and replied: "For now, no. But I think they will replace Taiwanese eventually." But this was not a problem that concerned her. She intended to find a white-collar job as soon as she was out of school.

It was middle-aged women workers who revealed the most anxiety over the presence of foreign labor, especially if they observed a gradual substitution of Taiwanese with foreign workers in their workplaces. This was the group of people who formed the core workforce in Taiwan's earlier export-oriented industrialization. Without much education and skills needed for jobs in Taiwan's fast growing service sector, these women do not have many alternatives if they are pushed out of their current jobs. Thus they are the most vulnerable group of industrial workers. In one interview my informant, a weaver in her late thirties, repeatedly pleaded for an answer to the impact of foreign labor. She was very anxious to know whether employment of foreign workers would one day reach a point whereby all Taiwanese would lose their jobs to foreigners. In her workplace, the Thai had gradually become the main labor force. She said that the owner of her company had explicitly expressed his preference of foreign workers over Taiwanese:

> He said that the Taiwanese take jobs only when their families have extra needs. When the extra needs are met, they quit their

jobs immediately. He feels it takes too much out of him just to keep up with all these hassles. It's much simpler to deal with foreign workers. Now my manager relies on us to teach the foreign workers. He will fire us all as soon as the foreign workers have learned what we know. I no longer feel I have any job security.

To stipulate the cost for hiring a foreign worker became a favorite exercise for people at Treasure Island and me. According to our calculation, despite the fact that a foreign worker was paid a monthly wage of NT$14,000, the total cost to hire a foreign worker was almost as much as that for a Taiwanese worker. An employer has to pay for their foreign employees' lodging, food, health insurance, airline tickets for home visit once or twice during their two-year contracts, and a special fee to the Council of Labor Affairs. In the end it would amount to at least NT$20,000 per month to hire a foreign worker, not much cheaper than hiring a local Taiwanese. Yet, there are other benefits. From an employer's viewpoint, it saves him/her from the headache of labor shortages. It also assures the stability of his/her workforce for at least two years, during which foreign workers would and could not change jobs; they have to stay where they were hired. Also, it might be easier for Taiwanese employers to enforce a strict discipline code when their employees are foreign, since they are under a constant threat of being sent back. Finally, it saves employers from workers' retirement pensions as well as annual bonuses. The pension issue has increasingly become a problem for many Taiwanese companies established in the 1970s, because they have an aging labor force, but until now failed to save for their workers.

Strategies for Capital Accumulation

The introduction of foreign labor to Taiwan, first and foremost, resonates with the global strategy for capital accumulation that sees women as secondary wage earners and disposable laborers who can be paid less than males. While young Taiwanese single women are no longer available to fill the needs for labor in the industrial sector, Taiwanese manufacturers turn to women from less industrialized countries as a source of cheap labor. It increases the employer's profit by lowering workers' wages from separating labor renewal processes and those of maintenance, thus externalizing certain costs of labor reproduction to the countries where these foreign workers came from. The introduction of foreign workers also parallels an age-old strategy of capital to control labor, facilitated by the state. The Taiwan government's legal and political measures to prevent foreign workers from becoming permanent residents, and denying them the rights of geographical and occupational mobility as well as to organize unions further extends the power of Taiwanese employers. Foreign workers are under constant threat of "deportation," if they do not comply with the employers' needs and demand. The government's tight regulation over foreign labor also gives the larger society a sense of security and control, although it has been increasingly criticized as being insufficient and inefficient. The fear of labor displacement and the presence of unfamiliar faces have made newspaper headlines from time to time, yet for the time being, these largely remain latent social concerns rather than a public outcry.

The introduction of foreign labor to Taiwan, however, is more than a simple replication of an old strategy. It signifies a new phase of articulation between international capital and labor flows (Sassen-Koob 1984:185). On the one hand, there has been an acceleration of direct foreign investment of Taiwanese enterprises to China and Southeast Asia, primarily in the form of manufacturing capital, and on the other hand, there has been a large influx of Southeast Asian migrant workers to Taiwan. Both of these are strategies developed by Taiwanese industrial producers in hopes of maintaining their competitiveness in the global economy. Notably, in an increasingly sophisticated world system of production, there is no clear demarcation between those who invest overseas, thus directly exploiting cheaper labor in other countries, and those who continue to produce in Taiwan, thus hiring foreign workers to reduce production costs in their own country. Many Taiwanese manufacturers have carefully segmented production to be distributed to different sites, in order to maximize the comparative advantage provided by each locality. Labor is thereby contracted to move in multiple directions in this intensified process of capital accumulation.

CHAPTER 7

Bridging the Global and the Local: Understanding Taiwan's Economic Restructuring

In his assessment of the present state as well as the future of the capitalist world economy, Blim (1996, 1997, 2000) drew examples from East Asia and proposed intriguing questions: Can we say that there is a plurality of capitalisms built on national or cultural differences such as kuan-hsi or relationship that we observe in East Asia? Given a minimal definition of capitalism, "which consists of the organization and utilization of labor and effort for profit" (Blim 2000:32–33), are these national or cultural differences "expressions of institutional practices that are fundamentally different from the current standards of capitalism" (Blim 1997:358)? To answer these questions, Blim (1997, 2000) suggests that we look for inspiration from China, a surging global economic player based on an alternative logic thus far. The overall size and strength exhibited by China suggests that it may have the potential to assimilate or transform the capitalist world economy currently championed by the United States in the international struggle for hegemony (Blim 1996:88). By so doing, he also cautioned against the recent trend of viewing East Asian economies including Taiwan as representing many new and distinct types of capitalism.

From a separate venue, Dirlik (1997, 1998) and Pinches (1999) demystified the culturalist claim of "Chineseness" as the key to the East Asian economic prosperity and that among Southeast Asian Chinese diasporas. Dirlik (1997:311) contends that governments in the Asian Pacific region have been propagating the discourse of "Chinese Capitalism" to advance a nationalist cause. Pinches (1999:18) added that the ideology of Confucianism, which forms the cultural core of "Chinese Capitalism," helped to constitute a transnational Chinese identity that assisted to elevate the status of ethnic Chinese minorities across Southeast Asia. Like Blim, they both see these as struggles for hegemony against the West, albeit in an ideological front instead of a material/institutional one.

This book engages in the issues raised by both of these authors and tries to combine the insight of both, yet at the same time approaches the issues from a different angle as well as from a middle ground. On the one hand, the subject of foreign labor discussed in Chapter Six shows a keen economic calculation on the part of all interested parties including industrial producers/employers and shop-floor workers, although they each have their own concerns according to their economic positioning. This should make clear the Taiwanese' conformity to the capitalist logic. Besides, the overall scale of the Taiwan economy is probably too small to fundamentally shake the institution and practice of capitalism. On the other hand, however, the language utilized by the Taiwanese to describe, explain, and rationalize the recent economic restructuring was certainly influenced by their culture. Cultural patterns, inscribed in social interactions and institutional arrangements, define one's sense of self, thereby where and how one should place oneself in the social universe. Culture may be a dependent variable in relation to capitalism and the state, but cultural commitments can guide an individual's practice in pervasive ways that are only evident when focus is on the process rather than the outcome (Creed 2000:332). Furthermore, while political economic factors weigh heavily in my analysis, I also feel we often forget too easily that a discourse or ideology can also be based on something genuine to one's lived experience, however powerful or powerless one is in social system. We need to give personal initiatives more credit, for, ultimately, it is through individual emotion and actions that a reality is created, realized, and reproduced, and that seeds for alteration and transformation are planted.

Now let us return to the immediate issue of Taiwan's economic restructuring. The processes set in motion by global industrialization articulate with local culture and history to produce distinct contours for each locality and society (Nash 1981). New kinds of labor processes and relations have proliferated as a result of the merging of global economic forces, and indigenous values and practices (Cairoli 1998). In order to understand the centrality of labor in the discourse and practice of Taiwan's recent economic restructuring, it is essential to look at the local production systems, which have been dominated by small businesses particularly in the export forefront. Exemplified by the development of Homei's textile industry, the specific production relations, themselves a historical product, have created a set of dispositions within which Taiwanese factory owners and workers draw their understanding and strategies; and these in turn become the foundation for later change. As the current disjuncture in the Taiwan economy entails a disruption of previous social stability, thus opening up new possibilities for configuring a new kind of social order, it provides a perfect opportunity to study the intersection of global capitalism and local cultural politics as well as the multiple layers of the global economic process's impact.

Marketing Dependency and Precedence of Labor Issues

> *During my stay at Treasure Island, the general manager appeared somber on several occasions because another factory of his was constantly short of labor. On one such occasion, he told me that he desperately needed to find two workers. "Two?" I recall my own disbelief after hearing him saying so: "That's all you need, and you can't find them?" He gave me a firm nod and began to groan that he would be forced to shut down the entire operation if he could not find two workers soon. The general manager was indeed telling the truth. This other factory of his had recently upgraded its machines, in order to save labor and to improve the quality of its products as well as to broaden its varieties. There were sixty-four looms in this factory, and the factory hired a total of six workers of three shifts, with two on each shift, to take care of these machines. Given the small scale of this factory, lacking two workers would mean to drop one-third of the total production. It was indeed a great disaster.*

To be sure, labor has always been an overriding issue in the discussion of global economic transformation. Even in the current stage of capitalist development, which involves an internationalization of productive, commodity, and financial capital, and in which cheap labor is no longer the only reason for capital movement (Elson 1989:189),[1] labor remains a major concern both economically and politically. The growing significance of commodity and financial capital does not diminish the importance of industrial production, but only brings new dynamics to the shop floor around the world.

Taiwanese industrial producers share the concern with their counterparts around the world about minimizing production cost in order to maximize profit. Many of their claims and tactics mentioned in this book reveal this concern. In spite of this common interest, however, Taiwanese manufacturers have their own reason to discipline labor and keep down the labor cost due to their "marketing dependency"

(Skoggard 1996:70), the special pattern of linkage that they have with the world economy.

Marketing dependency refers to the distinct arrangement "in which Taiwanese-owned factories manufactured commodities to be sold under the brand names of transnational corporations or large retailing companies," leaving design work, product development, and marketing to foreign agencies (Skoggard 1996:70). This pattern of development has allowed Taiwan's capital-deficient small enterprises to take a quick and low-cost course to industrialization and an invaluable ready-made access to the international market. Nevertheless, the lack of technological supremacy and marketing ability also made Taiwanese capital vulnerable to economic circumstances, such as world recessions, oil crises, trade restrictions and negotiations, and competition from countries with the ability to produce similar commodities with cheaper prices. Uncertainties in the marketplace have discouraged Taiwanese entrepreneurs from making any large, long-term investment, but oblige them to make business decisions based on short-term product cycle and quick profit return (Skoggard 1996:70). To remain small is thus adaptive, as it enables them to be flexible and to spread the business risk broadly through a decentralized industrial system. Nonetheless, precisely because of their small size, Taiwanese firms lost their power to command prices in the marketplace (Skoggard 1996:70). Their small size also impeded their access to domestic as well as international financial institutions. Furthermore, the respective decentralized nature of Taiwan's industrial production prevented the government from intervening directly and effectively, particularly in times of economic difficulty.

Without the ability to command either the price or the market, small firms in Taiwan largely realize their profit through labor, the factor over which they have the most control. As a result, wages and the access to cheap labor are their principle concerns. Skoggard (1996:81–85) observed that in Taiwan's shoe industry small manufacturers realized profit mainly by hiring women and through their ability to manipulate the piece-rate system. Specifically, piecework enabled factory owners to change the pay rate for each task involved from order to order. This flexibility allowed them to adjust the labor cost of each order, so as to guarantee profits at the same time that it fractured the ability of the labor force to organize. Neither of these tactics is unique to the shoe industry, but they are widely adopted by employers in Taiwan's manufacturing sector, including those in Homei's textile industry in which women workers are paid by the number of yards produced by the looms under their care. It is under these circumstances that we can begin to understand why Taiwanese manufacturers chose to prioritize the labor issue in the context of the recent economic exigency.

Harmony, Prosperity, and the Moral Discourse

Subsequently, the New New Generation moral discourse did not emerge by chance, but truthfully captured the manufacturers' anxiety over their inadequacy in capital accumulation. The New New Generation discourse, however, encompassed more than just the economic concern of small producers. Although challenged by some labor advocate groups (mainly on behalf of unemployed middle-aged workers), the moral discourse nonetheless succeeded in articulating "the overwhelming majority of ideological elements characteristic of a given social formation," therefore creating "a collective national-popular will" (Smart 1997:405–406). As such, it made its appeal to a larger audience in Taiwanese society.

> On that hot summer afternoon, after lamenting young people's declining work ethic, Mr. Lin, the foreman at Treasure Island, continued, "If we don't work hard, we [Taiwanese] will be like the Philippines very soon. Look at the Philippinos! They used to be the most industrialized and wealthy country in Asia, but now they have [to come to Taiwan] to work for us. [When you take a trip to the Philippines, you will see] the people there don't work. They indulge themselves and don't want to keep up with what they have accomplished. [Mr. Lin paused for a second, seemingly to convince himself before he went on.] No, we won't be like the Philippines. We're hard working, and we've built a much more solid foundation to fall back on."

Although I was initially taken aback by the Philippino analogy in the conversation I had with Mr. Lin, I soon discovered that the Philippines was a fairly common reference, when local residents wanted to reflect on their current economic predicament. Despite its racist undertone, the comparison to the Philippines implicated the Taiwanese' anxiety for failure. For many Taiwanese, the contrast in wealth—or rather, the similarity in developmental history—between Taiwan and the Philippines or other Southeast Asian countries is not simply a convenient imagination on their part. It becomes only too real when they step out of the country, travel to Southeast Asia or China, and witness the "backwardness" and rural character yet the thriving force for progress and success in these countries. This reminds them of Taiwan in their own childhood, only twenty or thirty years ago. The prosperity of Taiwan is still too recent to become a permanent part of the national memory. Nonetheless, Taiwan's worldwide acclaim for its swift economic development surely fosters the Taiwanese' sense of pride. Taiwan's ruling KMT party also propagated a developmental ideology, both rhetorically and institutionally, as a way to establish its five-decade governing legitimacy, until the party lost the presidential election in 2000. This further reinforced the importance of the economy in shaping Taiwan's self-image. Yet, given the profound degree of Taiwan's dependence on foreign trade, and the continued state of hostility and possibility for military action between Taiwan and China, Taiwanese self-confidence tends to be precarious. This mixture of pride and continuing feeling of insecurity, I contend, dictates the ideological construction of Taiwan's recent crisis of capital accumulation.

Equal opportunity and upward mobility are important validations for the developmental hegemony. In addition to the rapid economic growth, equally impressive to the world about Taiwan's post-WWII industrialization is its relatively equal income distribution, accompanied by a nearly full employment rate, increases in real wages, and improvement of material standard of living (Deyo 1987). The small income disparity in Taiwanese society can be in part attributed to the spatial and organizational dispersal of industrial production, which, instead of erecting large enterprises with high concentration of capital and labor, provided opportunities for the Taiwanese to become small business owners. Past literature has paid much attention to the specific life trajectory of Taiwanese male workers in conjunction with Taiwan's highly decentralized industrial structure. Gates (1979) describes Taiwanese workers—men and women alike—as "part-time proletariats," because few of them expect to remain somebody else's employee for all their lives. Young Taiwanese workers share a common goal that they will only work for wages for a few years, and they will one day own a business and become self-employed. Industrial employment is therefore "an entrepreneurial strategy" (Hu 1983; Niehoff 1987; Stites 1985), from which young workers learn the knowledge, skills, and business networks in preparation to establish their own firms. This was certainly the situation in Homei, where many factory owners I met started out as hired mechanics in weaving factories. With the help of their wives, they eventually became their own bosses.

Yet, hegemony can never be exhaustive in practice (R. Williams 1977:112). In Taiwan, the booming of small-scale enterprises is closely associated with Taiwan's role in the global economic system and determined by the quantity of manufacturing orders from overseas. As Taiwan gradually lost its edge in producing light consumer goods for the international market after the 1980s, the chance to achieve small business ownership has correspondingly diminished. In spite of this fact, the expectation to become one's own boss continues to remain high, if not in the traditional manufacturing sector. However, even in the heyday of export-led industrialization, when there were plentiful business orders, not every working-class Taiwanese male shared equal opportunity to become an entrepreneur. The chance for a male worker to become his own boss varies from industry to industry, depending upon how segmented the production process is and to what extent subcontracting is utilized (Shieh 1989:30–31). For instance, in the garment industry, those who specialize in cutting fabric pieces and pressing have a better chance than those who do packing to establish an independent operation, and knowing about both production and marketing gives one the best edge to become an entrepreneur (Shieh 1989:31). Capital is also a primary factor. Not only does each individual have a different ability to mobilize financial resources essential for success, it is comparably easier to start up a small factory in labor-intensive industries than in capital-intensive ones, or within the same industry in the less capital-concentrated segments of the production (Shieh 1989:30–31). Within the textile industry, for example, it is easier to begin a dyeing factory than a weaving factory because the latter is more capital intensive (Shieh 1989:31).

Similarly, as hegemony is at no time fully encompassing, there can be never a singular hegemonic discourse. The aspiration for success and prosperity is further strengthened by the ideology of harmony. In the late 1980s, when Taiwan began to feel the pressure of intensified global competition, and the society was witnessing a wave of burgeoning social activism, the sentiment that peace and social order needed to be restored in order to ensure a continuation of economic prosperity was appropriated particularly by the business circle. This was most evident in cases of labor disputes, when management of the disputed company and often government mediators stressed cooperation, instead of confrontation, between labor and management to create a "win-win" situation. Yet, hidden behind the benign face of harmony and the alleged result of prosperity was an attempt to pacify the disenfranchised (Nader 1990, 1997). It was a move away from concerns with root causes (in this case, the crisis of capital accumulation and the unequal relations between capital and labor) and toward valorization of status quo and vested interests (Nader 1997:713–714).

> Ch'un-mei, my roommate at Treasure Island, used to drive me around on her motorcycle to explore industrial establishments hidden among rice paddies in Homei. One day she took me to the

factory of the son of her father's brother where she started her first job as a young weaving apprentice. She told me that this cousin of hers made a lot of money for being a shrewd businessman. Like many of his cohorts, he began his career as a hired mechanic, but soon saved enough money to open his own factory. He always knew what to produce and had invested his money wisely. Ch'un-mei, however, did not have good memory about his factory. "My cousin-in-law always told me to be a role model," she said, "I was always the first one who had to sign up for working overtime, and I was told to shut my mouth when employees were having complaints. They told me I was one of the family." "So were you treated differently?" I was curious. "I was only one of their family when they needed me," Ch'un-mei answered.

On the day of our visit, Ch'un-mei's cousin-in-law was working alone on the shop floor. Like many of their counterparts in Homei, the factory had a hard time finding and retaining workers. There were a few looms left, however. As shrewd as Ch'un-mei's cousin was, he had sold most of his machines and invested much of his money on real estate. Nevertheless, textile manufacturing remained the root of the family business. That's what they did the best, after all! Ch'un-mei told me that her cousin, himself a junior high school graduate, sent all his children to vocational high school: "One of my nieces studied commercial design; that's quite useful these days. And she found a nice job after graduation, too. But my cousin-in-law persuaded her to come back to work for the family factory. She told her daughter she would give her $15,000 a month, just like she would make working for others. I don't think it's right." Echoing her own experience and ambition, Ch'un-mei continued: "They shouldn't keep her at home. They should let her go. The world has changed now. It would be better for a girl if she has a job of her own."

The coercive power of the harmony ideology is most pervasive in the Taiwanese family. Ideas of gender and family are essential to the ideological construction of Taiwanese economy. Whereas the past success of Taiwan's export-led industrialization was closely related to the belief in and practice of entrepreneurship, the attainment of such status was supported by the roles of men and women in the family. There is no distinction made between the opportunity of men and women to become economically independent and successful in the developmental ideology. In reality, however, men are considered the household heads and breadwinners and are encouraged both ideologically and institutionally to be self-employed bosses. Women, on the contrary, are at most auxiliary, in that their contribution enables the men in their families to accomplish the goal of entrepreneurship (Hsiung 1996). Assumed to be the unit of production, accumulation, consumption, and distribution, the family forms the foundation of entrepreneurship. All members of a family presumably share the same inspiration, have equal access to resources, equal opportunity to pursue personal interests (which, once again, are assumed to coincide with the collective interests of the family), and equal share to the wealth accumulated. Yet, under the framework of patriliny and patrilocality, men and women secure their share through very different and highly unequal means. Men as sons are born lifelong members of their fathers' families. Whether married or not, they both contribute to and obtain benefits from the same social unit in which they acquire rights through birth. In the case of Taiwanese women, however, as daughters they are not considered permanent members of their natal families. Under Taiwan's export-led industrialization, they have likely contributed to the wealth of their parents' families, which forms the basis for their brothers' future prospects. A daughter may have helped to build, and also enjoyed, the property and prosperity of her natal family while she is single, but she has no claim over it. Her future rests with her husband's family. A Taiwanese woman does not and cannot attain full status through birth. Her marital status is the primary determinant of her social and economic privileges as well as her cultural and personal identity.

Gender and the Meaning of Work

Labor is never simply an economic term associated with only the human body, physical strength, individual output, or productivity. Rather, it has always been a concept laden with cultural meanings and social connotations. Members of a society are designated to various kinds of labor, which are often given different values. Any individual's claim over others' labor has to be recognized—if not legitimized—through a socially approved system of labor division. Therefore, to grasp the full ramification of Taiwan's recent discussion of labor, one needs to look beyond the immediate economic reasoning and ask questions regarding the construction and conceptualization of labor appropriation. Specifically, the culturally constructed gender has to be taken into account, for it is a defining factor in the segmented division of labor in Taiwan's postwar economic development.

As fieldworkers, we all want to be the best friend of and liked by as many people as possible. One morning while I was sauntering on the shop floor of Treasure Island with Ah-fong, who was doing her daily inspection as a line leader, Shu-fen, my roommate and a single senior high school graduate in her early twenties who worked as a technician preparing dyes at the company's laboratory, walked by. I hardly saw Shu-fen on the shop floor, for the lab was located on the second floor of a building in the far back of the company. It was a rare pleasure to run into her this way. I eagerly said hi to her and continued to accompany Ah-fong on her daily routine. As soon as Shu-fen was out of earshot, Ah-fong turned to me and said: "Look at her, see how arrogant she is. She thinks she's one cut above us. I would never want to initiate a conversation with her. We don't want to curry favor with somebody [who's better than we]." I was surprised, wondering what on earth Shu-fen, one of the most sincere persons I had met in Homei, could have done to invite such a vehement comment? As days went by, I discovered that Ah-fong made similar comments to nearly everyone who worked in the office or other nonshop floor departments, or who was slightly younger or went to school longer. It was not who these individuals were but what they represented that she was commenting on. Ah-fong thought that she and these people lived in two different worlds.

Young single women have been the favored labor force in the industrial sector. However, rather than seeing the sexual division of labor as a given, we should acknowledge it as an ever-changing product of the socioeconomic processes. This is revealed in the various contending voices in the New New Generation moral discourse. The competing views about the moral discourse elucidate in clear ways the contradiction between gender prescriptions and women workers' lived experience in a world of need, obligation, and opportunity. The apprehension of industrial employers and the society over young people's putative declining work ethic is thus an example of the inability or unwillingness of those who engage in, profit by, or contemplate women's industrial labor to give up their deeply ingrained ideas about men and women (cf. French and James 1997).

Still, there is more to be considered. Central to Taiwan's labor debate is the discordance of accounts not only between individuals of distinct economic interests (e.g., capital owners and workers) or between men and women, but also among women of different generations. This leads us to two important theoretical issues that are not only relevant in understanding the particular dynamics in Taiwan's recent economic restructuring, but also crucial in advancing our general knowledge about labor and gender in the current global economy.

The first issue regards the intersection of gender and other social institutions that defines women in the same society as groups of diverse obligations, rights, and interests. Gender has been acknowledged as a primary category for the allocation of political, social, and economic power. It is specifically identified as a key factor to understand the processes of economic globalization insofar as it is fundamental to the organization of production and labor (Fernandez-Kelly 1989b, 1994; Nash 1988; Nash and Fernandez-Kelly 1983). Built on the contribution made by previous studies, we now affirm that gender as a category by itself is not sufficient to explain the experiences of women. Rather, it is the articulation of gender and other social institutions that has to be examined. Also, similar to the concept of labor, gender is not a system of essentialized cultural beliefs and social interactions, but a process characterized by heterogeneity and instability that changes overtime (Ginsburg and Tsing 1990).

To study the relationship of economy and the formation of subjectivity, we thus have to have a plural understanding of the subject matter. Women as well as men do not exist as a group with monolithic interests. It may be difficult to find a single set of collective consciousness and action among each of them. Multiple patterns of capitalist accumulation coexist in each social formation by appropriating a population segmented by varied productive and reproductive roles. Women are thus labeled as different kinds of workers or potential labor force and integrated into the wage labor market—separately or concomitantly—at different stages of industrialization. This is particularly salient in societies like Taiwan, where patriarchy predates the penetration of capitalist enterprises in that gender intersects with kinship in these societies and designates individuals into a hierarchical order according to their gender, age, and generational category (Etienne and Leacock 1980; Nash 1988).[2] The meaning of gender is manifold, and only substantialized by daily contextualization, as comprehended and enacted by both workers and managers.

This was evident in Homei, where three distinct groups of women workers were found in the local textile industry. These three groups of women, as elucidated in the life stories of Yeh Ah-fong, Yang Ch'un-mei, and Lin Hsiao-fen, formed separate work and social groups on the shop floor as well as after work. The separation was not simply derived from differences in their age or marital status, but rather from the connotations these differences implied. Work in general, and industrial work in particular, covered a wide range of meanings for these three groups of women, who differed not only by generation but also by the time in their lives when they started working. Socialization of women in their gender roles fixed the parameters within which particular cultural and social responsibilities had to be fulfilled. This in turn affected their participation in the wage labor market. Concomitantly, they had different ideas about the causes and consequences of Taiwan's recent industrial restructuring, which indeed had a different impact on each group. They thus acted upon their ideas accordingly and differently.

Another important issue is the interplay of gender, ethnicity, and nationality in the global division of labor. One of the most distinctive features of Taiwan's recent restructuring is its rapidly transnationalized workforce, with an increasingly sizable number of Southeast Asian workers in its industrial sector. This coincides with the larger trend of intraregional migration in Asia, as Japan and other fast-growing Asian economies (e.g., Singapore, Malaysia, Hong Kong, and Taiwan) and oil-rich Middle East countries gradually become favored destinations of migration in addition to traditionally preferred Europe and North America (Raghaven 1996). A central cause of this wave of international migration is the unequal economic development between labor-sending and labor-receiving countries. It is a process by which individuals take advantage of economic opportunities distributed differentially across space (Kearney 1986:331). Yet, as embodied in Taiwan's strict foreign labor policy, it is also the intention of receiving countries to maximize the advantage of transnational labor while at the same time minimizing the cost of social reproduction in their countries (Kearney 1986:344). Furthermore, what needs to be addressed is the predominance of Asian women in the intraregional migration (Raghaven 1996). This reflects the important direction, and general pattern, of labor deployment globally. In Taiwan, industrial producers consider female foreign workers as a favorable source of cheap labor, as they exploit the latter's disadvantaged status as both female and non-national.

Nonetheless, the introduction of new labor and technology also introduced new ways of organizing work. Some of the textile employers in Homei have begun to assign their male Thai workers to tend looms. Clearly evinced in these cases was Taiwanese manufacturers' shrewd economic calculation, which was not considered as abhorrent within the context of preconceived cultural assumptions. As male and female foreign workers are paid the same wage, and since they are not obliged to follow Taiwanese cultural beliefs, there appeared to be little gain for Taiwanese factory owners to make loom-tending an exclusively woman's job. A job is gender specially labeled only when there are economic incentives and cultural sanctions or disinclination.

Workers' Identity and Women's Agency

Toward the end of my stay with the Wang family, Mei-ling drifted into my bedroom one after-midnight. She was very unhappy. She said her parents just had an argument over her. As Mei-ling had passed her thirtieth birthday, and her marriage prospects diminished not only due to her advanced age but also because of her stubbornness in not wanting to marry, "my father was thinking of giving me two million dollars so that I could have something to fall back on if I never get married; he's worried about me." I understood that it was the sum of money Mei-ling's father gave her brother when he took over the family factory. As such, culturally, it was like giving Mei-ling an equal share of the inheritance, although the brother would remain as the sole heir of the family farmland after their parents' death. "But my mother said no," Mei-ling continued, "She insisted there's no such thing that an unmarried daughter be given inheritance. She said it would be unfair to my brother." Mei-ling felt deeply hurt by her mother's words. It wasn't just about money.

When studying workers' identity and resistance in the current global industrialization, a fundamental question must be raised. Nonwestern experiences of capitalism have often been assessed in terms of "class consciousness," a concept largely based on western industrial experience with an emphasis on "the degree of recognition of class interests, organized action against capital, and even the goal of structural redistribution of power in society" (Ong 1997:77). Yet, capital has expanded to farther and farther corners of the world in the current global economic system and included increasingly heterogeneous groups of people in its workforce. Diverse forms of labor control have also developed, ranging from direct supervision on the shop floor, state intervention and suppression, to social and cultural regulations embodied in workers' kin and gender roles. Under these circumstances one needs to examine whether one can continue to use classic notions such as labor-capital conflict and class consciousness to conceptualize the effects of the latest capitalist expansion. As a matter of fact, instead of direct labor-capital confrontations, recent research often finds workers' resistance "in their oppositional tactics, embodied desires, and alternative interpretations and images" (Ong 1997:78).

Multiple sites of contradiction emerge in late capitalism, as diverse social formations are impacted by, and brought into tension with, the encroaching global economic processes (Lowe and Lloyd 1997:24–25). This is particularly the case of the competitive capitalist sector, such as that of Taiwan, where traditional family loyalty and responsibilities, as well as relationships between friends and neighbors, are drawn upon as a means for labor mobilization. Within such systems the emerging consciousness of young women workers is often an awareness of how their status as daughter and young woman is linked to domination by family, industry, and society. Therefore, in Taiwan, where class consciousness is denied as immoral for workers, women are able to reaccess and remake their identities and lives in important ways by manipulating, contesting, or rejecting their families' claims.

One important question remains, however. That is, how or under what circumstances is women's agency consciously constructed or enacted? In the attempt to answer this question, I would like to go back to my previous discussion of the concept of hegemony.

As discussed previously, whatever the hegemonic order may be in a society, it can never guide all aspects of social life, neither can it exhaust all possibilities of social dynamics. At most it can be a "partial hegemony" (Ortner 1996:18), leaving sites of alternative practices and perspectives that may become the bases for resistance and transformation. Accordingly, as Ortner (1996:17) has suggested, it is thereupon in "the lapses in social reproduction, the erosions of long-standing patterns, and at the moments of disorder and of outright anger and obstruction" that the subaltern agency, including that of women, is most likely discovered.

My research in Homei shows that women's agency was most expressive at the moment of disjunction when a young daughter broke away from the culturally sanctioned life trajectory to marriage and pursued a course of her own outside the traditional family spectrum. Against the background of patriliny, a woman's refusal to marry upsets the balance of obligations and rights that she and her natal family have over each other. This generally disrupts the formation of the ideal patrilineal family, as illuminated in the case of the Wang household, for the woman in question is subjected to a state of ambiguity and insecurity that often leads to her parents' concern about and need for special arrangements for her future.

This kind of cultural transgression is particularly meaningful under Taiwan's current economic circumstances. This is not simply because it shows Taiwanese women's desire and individual points of view, as opposed to the roles expected of them in the culture, though this fact is certainly in and of itself important. It is significant because the society's need for industrial labor provides a material base for women to be self-sufficient while remaining single. Moreover, it is crucial because through the need for special arrangements for unmarried daughters, we may begin to see Taiwanese parents' aberration from the patriarchal cultural ideal, forming a potential site for challenging the patrilineal hegemony. Last and most importantly, it elucidates the paradoxical yet dialectical relationship between the cultural ideal and practical economic consideration. Given the current tight labor market and the soaring international competition faced by Taiwanese manufacturers, parents and brother(s) in a small factory-owning family may feel ambivalent about their unmarried daughter-sister. On the one hand, the young woman's single status likely brings social pressure and stigma to the family, but on the other hand, she can make up their urgently needed production labor. As a result, a young woman who chooses to seek a future of her own may find herself caught in a dubious state of freedom while pursuing personal advancement, because of the pressure she has to endure due to the family's increasing need for workers. Both of these have a root in Taiwan's changing economy, and both of these reckon their claim through patriarchal family ideology.

Notes

Chapter 1

1. Labor activists who assisted me on this stage of my research included members of labor-advocate groups such as *Nu kung tuan chieh sheng ch'an hsien* (女工團結生產線), *Kung jun li fa hsing tung wei yuan hui* (工人立法行動委員會), *Lao kung chen hsien* (勞工陣線 [Taiwan Labor Front]), and of the former Labor Party (勞動黨). Most of them had prior experience in assisting workers in labor-management disputes due to plant closing and other causes. I thank them all for the help they provided me.

2. *Liberty Times U.S.A.*, October 13, 1997.

3. Although this newspaper article did not specify the sex of these unemployed workers, it is clear from the tone of the article, and the photo printed along with the article (featuring a middle-aged man sitting alone on a park bench, with a numbed look on his face), that idle males were the concern here.

4. *Free China Journal*, December 16, 1994.

5. I am grateful to the faculty and graduate students in the Department of Sociology at Tung-hai University (especially Feng Shu-chen, Fang Hsiao-ting, Wang Jenn Hwan, and Chao Kang), and my friend from college, K'o Yao-pi, for their help in directing me to Homei.

Chapter 2

1. The lantern festival takes place on lunar January fifteenth, the last day of the Chinese New Year. It symbolizes the end of the Chinese New Year celebration as well as the beginning of a new working season.

2. How the local businessmen in Homei were able to influence or even change the decision of the KMT government at a time of political turmoil such

as the late 1940s and 1950s is itself an interesting question. One explanation was that the KMT government was using this as an opportunity to cultivate a patron-client relationship with the local society of Taiwan (Huang 2000:49). The answer to this question would certainly lead us to a better understanding of the dynamics of an authoritarian regime (KMT) with the people it governed (the Taiwanese) at its founding stage. However, it is beyond the scope of this book to explore this issue.

3. Nonetheless, this issue remains controversial and far from being resolved. For example, Gold (1994) identifies the KMT-led party-state as one of the promoters of Taiwan's postwar economic development. He emphasizes characteristics such as "stable rule by a political-bureaucratic elite not acceding to political demands that would undermine economic growth; cooperation between political and private sectors under the overall guidance of a pilot planning agency; heavy and continuing investment in education for everyone, combined with policies to ensure the equitable distribution of the wealth created by high-speed growth; and a government that understands the need to use and respect methods of economic intervention based on the price mechanism" (Gold 1994:49).

4. The number of factories listed in Taiwan's official statistics are usually much lower than this, for many Taiwanese factories are nonregistered and unlicensed, and therefore are not included in the official record. The closest information I was able to gather came from the 1992 Statistics of Taiwan Textile and Apparel Industries (published by the Taiwan Textile Federation), in which the number of members of the Taiwan Weaving Industry Association in the whole country in that year was listed as only 296. This number should not be used to compare with that of Taiwan's weaving factories in its peak in the 1980s, for many manufacturers ended their businesses or relocated their productions overseas after the late 1980s. Nonetheless, the number may provide a gross estimate, showing the possible gap between the number of factories in the official record and those actually in operation.

5. The definition of small- and medium-scale businesses has changed over time, following the expansion of the scale of Taiwan's economy. Currently, small- and medium-scale businesses in the manufacturing sector refer to those whose paid-in capital does not exceed $80 million New Taiwan dollars or whose number of regular employees does not exceed 200 persons (Small and Medium Enterprise Administration, the Ministry of Economic Affairs, 2002).

6. Hsing (1998), Hu (1983, 1984), Ka (1993), and Shieh (1989, 1991, 1992) observed similar phenomena in other industries.

7. The national savings rate has always been high in Taiwan, even before the economy took off in the 1960s. For example, it was 15 percent of the GNP in 1952. The percentage of savings in the GNP continued to grow in later years and amounted to more than 30 percent in the 1970s and more than 35 percent after the 1980s (Yu 1993:105–106).

8. Taiwan held the second largest foreign reserves in the late 1980s, and the fourth largest in the world in the mid-1990s.

9. The mandatory education was extended from six to nine years in 1969, but in the first ten odd years after its implementation, parents in Homei largely ignored it. Girls were still urged by their parents to work upon elementary school graduation. This only began to change in the late 1970s.

10. *Free China Journal*, October 13, 1997.

11. Most of the Taiwanese investments in China have been routed through Hong Kong. The Taiwan government required that investment projects in the PRC of more than US$1 million be made through a company in a third country (Schive 1995:37), and Hong Kong appeared to be the most convenient broker for the Taiwan-China capital flows, at least before its handover to China on July 1, 1997.

Chapter 3

1. KTV, standing for "karoake TV," is an advanced derivation of sing-along bars. It is a club-like recreational place of booth-style private karaoke video rooms, with a big-screen TV and a computer-controlled selector box in each room (Boretz 2004). It can be considered as one of the most popular forms of entertainment not only in Taiwan but also where Taiwanese have migrated or Taiwanese manufacturers have expanded their production (Hsing 1998; Shen 2002).

2. Although in the following sections I discuss the changing pattern of interaction between industrial producers and their potential employees, in which young job seekers possess a certain amount of autonomy and choice, I do not by any means imply that Taiwanese workers now exert power over—or are equals to—their employers. As Shieh (1997) made it clear in his study, Taiwan's labor regime remains despotic in spite of recent changes in the economy. The despotic nature of Taiwan's labor regime is most evident in the occasion of labor dispute, when the state as the law maker yields neither authority nor willpower to mitigate, but leaves the disputed parties to reach a compromise, which often means to leave the worker(s) at the mercy of the employer, who has more money and powerful social connections, as well as better access to legal services (Shieh 1997:147–263).

3. Different from the "apprentice" mentioned by DeGlopper (1997), "apprentice" in this case is simply a colloquial way to refer to regular employees who get paid, albeit often in lower wages because they are not fully skilled.

Chapter 4

1. Although young single women were the preferred employees of industrial producers (particularly for the multinationals), this does not mean that older married women were not engaged in productive work but only staying home, conducting housework, and caring for their families. While homemaking was considered to be the primary role of married Taiwanese women, homemaking duties often combined with homework. Industrial producers actively sought married women as a source of low-paid labor intended to supplement factory output for the export sector (i.e., the putting-out system). Furthermore, "[w]hile homework is not uncommon in industrial nations, Taiwan is one of the few countries actively to pursue such cheap labor through state policies" (Appelbaum and Henderson 1992:228). Under the "Living Room is Factory" campaign, originated in 1968, the Taiwan government "[provided] special incentives for families to purchase sewing machines and learn sewing skills for homework. This simultaneously [increased] the supply of cheap female labor while reducing its cost, since expenditures [did] not have to be made on facilities, energy, dormitories, or management. Nor [were] women who [worked] at home provided with health insurance, minimum wage guarantees, or similar protections" (Appelbaum and Henderson 1992:228; also see Cheng and Hsiung 1992, Hsiung 1996).

2. This subheading came from Lamphere's (1987) book, *From Working Daughters to Working Mothers: Immigrant Women in a New England Industrial Community*. In this book she examines the transformation in the industrial labor market from one dominated by young daughters of immigrants to one by married women with children, as local industries evolved. A similar process has been observed in current Taiwan. I borrowed her title to indicate the fact that Ah-fong used to be a working daughter, but she continued working after marriage and childbirth, for reasons I will discuss below.

3. Many of those who declared themselves as farmers were in fact engaged in nonfarming economic activities, and they might derive most of their revenues from nonfarming sources. Nevertheless, they would continue to grow rice or other food crops even if only half-heartedly, mainly for the reason that they would be fined or even lose the title of their land if they left the land unattended.

4. Treasure Island provided three meals plus one late-night snack to its employees every day, to feed its three shifts of shop-floor workers. The meals were highly subsidized by the company. Employees paid almost nothing for the food they ate at work. At the time when I was lodging in the company, employees at Treasure Island paid NT$10 (roughly US$0.40) per day for the meals.

5. See note 2.

6. I do not have good statistical data to show the magnitude of men's drinking and gambling problems. Nonetheless, my conversation with local people, both men and women, seemed to confirm that the problem was fairly common.

Whether or not one spends excessively on drinking or gambling, these two are quite ordinary activities among male social gatherings not only in Homei but also nationwide. Boretz (2004) postulates in his research on Taiwanese masculinity that "there are, at a minimum, five tangible elements which no [Taiwanese males'] entertainment venue can be without: drinking, smoking, singing, and in one form or another, sex and gambling." These five elements "each and in combination are providing the actional context for the production of male subjectivity" (Boretz 2004).

7. Another important reason for their not hesitating to quit upon the birth of the first child is that their job as shop-floor workers is dead-end. Unlike their white-collar counterparts, whose career might be disrupted by quitting upon childbirth, female industrial workers stand no loss in promotion. They can always find another manufacture-related job, if they choose to return to the wage labor market.

8. Pei-chien-huo [賠錢貨], literally "commodities on which one loses money," is used in Chinese to describe women (daughters in particular) who consume their parents' resources (including dowry) but contribute their labor to and bear children for their husbands' families.

9. All of Ch'un-mei's siblings continued their education after elementary school.

10. Again, this seemingly benign work program for the convenience of night-school students can be considered as the petroleum company's strategy to attract a segment of the labor force who would have or be willing to work for less pay and with flexible working hours.

11. Sectarian religion has had its share of political persecution in Chinese history since the late imperial period (Naquin 1976, 1981; Overmyer 1976; Shek 1982, 1999). I-Kuan Tao as a modern sectarian religion has been no exception. It was considered by the Taiwan government as a threat to political stability and public safety, and banned as illegal and demonized as heterodox for nearly forty years until the suspension of the martial law in 1987. Largely due to this unpleasant and often dangerous history, I-Kuan Tao is organized as a secret sect, with temples located on the top floor of private homes. Believers are organized in temple cells of eight to ten core followers per temple (Bosco 1994:425); worship is largely clandestine. However, there are larger temples built for the purpose of major gatherings and public activities. The Sacred Heaven Fo-tang is one of the latter kind.

12. Women at Sacred Heaven who decided to remain single are not nuns. They are mainly dedicated I-Kuan Tao believers who chose to endow their time and income to spread the Tao. These women themselves use "sister," in a conventional and secular sense, to imply the bonding, intimacy, and affection developed among women who live under one roof and share their social and spiritual lives together.

13. There has been substantial literature published on the issue of gender and Chinese sectarianism (e.g., Jordan and Overmyer 1986; Naquin 1976, 1981; Sangren 1983; Shek 1982, 1999; Weller 1999:93–96).

14. For the organization of I-Kuan Tao lineage, see Jordan and Overmyer (1986:222–223).

15. *Szi-shu* (四書), which includes *Lun-yu* (論語, *the Analects of Confucius*), *Meng-tzu* (孟子, the Mencius), Ta-Hsueh (大學, the *Great Learning*), and *Chung-yung* (中庸, *the Doctrine of the Mean*). The Four Books have been considered as core to the learning of Chinese classics, thus fundamental to the education of Chinese intellectuals since early imperial times.

16. This is a commonly used term that the Taiwanese borrowed from Japanese since the colonial period. It means middle-aged or old women, or married women with children.

17. With all the talks of young workers being lazy and carefree, when it came to the decision of promotion, the management at Treasure Island still preferred the young and unmarried to the old and married, regardless of the latter's alleged diligence and sense of responsibility. Hsiao-fen's line leader, Li-ying, was one of the few exceptions. She was married but also had been working at Treasure Island since her early teens except for the several years right after her wedding when her children were very young. She was trusted because of her long-term relationship with the company, and her ability was well recognized. The other few married line leaders all shared similar backgrounds with Li-ying.

Chapter 6

1. Although in this chapter I focus my discussion on foreign workers in the industrial sector (namely the textile industry), they are not the only group recently introduced to Taiwan's wage labor market. There are also large numbers of foreign workers in the construction industry and in domestic service (Table 6.1), and they each have very different impacts on the preexistent native workforce in the sectors concerned.

2. The causes of the runaway problem are more complex than Mrs. Lin had explained. Lee and Wang (1996: 294–295, in Tierney n.d.:20) posit several hypotheses including "the failure to pass health check-ups or probationary periods, the desire to secure higher wages and/or improved personal relations with co-workers, and the frustration experienced after discovering that wages and conditions are highly contrary to those promised prior to departing their home countries." Nonetheless, the runaway workers were often disappointed, as illustrated in the result of this incident.

Chapter 7

1. At the present time, in many cases, international capital investment carries the mission to penetrate the local market of invested countries. To increase profit, investors may withdraw from production and concentrate on marketing goods produced by others. Another commonly used strategy along the same line is to compete through acquisitions, taking over potential rivals and buying market share (Elson 1989:189).

2. In order to clarify the specific historical circumstances in which gender was forged to become a decisive factor in the world systems, Nash (1988) urges a distinction to be made between forms of male dominance—those that rest upon patriarchy, and those whose male hegemony is imposed. Patriarchy refers to "elder male authority in a gerontocracy. It provides reciprocal benefits to the subordinate females and youths in the society where it prevails, and it implies persistence from past institutions" (Nash 1988:15). This process differs from the promotion of male dominance in Third World countries, where gender hierarchy was originally lacking but was fostered in the introduction of capitalist enterprises (Nash 1988:12).

References

Aberbach, Joel D., David Dollar, and Kenneth L. Sokoloff. Eds. 1994. *The Role of the State in Taiwan's Development.* Armonk, NY: M. E. Sharpe.

Appelbaum, Richard P., and Jeffrey Henderson. Eds. 1992. *States and Development in the Asian Pacific Rim.* California: Sage.

Arrigo, Linda Gail. 1980. "The Industrial Work Force of Young Women in Taiwan." *Bulletin of Concerned Asian Scholars* 12(2):25–38.

———. 1984. "Taiwan Electronics Workers." In *Lives: Chinese Working Women*, eds. Mary Sheridan and Janet Salaff. Pp. 123–145. Bloomington: Indiana University Press.

———. 1985. "Control of Women Workers in Taiwan." *Contemporary Marxism* 11:77–95.

Berger, Peter, and Hsin Huang Hsiao. Eds. 1988. *In Search of an East Asian Development Model.* New Brunswick: Transaction Books.

Blim, Michael L. 1992. "Introduction: The Emerging Global Factory and Anthropology." In *Anthropology and the Global Factory: Studies of Industrialization in the Late Twentieth Century*, eds. Frances A. Rothstein and Michael L. Blim. Pp. 1–30. New York: Bergin & Gavrey.

———. 1996. "Cultures and the Problems of Capitalism." *Critique of Anthropology* 16:79–93.

———. 1997. "Can NOT-capitalism Lie at the End of History, or Is Capitalism's History Drawing to an End?" *Critique of Anthropology* 17:351–364.

———. 2000. "Capitalisms in Late Modernity." *Annual Review of Anthropology* 29:25–38.

Bo Lan Chi (柏蘭芝). 1993. *Ching chi tsai chieh kou chung to fu nu chiu yeh pien ch'ien yu ti yu k'ung chien chuan hua: Tai-pei hsien ch'eng yi yeh kuan ch'ang nu kung tsai chiu yeh to ko an yen chiu* (經濟再解構中的婦女就業變遷與地域空間轉化：台北縣成衣業關廠女工再就業的個案研究 [Changes in Space Management and Women's Employment under Taiwan's Economic Restructuring: A Case Study of the Garment Industry in Taiwan County]). Master thesis. Taipei: National Taiwan University.

Bonacich, Edna, Lucie Cheng, Norma Chinchilla, and Paul Ong. Eds. 1994. *Global Production: The Apparel Industry in the Pacific Rim*. Philadelphia: Temple University Press.

Boretz, Avron. 2004. "Wine, Women, and (especially) Song: Carousing, Karaoke, and Machismo in Taiwan." In *Women in the New Taiwan: Gender Roles and Gender Consciousness in a Changing Society*, eds. Catherine Farris, Anru Lee, and Murray A. Rubinstein. Armonk, NY: M. E. Sharpe.

Bosco, Joseph. 1990. *Family and State in Taiwan's Rural Industrialization*. Ph.D. Dissertation. New York: Columbia University.

———. 1994. "Yiguan Dao: 'Heterodoxy' and Popular Religion in Taiwan." In *The Other Taiwan: 1945 to the Present*, ed. Murray A. Rubinstein. Pp. 423–444. Armonk, NY: M. E. Sharpe.

Bourdieu, Pierre. 1977. *Outline of a Theory of Practice*. Translated by R. Nice. Cambridge, MA: Harvard University Press.

———. 1984. *Distinction: A Social Critique of the Judgment of Taste*. Translated by R. Nice. Cambridge, MA: Harvard University Press.

Burawoy, Michael. 1976. "The Functions and Reproduction of Migrant Labor: Comparative Material from Southern Africa and the United States." *American Journal of Sociology* 81:1050–1087.

Cairoli, M. Laetitia. 1998. "Factory as Home and Family: Female Workers in the Moroccan Garment Industry." *Human Organization* 57(2):181–189.

Castells, Manuel. 1996. *The Rise of the Network Society*. Oxford: Blackwell.

Ch'ai Sung Ling, and Hsieh Chin Ho (柴松林與謝金河). Eds. 1988. *Chin ch'ien yu hsi: I chiu pa ch'i T'ai-wan ts'ai ching p'i p'an* (金錢遊戲 [The Money Games]). Taipei: Tun li.

Chang Chin Fen (張晉芬). 1995. "Kung tsuo ch'uan: Mien mien ts'i hen, ko yu chuen ch'i?" (工作權：綿綿此恨，可有絕期？[The Right to Work]). Paper presented in the first annual conference of Association for Women's Studies, Taipei.

Chang Ch'ing Hsi (張清溪). 1995. "Pa ling nien tai hou ch'i lao kung tuan ch'ueh yu hsiang kuan to lao tung shi ch'ang wen t'i" (八零年代後期勞工短缺與相關的勞動市場問題 [The Labor Shortage and Other Issues Relating to the Labor Market after the Late 1980s]). In *T'aiwan jen li tsi yuan lun wen chi* (台灣人力資源論文集 [Essays on Taiwan's Human Resources]), ed. Liu K'o Chi. Taipei: Lien ching.

Chang, Raymond J. M., and Pei-chen Chang. 1992. "Taiwan's Emerging Economic Relations With the PRC." In *Taiwan: Beyond the Economic Miracle*, eds. D. Simon and Y. M. Kau. Pp. 275–298. Armonk, NY: M. E. Sharpe.

Chen Chieh Hsuan (陳介玄). 1994. *Hsieh li wang luo yu sheng huo chieh kou: T'ai-wan chung hsiao ch'i yeh to sho hui ching chi fen hsi* (協力網絡與生活結構:台灣中小企業的社會經濟分析 [The Subcontracting Networks: A Socioeconomic Analysis of Taiwan's Small- and Medium-Sized Businesses]). Taipei: Lien ching.

———. 1995. *Huo pi wang luo yu sheng huo wang luo: Ti fang ching jung, chung shiao ch'i yeh yu T'ai-wan shi su hua sho hui chi chuan hua* (貨幣網絡與生活網絡:地方金融,中小企業與台灣世俗社會之轉化 [The Fiscal and Social Networks: Transformations in Taiwan's Local Financial Sector, Small- and Medium-Sized Businesses, and the Secular Society]). Taipei: Lien ching.

———. 1999. *T'ai-wan ch'an yeh to sho hui hsueh yen chiu: Chuan hsing chung to chung hsiao ch'i yeh* (台灣產業的社會學研究:轉型中的中小企業 [A Sociological Study of Taiwan's Manufacturing Industries: Small- and Medium-Sized Businesses in Transition]). Taipei: Lien ching.

Chen Chieh Ying (陳介英). 2001. "Chia tsu ch'i yeh yu T'ai-wan ching chi" (家族企業與台灣經濟 [Family Businesses and Taiwan's Economy]). In *Ching chi yu sho hui: Liang an san ti sho hui wen hua to fen hsi* (經濟與社會:兩岸三地社會文化的分析 [Economy and Society: Analyses of the Society and Culture in Taiwan, Hong Kong, and the People's Republic of China]), eds. Yen Hua Chu and Wei An Chang. Pp. 37–50. Taipei: Sheng chi.

Cheng, Lucie, and Gary Gereffi. 1994. "U.S. Retailers and Asian Garment Production." In *Global Production: The Apparel Industry in the Pacific Rim*, eds. Edna Bonacich et al. Pp. 63–79. Philadelphia: Temple University Press.

Cheng, Lucie, and Ping-chun Hsiung. 1992. "Women, Export-Oriented Growth, and the State: The Case of Taiwan." In *States and Development in the Asian Pacific Rim*, eds. Richard Appelbaum and Jan Henderson. Pp. 233–266. Beverly Hills: Sage Publications.

Cheng, Shu-ju Ada. 1999. "Labor Migration and International Sexual Division of Labor: A Feminist Perspective." In *Gender and Immigration*, eds. Gregory A. Kelson and Debra L. DeLaet. New York: New York University Press.

Chou, Bi-er, Cal Clark, and Janet Clark. 1990. *Women in Taiwan Politics: Overcoming Barriers to Women's Participation in a Modernizing Society*. Boulder, CO: Lynne Rienner Publishers.

Chou Tien Cheng, and Lin Chi Ch'eng (周添城與林志誠). 1999. *T'ai-wan chung hsiao ch'i yeh to fa chan chi chi* (台灣中小企業的發展機制 [The Mechanism for Development of Taiwan's Small- and Medium-Sized Businesses]). Taipei: Lien ching.

Chu Yen Hua, and Chang Wei An (朱燕華與張維安). 2001. Ching chi yu sho hui: Liang an san ti sho hui wen hua to fen his (經濟與社會：兩岸三地社會文化的分析 [Economy and Society: Analyses of the Society and Culture in Taiwan, Hong Kong, and the People's Republic of China]). Taipei: Sheng chi.

Chuang Ying Chang (莊英章). 1994. *Chia tsu yu hun yin* (家族與婚姻 [Family, Kinship, and Marriage]). Taipei: Institute of Ethnology, Academia Sinica.

Cohen, Myron. 1976. *House United, House Divided: The Chinese Family in Taiwan*. New York: Columbia University Press.

———. 1978. "Developmental Process in the Chinese Domestic Group." In *Studies in Chinese Society*, ed. Arthur P. Wolf. Pp. 183–198. Stanford, CA: Stanford University Press.

———. 1992. "Family Management and Family Division in Contemporary Rural China." *China Quarterly* 130:357–377.

Council of Labor Affairs. 1995. *Monthly Bulletin of Labor Statistics*. Taipei: Executive Yuan, Republic of China.

———. 2002. *The Republic of China Yearbook—Taiwan 2001* [html document]. Available from: http://www.gio.gov.tw/Taiwan.

Creed, Gerald W. 2000. "'Family Values' and Domestic Economies." *Annual Review of Anthropology* 29:329–355.

Deglopper, Donald. 1997. Personal communication.

Deyo, Frederic C. ed. 1987. *The Political Economy of the New Asian Industrialism*. Ithaca, NY: Cornell University Press.

Diamonod, Norma. 1979. "Women and Industry in Taiwan." *Modern China* (3):317–340.

Directorate-General of Budget, Accounting, and Statistics (DGBAS). 2001. "Ba shi chiu nien T'ai-wan ti ch'u fu nu hun yu yu jiu yeh tiao ch'a chieh kuo chai yao" (八十九年台灣地區婦女婚育與就業調查結果摘要 [Marriage Reproduction, and Employment of Women in Taiwan, 2000]) [html document]. Available from: http://www.dgbas.tw.

———. 2002. "National Statistics: Social Indicators" [html document]. Available from: http://www.dgbas.gov.tw.

Dirlik, Arif. 1997. "Critical Reflections on 'Chinese Capitalism' as Paradigm." *Identities: Global Studies in Culture and Power* 3(3):303–330.

References

———. ed. 1998. *What Is In a Rim? Critical Perspectives on the Pacific Region Idea.* 2nd edition. New York: Rowman & Littlefield.

Elson, Diane. 1989. "Bound by One Thread: The Restructuring of UK Clothing and Textile Multinationals." In *Instability and Change in the World Economy*, eds. Arthur MacEwan and William K. Tabb. Pp. 187–204. New York: Monthly Review.

Employment and Vocational Training Administration (EVTA). 2000a. "Foreign Labor" [html document]. Available from: http://www.evta.gov.tw.

———. 2000b. "Statistic Indice" [html document]. Available from: http://www.evta.gov.tw.

Enloe, Cynthia. 1989. *Bananas, Beaches, and Bases: Making Feminist Sense of International Politics.* Berkeley: University of California Press.

Etienne, Mona, and Eleanor Leacock. 1980. "Introduction." In *Women and Colonization: Anthropological Perspectives*, eds. Mona Etienne and Eleanor Leacock. Pp. 1–24. New York: Praeger.

Fernandez-Kelly, M. Patricia. 1983. *For We Are Sold, I and My People: Women and Industry in Mexico's Frontier.* Albany: State University of New York Press.

———. 1989a. "International Development and Industrial Restructuring: The Case of Garment and Electronics Industries in Southern California." In *Instability and Change in the World Economy*, eds. Arthur MacEwan and William K. Tabb. Pp. 147–165. New York: Monthly Review.

———. 1989b. "Broadening the Scope: Gender and International Economic Development." *Sociological Forum* 4(4):611–635.

———. 1994. "Making Sense of Gender in the World Economy: Focus on Latin America." *Organization* 1(2):249–276.

Freeman, Maurice. 1966. *Chinese Lineage and Society: Fukien and Kwangtung.* London: The Athlone Press.

French, John D., and Daniel James. 1997. "Squaring the Circle: Women's Factory Labor, Gender Ideology, and Necessity." In *Gendered Worlds of Latin American Women Workers: From Household and Factory to the Union Hall and Ballot Box*, eds. John D. French and Daniel James. Pp. 1–30. Durham, NC: Duke University Press.

Gallin, Bernard. 1966. *Hsin Hsing, Taiwan: A Chinese Village in Change.* Berkeley: University of California Press.

Gallin, Bernard, and Rita Gallin. 1985. "Matrilateral and Affinal Relationships in Changing Chinese Society." In *The Chinese Family and Its Ritual*

Behavior, eds. Hsieh Jih-chang and Chuang Ying-chang. Pp. 101–127. Taipei: Institute of Ethnology, Academia Sinica.

Gallin, Rita. 1984a. "Rural Industrialization and Chinese Women: A Case Study from Taiwan." Michigan State University, Women in International Development, Working Paper, No. 47.

———. 1984b. "Women, Family and the Political Economy in Taiwan." *Journal of Peasant Studies* 12(1):76–92.

———. 1990. "Women and the Export Industry in Taiwan: The Muting of Class Consciousness." In *Women Workers and Global Restructuring*, ed. Katherine Ward. Pp. 179–192. New York: ILR Press.

Gates, Hill. 1979. "Dependency and the Part-time Proletariat." *Modern China* 5:381–407.

———. 1987. *Chinese Working Lives: Getting By in Taiwan*. Ithaca, NY: Cornell University Press.

Gereffi, Gary, and Mei-lin Pan. 1994. "The Globalization of Taiwan's Garment Industry." In *Global Production: The Apparel Industry in the Pacific Rim*, eds. Edna Bonacich et al. Pp. 126–146. Philadelphia: Temple University Press.

Ginsburg, Faye, and Anna L. Tsing. 1990. "Introduction." In *Uncertain Terms: Negotiating Gender in American Culture*, eds. Faye Ginsburg and Anna L. Tsing. Pp. 1–16. Boston: Beacon Press.

Gold, Thomas. 1986. *State and Society in the Taiwan Miracle*. Armonk, NY: M. E. Sharpe.

———. 1994. "Civil Society and Taiwan's Quest for Identity." In *Cultural Change in Postwar Taiwan*, eds. Stevan Harrell and Huang Chun-chieh. Pp. 47–68. Boulder, CO: Westview.

Goss, J. D., and Bruce Lindquist. 1995. "Conceptualizing International Labor Migration: A Structuration Perspective." *International Migration Review* 29(2):317–351.

Greenhalgh, Susan. 1985. "Sexual Stratification: The Other Side of 'Growth with Equity.'" *East Asia Population and Development Review* 11(2):265–314.

———. 1990. "Families and Networks in Taiwan's Economic Development." In *Contending Approaches to the Political Economy of Taiwan*, eds. Edwin Winckler and Susan Greenhalgh. Pp. 224–248. Armonk, NY: M. E. Sharpe.

———. 1994. "De-Orientalizing the Chinese Family Firm." *American Ethnologist* 21(4):746–775.

References

Hamilton, Gary. 1998. "Culture and Organization in Taiwan's Market Economy." In *Market Cultures: Society and Morality in the New Asian Capitalisms*, ed. Robert W. Hefner. Pp. 41–77. Boulder, CO: Westview.

Harrell, Stevan. 1982. *Ploughshare Village: Culture and Context in Taiwan*. Seattle: University of Washington Press.

———. 1985. "Why Do the Chinese Work So Hard? Reflections on An Entrepreneurial Ethic." *Modern China* 11(2):203–226.

Harvey, David. 1989. *The Condition of Postmodernity*. Oxford: Blackwell.

Hefner, Robert W. ed. 1998. *Market Cultures: Society and Morality in the New Asian Capitalisms*. Boulder, CO: Westview.

Ho, Samuel P. S. 1978. *Economic Development of Taiwan, 1860–1970*. New Haven, CT: Yale University Press.

Ho-mei Chen Kung Suo (和美鎮公所 [Ho-mei Township]). 1989. *Ho-mei Chen Chi* (和美鎮志 [The History of Ho-mei Township]). Changhua, Taiwan: Ho-mei Chen Kung Suo.

Hochschild, Arlie. 1983. *The Managed Heart: Commercialization of Human Feeling*. Berkeley: University of California Press.

Ho Yen Tang (何燕堂). 1992. *Lao kung chi ti kang cheng to hsing shi yu tung yuan: Hsin Kuang kuan ch'ang kang cheng to ko an yen chiu* (勞工集體抗爭行動的形式與動員：新光士林廠關廠抗爭的個案研究 [Patterns of Mobilization in Collective Labor Struggle: A Case Study of Plant Closing at Hsin-kuang, Shi-lin]). Master thesis. Taipei: Soochow University.

Hsia Lin Ching (夏林清). 1993. *Tai-pei hsiang kuan ch'ang wen t'i tiao ch'a pao kao* (台北縣關廠問題調查報告 [An Investigating Report on the Plant Closing in Taipei County]). Taipei: Center for Labor Education, Taipei County Government.

Hsiao Hsin Huang et al. (蕭新煌等). Eds. 1992. *Chieh p'o Tai-wan ching chi: Wei ch'uan t'i chi hsia to lung tuan yu po hsueh* (解剖台灣經濟：威權體制下的壟斷與剝削 [Dissecting Taiwan's Economy: Monopolies and Exploitation under Taiwan's Authoritarian Regime]). Taipei: Ch'ien wei ch'u pan sho.

Hsing, You-tien. 1998. *Making Capitalism in China: The Taiwan Connection*. Oxford: Oxford University Press.

Hsiung, Ping-chun. 1996. *Living Rooms as Factories: Class, Gender, and the Satellite Factory System in Taiwan*. Philadelphia: Temple University Press.

Hsu Cheng Kuang, and Sung Wen Li (徐正光與宋文里). Eds. 1989. *T'ai-wan Hsin Hsing Sho Hui Yun Tung* (台灣新興社會運動 [The Emerging Social Movements in Taiwan]), Taipei: Chu liu tu shu kung shi.

Hu, Tai-li (胡台麗). 1983. "The Emergence of Small-Scale Industry in a Taiwanese Rural Community." In *Women, Men, and the International Division of Labor*, eds. June Nash and M. P. Fernandez-Kelly. Pp. 387–406. Albany: State University of New York Press.

———. 1984. *My Mother-In-Law's Village: Rural Industrialization and Change in Taiwan*. Taipei: Institute of Ethnology, Academia Sinica.

———. 1985. "T'ai-wan nung ts'un kung yeh hua tui fu nu ti wei to ying hsiang" (台灣農村工業化對婦女地位的影響 [The Impact of Rural Industrialization on Women's Status in Taiwan]). In *Proceedings of the Conference on the Role of Women in the National Development Process in Taiwan*. Pp. 337–356. Taipei: Population Studies Center, National Taiwan University.

Huang Chi Liang (黃志亮). 2000. *Shou lieh Ho-mei san shi nian* (狩獵和美三十年 [Thirty Years of Journalism on Ho-mei]). Lukang, Taiwan: Tsuo yang.

Jaschok, M. 1984. "On the Lives of Women Unwed by Choice in Pre-Communist China: Research in Progress." *Republican China* 10(1A):42–55.

Jordan, David K., and Daniel L. Overmyer. 1986. *The Flying Phoenix: Aspects of Chinese Sectarianism in Taiwan*. Princeton, NJ: Princeton University Press.

Ka Chih Ming (柯志明). 1993. *T'ai-wan tu shi hsiao hsing chi chao ye te chuang ye, ching ying yu shen chan tsu chih* (台灣都市小型製造業的創業，經營與生產組織：以五分埔成衣製造業為案例的分析 [Market, Social Networks, and the Production Organization of Small-Scale Industry in Taiwan]). Taipei: Institute of Ethnology, Academia Sinica.

Kao Ch'eng Shu (高承恕). 1999. *T'ou chia niang: T'ai-wan chung hsiao ch'i yeh "t'ou chia niang" to ching chi huo tung yu sho hui yi yi* (頭家娘：台灣中小企業'頭家娘'的經濟活動與社會意義 [The Economic Activities and Social Meanings of "the Boss's Wife" in Taiwan's Small- and Medium-Sized Businesses]). Taipei: Lien ching.

Kearney, Michael. 1986. "From the Invisible Hand to Visible Feet: Anthropological Studies of Migration and Development." *Annual Review of Anthropology* 15:331–361.

Kim, Seung-kyung. 1992. "Women Workers and the Labor Movement in South Korea." In *Anthropology and the Global Factory*, eds. Frances A. Rothstein and Michael Blim. Pp. 220–238. New York: Bergin and Garvey.

———. 1997. *Class Struggle or Family Struggle? The Lives of Women Factory Workers in South Korea*. Cambridge: Cambridge University Press.

Klein, Donald W. 1992. "The Political Economy of Taiwan's International Commercial Links." In *Taiwan: Beyond the Economic Miracle*, eds. Denis Fred Simon and Michael Y. M. Kau. Pp. 257–274. Armonk, NY: M. E. Sharpe.

References

Knauft, Bruce M. 1996. *Genealogies for the Present in Cultural Anthropology.* New York: Routledge.

Kung, Lydia. 1981. "Perceptions of Work among Factory Women." In *The Anthropology of Taiwanese Society*, eds. Emily Martin Ahern and Hill Gates. Pp. 184–211. Stanford, CA: Stanford University Press.

———. 1994. *Factory Women in Taiwan.* New York: Columbia University.

Kuo, Cheng-tien. 1995. *Global Competitiveness and Industrial Growth in Taiwan and the Philippines.* Pittsburgh: University of Pittsburgh Press.

Kurtz, D. 1996. "Hegemony and Anthropology." *Critique of Anthropology* 16(2): 103–135.

Lamphere, Louise. 1987. *From Working Daughters to Working Mothers: Immigrant Women in a New England Industrial Community.* Ithaca, NY: Cornell University Press.

Lee, Ching Kwan. 1998. *Gender and the South China Miracle: Two Worlds of Factory Women.* Berkeley: University of California Press.

Lee, Joseph S., and Su-wen Wang. 1996. "Recruiting and Managing Foreign Workers in Taiwan." *Asian and Pacific Migration Journal* 5(2–3):280–301.

Lee, Teng-hui. 1971. *Intersectoral Capital Flows in the Economic Development of Taiwan, 1895–1960.* Ithaca, NY: Cornell University Press.

Li Yueh Tuan, and Ka Chih Ming (李悦端與柯志明). 1994. "Hsiao hsing ch'i yeh to ching ying yu hsing pieh fen kung: Yi Wu-fen-pu ch'eng yi yeh sheng ch'an chu chi wei an li to fen hsi" (小型企業的經營與性別分工：以五分埔成衣業生產組織為案例的分析 [Sexual Division of Labor and Production Organization in Wufepu's Small-Scale Industries]). *Tai-wan sho hui yen chiu chi kan* 17:41–81.

Liberty Times, U.S.A. 1998. "Wai lao wei ch'i suo. Cheng yuan t'ung kuo." February 20.

Lin Chung Cheng (林忠正). 1994. "T'ai-wan fang chi kung yeh fa chan chi yen chiu" (台灣紡織工業發展之研究 [A Study on the Development of Taiwan's Textile Industry]). Unpublished paper.

Liu Ching Ching (劉進慶). 1992. *T'ai-wan chan hou ching chi fen hsi* (台灣戰後經濟分析 [An Analysis of Taiwan's Post-World-War-II Economy]). Taipei: Jen chan chu pan sho.

Low, Setha M. 1999. "Introduction: Theorizing the City." In *Theorizing the City: The New Urban Anthropology Reader*, ed. Setha M. Low. Pp. 1–36. New Brunswick, NJ: Rutgers University Press.

Lowe, Lisa, and David Lloyd. 1997. "Introduction." In *The Politics of Culture in the Shadow of Capital*, eds. Lisa Lowe and David Lloyd. Pp. 1–32. Durham, NC: Duke University Press.

Mainland Affairs Council. 2002. *The Republic of China Yearbook—Taiwan 2001* [html document]. Available from: http://www.gio.gov.tw.

Massey, D. S., J. Arrango, G. Hugo, A. Kouaouci, A. Pellegrino, and J. E. Taylor. 1993. "Theories of International Migration: A Review and Appraisal." *Population and Development Review* 19(3):431–466.

Mills, Mary Beth. 1997. "Contesting the Margins of Modernity: Women, Migration, and Consumption in Thailand." *American Ethnologist* 24(1):37–61.

———. 1999. *Thai Women in the Global Labor Force: Consuming Desires, Contested Selves*. New York: Routledge.

Moore, Henrietta L. 1994. *A Passion for Difference: Essays in Anthropology and Gender*. Bloomington: Indiana University Press.

Nader, Laura. 1990. *Harmony Ideology: Justice and Control in a Mountain Zapotec Village*. Stanford, CA: Stanford University Press.

———. 1997. "Controlling Processes: Tracing the Dynamic Components of Power." *Current Anthropology* 38(5):711–737.

Naquin, Susan. 1976. *Millenarian Rebellion in China: The Eight Trigrams Uprising of 1813*. New Haven, CT: Yale University Press.

———. 1981. *Shantung Rebellion: The Wang Lun Uprising of 1774*. New Haven, CT: Yale University Press.

Nash, June. 1981. "Ethnographic Aspects of the World Capitalist System." *Annual Review of Anthropology* 10:393–423.

———. 1985. "Deindustrialization and the Impact on the Labor Control System." *Urban Anthropology* 14(1):151–182.

———. 1988. "Cultural Parameters of Sexism and Racism in the International Division of Labor." In *Racism, Sexism, and the World System*, eds. Joan Smith, Jane Collins, Terence K. Hopkins, and Akbar Muhammad. Pp. 11–38. New York: Greenwood Press.

———. 1989. *From Tank Town to High Tech: The Clash of Community and Industrial Cycles*. Albany: State University of New York Press.

———. 2000. "Labor Struggles, Gender, Ethnicity, and the New Migration." In *Cultural Diversity in the United States: A Critical Reader*, eds. Ida Susser and Thomas Carl Patterson. Pp. 206–228. London: Blackwell.

References

Nash, June, and M. Patricia Fernandez-Kelly, eds. 1983. *Women, Men, and the International Division of Labor.* Albany: State University of New York Press.

Niehoff, Justin D. 1987. "The Villager as Industrialist: Ideologies of Household Manufacturing in Rural Taiwan." *Modern China* 13(3):278–309.

Ong, Aihwa. 1987. *Spirits of Resistance and Capitalist Discipline.* Albany: State University of New York Press.

———. 1997. "The Gender and Labor Politics of Postmodernity." In *The Politics of Culture in the Shadow of Capital*, eds. Lisa Lowe and David Lloyd. Pp. 61–97. Durham, NC: Duke University Press.

Ortner, Sherry. 1984. "Theory in Anthropology Since the Sixties." *Comparative Studies in Society and History* 26(1):126–166.

———. 1989. *High Religion: A Cultural and Political History of Sherpa Buddhism.* Princeton, NJ: Princeton University Press.

———. 1996. *Making Gender: The Politics and Erotics of Culture.* Boston: Beacon Press.

———. 1999. *Life and Death on Mt. Everest: Sherpas and Himalayan Mountaineering.* Princeton, NJ: Princeton University Press.

Overmyer, Daniel L. 1976. *Folk Buddhist Religion: Dissenting Sects in Late Traditional China.* Cambridge: Harvard University Press.

Oxfeld, Ellen. 1993. *Blood, Sweat, and Mahjong: Family and Enterprises in an Overseas Chinese Community.* Ithaca, NY: Cornell University Press.

Parish, William I., and Robert J. Willis. 1993. "Daughters, Education, and Family Budgets: Taiwan Experiences." *The Journal of Human Resources*, 28(4): 863–898.

Pasternak, Burton. 1972. *Kinship and Community in Two Chinese Villages.* Stanford, CA: Stanford University Press.

———. 1983. *Guests in the Dragon: Social Demography of a Chinese District, 1895–1946.* New York: Columbia University Press.

Pasternak, Burton, and Janet Salaff. 1993. *Cowboys & Cultivators: The Chinese Inner Mongolia.* Boulder, CO: Westview.

Pinches, Michael. 1999. "Cultural Relations, Class and the New Rich of Asia." In *Culture and Privilege in Capitalist Asia*, ed. Michael Pinches. Pp. 1–55. London: Routledge.

Raghaven, Chakravarthi. 1996. "Asian Female Migrant Workers Require Protection, Says ILO." *Third World Resurgence* 67:32–34.

Redding, S. G. 1990. *The Spirit of Chinese Capitalism*. New York: Walter de Gruyter.

Reinharz, Shulamit. 1992. *Feminist Methods in Social Research*. New York: Oxford University Press.

Robinson, Richard, and David S. G. Goodman. Eds. 1996. *The New Rich in Asia: Mobile Phones, McDonald's and Middle-Class Revolution*. London: Routledge.

Rofel, Lisa. 1994. "Liberation Nostalgia and a Yearning for Modernity." In *Engendering China: Women, Culture, and the State*, eds. Christina K. Gilmartin et al. Pp. 226–249. Cambridge, MA: Harvard University Press.

———. 1999. *Other Modernities: Gendered Yearnings in China after Socialism*. Berkeley: University of California Press.

Rubinstein, Murray A. ed. 1999. *Taiwan: A New History*. Armonk, NY: M. E. Sharpe.

Safa, Helen I. 1983. "Women, Production, and Reproduction in Industrial Capitalism: A Comparison of Brazilian and U.S. Factory Workers." In *Women, Men and the International Division of Labor*, eds. June Nash and M. Patricia Fernandez-Kelly. Pp. 95–116. Albany: State University of New York Press.

———. 1995. *The Myth of the Male Breadwinner: Women and Industrialization in the Caribbean*. Boulder, CO: Westview.

Salaff, Janet. 1990. "Women, the Family, and the State: Hong Kong, Taiwan, Singapore—Newly Industrialized Countries in Asia." In *Women, Employment and the Family in the International Division of Labor*, eds. Sharon Stichter and Jane L. Parpart. Pp. 98–136. Philadelphia: Temple University Press.

———. 1992. "Women, the Family, and the State in Hong Kong, Taiwan, and Singapore." In *States and Development in the Asian Pacific Rim*, eds. Richard P. Appelbaum and Jeffrey Henderson. Pp. 267–288. Newbury Park, CA: Sage.

———. 1995. *Working Daughters of Hong Kong*. New York: Columbia University Press.

Sangren, P. Steven. 1983. "Female Gender in Chinese Religious Symbols: Kuan Yin, Ma Tsu, and the 'Eternal Mother.'" *Signs* 9:4–25.

Sankar, Andrea. 1984. "Spinster Sisterhoods. Jing Yih Sifu: Spinster-Domestic-Hun." In *Lives: Chinese Working Women*, eds. Mary Sheridan and Janet W. Salaff. Pp. 51–70. Bloomington: Indiana University Press.

Sassen-Koob, Saskia. 1984. "Labor Migrations and the New International Division of Labor." In *Women, Men, and the International Division of Labor*, eds. June Nash and M. Patricia Fernandez-Kelly. Pp. 175–204. Albany: State University of New York Press.

———. 1988. *The Mobility of Labor and Capital: A Study in International Investment and Labor Flow.* Cambridge: Cambridge University Press.

Schive, Chi. 1992. "Taiwan's Emerging Position in the International Division of Labor." In *Taiwan: Beyond the Economic Miracle*, eds. Denis Fred Simon and Michael Y. M. Kau. Pp. 101–122. Armonk, NY: M. E. Sharpe.

———. 1995. *Taiwan's Economic Role in East Asia.* Washington, D.C.: The Center for Strategic & International Studies.

Shek, Richard. 1982. "Millenarianism without Rebellion: The Huangtian Dao in North China." *Modern China* 8:305–336.

———. 1999. "Challenge to Orthodoxy: Beliefs and Values of the Eternal Mother Sects in Sixteenth- and Seventeenth-Century China." *Journal of Early Modern History* 3(4):355–393.

Shen, Hsiu-hua. 2002. *Crossing the Taiwan Strait: The Gender and Sexual Politics of Identity Construction in the Global Economy.* Ph.D. dissertation. University of Kansas.

Shieh, Gwo-shyong (謝國雄). 1989. "Hei shou pien tou chia: T'ai-wan chi tsao yeh to chieh chi liu tung" (黑手變頭家：台灣製造業的階級流動 ['Blackhands Becoming Their Own Bosses': Class Mobility in Taiwan's Manufacturing Sectors]). *T'ai-wan sho hui yen chiu chi kan* 2(2):11–54.

———. 1991. "Wang luo shi sheng ch'an tsu chi: T'ai-wan wai hsiao kung yeh chung to wai pao chi tu" (網絡式生產組織：台灣外銷工業中的外包制度 [Network Labor Process: The Subcontracting Networks in the Manufacturing Industries of Taiwan]). *Bulletin of the Institute of Ethnology, Academia Sinica* 71:161–182.

———. 1992. *"Boss" Island: The Subcontracting Network and Micro-Entrepreneurship in Taiwan's Development.* New York: Peter Lang.

———. 1997. *Ch'un lao tung: T'ai-wan lao tung t'i chi hsu lun* (純勞動：台灣勞動體制緒論 [Labor Only: Essays on the Labor Regime in Taiwan]). Taipei: Institute of Sociology, Academia Sinica.

Siu, F. Helen. 1990. "Where Were the Women? Rethinking Marriage Resistance and Regional Culture in South China." *Late Imperial China* II(2)12:32–62.

Skinner, G. William. 1957. "Livelihood in a New Land: The Chinese Position in the Thai Economy Through the Fifth Reign." In *Chinese Society in Thailand: An Analytical History.* Pp. 91–125. Ithaca, NY: Cornell University Press.

Skoggard, Ian. 1996. *The Indigenous Dynamic in Taiwan's Postwar Development: The Religious and Historical Roots of Entrepreneurship.* Armonk, NY: M. E. Sharpe.

Small and Medium Enterprise Administration, Ministry of Economic Affairs. 2002. "Appendix I: Standards for Identifying a Small or Medium-Sized Enterprise" [html document]. Available from: http://www.moeasmea.gov.tw/English.

Smart, Alan. 1997. "Capitalist Story-Telling and Hegemonic Crises: Some Comments." *Identities: Global Studies in Culture and Power* 3(3):399–412.

Smithsonian Institute. 1999. "Between a Rock and a Hard Place: A History of American Sweatshops" [html document]. Available from: http://www.si.edu/nmah/ve/sweatshops.

Sobieszczyk, Teresa. 1999. "Official and Unofficial Methods of Recruitment of Thai Labor for Overseas Employment." Paper presented at the Association for Asian Studies annual meeting, Boston.

Stites, Richard W. 1982. "Small-Scale Industry in Yingge, Taiwan." *Modern China* 8(2):247–279.

———. 1985. "Industrial Work as an Entrepreneurial Strategy." *Modern China* 11(2):227–246.

Stockard, Janice E. 1989. *Daughters of the Canton Delta: Marriage Patterns and Economic Strategies in South China, 1860–1930.* Stanford, CA: Stanford University Press.

Sung Kuang Yu (宋光宇). 1983. *T'ien tao kou ch'en: I-Kuan Tao tiao ch'a pao kao* (天道鉤沈：一貫道調查報告 [An Investigative Report on Taiwan's I-Kuan Tao]). Taipei: T'ien-yu Publishing Company.

———. 2000. "I-Kuan Tao tsai T'ai-wan to fang chan chi ch'i ts'o lueh chi t'an t'ao" (一貫道在台灣的發展及其策略之探討 [A Discussion on the Development of I-Kuan Tao and its Strategies in Taiwan]). Paper presented at the Third International Conference on Sinology, Academia Sinica, Taipei, June 29–July 1.

Tai, Hung-chao. Ed. 1989. *Confucianism and Economic Development.* Washington, D.C.: Washington Institute Press.

Thornton, Arland, and Hui-sheng Lin. 1994. *Social Change and the Family in Taiwan.* Chicago: University of Chicago Press.

Tierney, Robert. n.d. "Foreign Workers and Capitalist Class Relations in Taiwan: A Study of Economic Exploitation and Political Isolation." Unpublished manuscript.

Tilly, Louise A., and Joan W. Scott. 1978. *Women, Work, and Family.* New York: Holt, Rinehart and Winston.

Topley, Marjorie. 1975. "Marriage Resistance in Rural Kwangtung." In *Women in Chinese Society*, eds. Margery Wolf and Roxane Witke. Pp. 67–88. Stanford, CA: Stanford University Press.

Wade, Robert. 1990. *Governing the Market: Economic Theory and the Role of Government in East Asian Industrialization.* Princeton, NJ: Princeton University Press.

Wang, Jenn Hwan (王振寰). 1995. "Yu nan hsiang cheng tzo, wo men ko yi kan tao sho mo?" (由南向政策，我們可以看到什麼？[What Did We See from the 'South-Bound Policy'?]). *T'ai-wan sho hui yen chiu chi kan* 18:225–230.

Ward, Kathryn, ed. 1990. *Women Workers and Global Restructuring.* Ithaca, NY: ILR Press.

Warren, Kay B., and Susan C. Bourque. 1989. "Women, Technology, and Development Ideologies: Frameworks and Findings." In *Gender and Anthropology: Critical Reviews for Researching and Teaching*, ed. Sundra Morgen. Pp. 382–410. Washington, D.C.: American Anthropological Association.

———. 1991. "Women, Technology, and International Development Ideologies: Analyzing Feminist Voices." In *Gender at the Crossroads of Knowledge: Feminist Anthropology in the Postmodern Era*, ed. Micaela di Leanardo. Pp. 278–311. Berkeley: University of California Press.

Weller, Robert P. 1994. "Capitalism, Community, and the Rise of Amoral Cults in Taiwan." In *Asian Visions of Authority: Religion and the Modern States of East and Southeast Asia*, eds. C. F. Keyes, L. Kendall, and H. Hardacre. Pp. 141–164. Honolulu: University of Hawaii Press.

———. 1998. "Divided Market Cultures in China." In *Market Cultures: Society and Morality in the New Asian Capitalisms*, ed. Robert W. Hefner. Pp. 78–103. Boulder, CO: Westview.

———. 1999. *Alternate Civilities: Democracy and Culture in China and Taiwan.* Boulder, CO: Westview.

Williams, Gwynn A. 1960. "Gramsci's Concept of Hegemony." *Journal of the History of Ideas* 21:586–599.

Williams, Raymond. 1977. *Marxism and Literature.* Oxford: Oxford University Press.

Willis, Paul. 1977. *Learning to Labor: How Working Class Kids Get Working Class Jobs.* New York: Columbia University Press.

Winkler, Edwin A., and Susan Greenhalgh, eds. 1990. *Contending Approaches to the Political Economy of Taiwan.* Armonk, NY: M. E. Sharpe.

Wolf, Margery. 1972. *Women and the Family in Rural Taiwan*. Stanford, CA: Stanford University Press.

World I-Kuan Tao Headquarters. 2001. "Taiwan 921 Earthquake Relief" [html document]. Available from: http://www.with.org/tw921quake.html.

Wu, Tien Chuan (吳田泉). 1993. *T'ai-wan nung yeh shi* (台灣農業發展史 [A History of Taiwan's Agricultural Development]). Taipei: Tsu li wan pao wen hua chu pan sho.

You, Su Fen (尤素芬). 1994. *T'ai-wan min ying ch'i yeh kuan ch'ang wen ti chi yen chiu: Kuan ch'ang kui fan chi fa li chi ch'u tan tao* (台灣民營企業關廠問題之研究：關廠規範之法理基礎探討 [A Discussion on the Jurisprudence of Taiwan's Plant-Closing Laws]). Master's thesis. Taipei: Chinese Culture University.

Yu, Tsong Hsien (于宗先). 1993. *Tui pien chung to T'ai-wan ching chi* (蛻變中的台灣經濟 [Taiwan's Economy in Transition]). Taipei: Sun min Publishing Co.

Index

Aberback, Joel D., 30
Agency, 163–165
Agriculture. *See* Taiwan, economy of, shift from agriculture to industry
Appelbaum, Richard P., 170n1
Arrango, J., 132
Arrigo, Linda Gail, 10, 77, 81, 116
ASEAN (Association of Southeast Asian Nations), 43

Berger, Peter, 54
Blim, Michael, L., xv, 9, 151
Bo, Lan Chi, 5
Bonacich, Edna, 40
Boretz, Avron, 169n1, 171n6
Bosco, Joseph, 9, 171n11
Bourdieu, Pierre, 19, 60
Bourque, Susan C., 78
Burawoy, Michael, 132–133

Cairoli, M. Laetitia, 9, 10, 78, 152
Capital accumulation, 30, 32–33
Capital flight, 4, 41–43. *Also see* Plant closure
Capitalism, 9, 151–152
Castells, Manuel, 70
Ch'ai, Sung Ling, 4, 37
Chang, Chin Fen, 60

Chang, Ch'ing Hsi, 133
Chang, Pei-Chen, 40
Chang, Raymond J. M., 40
Chang, Wei An, 45
Chen, Chieh Hsuan, 45, 70
Chen, Chieh Ying, 45
Cheng, Lucie, 10, 31, 40, 116, 170n1
Cheng, Shu-ju Ada, 132
China, People's Republic of, 42–43, 151
Chinchilla, Norma, 40
Chinese capitalism. *Also see* Network capitalism
  and Confucianism, 151
  critique of, 151
Chinese family:
  and tactics of resistance, 127–128
  as control strategy, 157–159
  as corporate unit, 111–112, 115
  feminist critique of, 116
  divergent interests in, 115–116
  embedded in practices of production, 119
  inheritance in, 120
  literature on, 115
  patriarchy and, 120
Chinese sectarianism, 171n11
  gender in, 172n13
Chou, Bi-er, 39
Chu, Yen Hua, 45

Chuang, Ying Chang, 115
Clark, Cal, 39
Clark, Janet, 39
Class conflicts:
    as familial matters, 115–116, 125–126
    suppression of, 63–65, 70–71, 156, 157–158
Class mobility. *See Hei shou pien t'ou chia* ("Black-hand becoming boss")
Cohen, Myron, 115
Council of Labor Affairs, 8
Creed, Gerald W., 152

Decentralized production system, 35–36. *Also see* Small-scale factories
DeGlopper, Donald, 63, 169n3
Democratization, in Taiwan, 2
Deyo, Frederic C., 9, 156
Diamond, Norma, 10, 81, 116
DBGAS (Directorate-General of Budget, Accounting, and Statistics), 75
Dirlik, Arif, 151
Division of labor in Taiwan, by nationality, 135, 139–140
Dollar, David, 30
Dowry, 120, 163
DPP (Democratic Progressive Party), 2

East Asia, Newly Industrializing Nations (NICs) in, 9
Elson, Diane, 153, 173n1
Empowerment of women, 99–101
EVTA (Employment and Vocational Training Administration), 132, 134
Enole, Cynthia, 62
Etienne, Mona, 161

Factory jobs:
    and social mobility, *see Hei shou pien t'ou chia*
    appeal to Taiwanese women, 81–82
Fernandez-Kelly, M. Patricia, 10, 20, 161
Flexible accumulation, 31
Foreign labor. *Also see* Foreign workers
    and capital accumulation, 132, 148–149
    state policy on, Taiwanese, 133–134
Foreign workers, 44
    discourse of, in Taiwan, 133, 145–148
    monitoring of, 141–143
    at Treasure, 143
    Taiwanese workers compared to, 137–138
Freeman, Maurice, 115
French, John D., 160

Gallin, Bernard, 115
Gallin, Rita, 10, 77, 81, 115, 116
Gates, Hill, 46, 115, 156
Gender, 45, 54, 72–73, 81–82, 85–86, 103, 108, 115–117, 127–128
    differentiation in education by, in Taiwan, 90, 104
    and global industrialization, literature on, 10
Gereffi, Gary, 9, 31, 35, 42, 119
Ginsburg, Faye, 161
Gold, Thomas, 9, 168n3
Goodman, David S. G., 60
Goss, J. D., 132
Greenhalgh, Susan, 9, 10, 115, 116

Hamilton, Gary, 9, 70
Harmony, 157–159
Harrell, Stevan, 9, 45, 115
Harvey, David, 10, 31

Index

Hefner, Robert W., xvi, 9, 44, 70
Hegemony, 50
Hei shou pien t'ou chia ("Black-hand becoming boss"), 23
   and Chinese family, 45 158–159
   and male subjectivity, 46
   and social mobility, 46–47, 156
Henderson, Jeffrey, 170n1
Ho, Samuel P. S., 26, 30, 80, 81, 82
Ho, Yen Tang, 5
Homei, textile manufacturing in:
   appeal to women, 51
   cottage industry in, before WWII, 24
   decentralized production system in, 36
   disfavored by women, 55–57
   effects of, on local population, 34–35
   plaid production in, 28
   recent restructuring in, 43–44
   standardization of, 32
Ho-mei Chen Kung Suo (The Township of Homei), 26
Hochschild, Arlie, 59
Hsia, Lin Ching, 5, 6
Hsiao, Hsin Huang, 25, 54
Hsieh, Chin Ho, 4, 37
Hsin hsin ren lei ("New new generation"):
   and consumption, 105–106
   and work ethics, 7, 53–54
   definition of, 8
   labor market participation of, 52–54, 59–60
   moral discourse of, 50
Hsing, You-tien, 43, 169n1
Hsiung, Ping-chun, 10, 35, 45, 116, 159, 170n1
Hsu, Cheng Kuang, 2
Hu, Tai-li, 35, 81, 115, 156
Huang, Chi Liang, 28, 31, 38, 56, 168n2
Hugo, G., 132

I-Kuan Tao, 93, 94, 171n11. *Also see* Sacred Heaven Fo-tang
   and industrialization, 93
   celibacy in, 95, 171n12
   organization of, 172n14

James, Daniel, 160
Jaschok, M., 97
Jen-ching ("human emotion"), 70
Jordan, David K., 94, 172n13

Ka, Chih Ming, 115, 116
Kao, Ch'eng Shu, 45–46
Kearney, Michael, 132, 162
Kim, Seung-kyung, 10, 60
Klein, Donald W., 40
KMT (Nationalist Party), 1, 24, 25–26, 42, 80–81
Knauft, Bruce M., xv, 19
Kouaouci, A., 132
Kuan-hsi ("relationship"), 70
Kung, Lydia, 10, 60, 75, 77, 81, 82, 90, 105, 115, 116
Kuo, Cheng-tien, 27

Labor, 4–5, 9–10, 63–66, 71
Labor market: 39
   and bubble economy, 38
   and labor recruitment, 68–69
Labor shortage, definition of, in Taiwan, 52–53
Labor Standards Law, 6
Lamphere, Louise, xiii, 170n2
Land reform, 80
Leacock, Eleanor, 161
Lee, Ching Kwan, 10, 63
Lee, Joseph S., 172n2
Lee, Teng-hui, 80
Li, Yueh Tuan, 116
Liberty Times, U.S.A., 133

Lin, Chung Cheng, 31
Lin, Hui-sheng, 86
Lindquist, Bruce, 132
Liu, Ching Ching, 25–26, 80–81
Living Room as Factory, 170n1
Lloyd, David, xv, 164
Lowe, Lisa, xv, 164

Marriage, 123, 124–125
  delayed transfer, 96–98
  effects of industrialization on, 93–94, 98
  and employment patterns in Taiwan, 54–55
  postponement of, 97
  rejection of, as resistance strategy, 97–98, 124–125
Married women:
  and homework, 170n1
  as factory workers, 54–55, 86
  single women compared to, 55–56, 160–162
Massey, D. S., 132
Migration, 131–132, 162
Mills, Mary Beth, 10, 62
Modernity, concept of, 61–62
  and industrial employment, 63, 83–84
  and service sector, 61–62, 159–160
Moore, Henrietta L., 62

Nader, Laura, 157
Naquin, Susan, 171n11, 172n13
Nash, June:
  on global economy and local history, 9, 14, 152
  on patriarchy, 161, 173n2
  on segmentation of industrial sectors, 14
  on women and the international division of labor, 10, 78, 161
  on women's productive and reproductive roles, 86
  on world migration, 132, 133
Native anthropology, 15–16
Network capitalism, 44
  and *kuan-hsi* ("relationship"), 70
  literature on, 9
New Taiwan (NT) dollars, appreciation of, 40
Niehoff, Justin D., 9, 115, 156

Ong, Aihwa, 10, 81, 163–164
Ong, Paul, 40
Ortner, Sherry, xv, 19, 164
Overmyer, Daniel L., 94, 171n11, 172n13
Oxfeld, Ellen, 115

Pan, Mei-lin, 9, 31, 35, 42, 119
Parish, William I., 90
Pasternak, Burton, 115
Pellegrino, A., 132
Pinches, Michael, 19, 151
Plant closure, 4, 6
  effects of, on workers, 5, 7
Practice, theory of, 19
Prosperity, as developmental ideology, 155–157

Raghaven, Chakarvarthi, 132, 162
Redding, S. G., 54
Reinharz, Shulamit, 129
Reproduction, social, 152
Robinson, Richard, 60
Rofel, Lisa, 73
Rubinstein, Murray A., 31

Sacred Heaven Fo-tang (pseud., I-Kuan Tao temple):
  activities in, 99–101
  and marriage, 95
  history of, 94–95

Index

residents of, 95
Safa, Helen I., 10, 86–87, 108
Salaff, Janet, 10, 60, 76, 77, 81, 83, 90, 115, 116
Sangren, P. Steven, 172n13
Sankar Andrea, 97
Sassen-Koob, Saskia, 51, 132, 149
Schive, Chi, 40, 41
Scott, Joan W., xiii
Service sector:
  appeal to Taiwanese women, 58–59, 60
  considered low status, 102
  gender and labor control in, 59
  gender constructions of jobs in, 60
  growth in, in Taiwan, 39–40
  wages in, 59
Shek, Richard, 171n11, 172n13
Shen, Hsiu-hua, 169n1
Shieh, Gwo-shyong, 23, 157, 169n2
Siu, F. Helen, 97
Skinner, G. William, 115
Skoggard, Ian, 9, 31, 93, 94, 118, 153–154
SMEA (Small and Medium Enterprise Administration, the Ministry of Economic Affairs), 168n5
Small-scale factories. *Also see* Decentralized production system
  and network capitalism, 44
  characteristics of, 35
  competitive flexibility based on, 35
  definition of, 33
  effects of, on women, 29
  family-centered aspects of, 118–119
  place of, in economy, 30, 33
Smart, Alan, 47, 155
Smithsonian Institute, 41
Sokoloff, Kenneth L., 30
South Bound policy, 42–43
Stites, Richard W., 9, 156
Stockard, Janice E., 97–98
Sung, Kuang Yu, 94
Sung, Wen Li, 2
Sunset industries, 12

Tai, Hung-chao, 54
Taiwan, economy of:
  bubble economy, 37–38
  current problems in, 39–41
  and female workers, 39
  and small-scale factories, 38, 50, 153–154
  export-oriented industrialization (EOI), 30
  market dependency, 153
  offshore investment, 41–43
  shift from agriculture to industry, 80–81, 117
Taiwan, history of, 1–2
Taylor, J. E., 132
Textile manufacturing:
  and Hong Kong, 25
  and U.S. aid, 26
  cotton in, 26
  gender constructions of jobs in, 51–52
  KMT policy on, 25–26
  sexual division of labor in, 29–30, 33
  standardization of production in, 32
  wages in, 59
Thornton, Arland, 86
Tilly, Louise A., xiii
Topley, Marjorie, 97–98
T'ou chia niang ("boss's wife"), 45–46
Treasure (pseud., textile factory):
  daily production at, 92
  fieldwork at, 12–13, 15–16
  foreign workers at, 135–138, 143–144
  hiring at, 68–70, 85
  labor force of, 58–59
  overview of, 12
  physical structure of, 61
  the Wang family compared to, 14
Triangle manufacturing, 42
Tsing, Anna L., 161

Uterine family, 115–116

Wade, Robert, 9
Wang family (pseud., textile factory):
  family relations in, 113–114, 123, 125–127
  fieldwork at, 11
  division of labor in, 119
  overview of, 117
  perception of daughters in, 120
  Treasure compared to, 14
Wang, Jenn Hwan, 41
Wang, Su-wen, 172n2
Ward, Kathryn, 10
Warren, Kay B., 78
Weller, Robert P., 38, 172n13
Williams, Gwynn A., 47
Williams, Raymond, 50–51, 156
Willis, Robert J., 90
Winkler, Edwin A., 9
Wolf, Margery, 115
Work ethics:
  and bubble economy, 37–38
  Also see Hsin hsin ren lei ("New new generation")
World I-Kuan Tao Headquarters, 100
Wu, Tien Chuan, 116

You, Su Fen, 6
Yu, Tsong Hsien, 4, 37, 168n7